"This book is the exploration of th ...
a reflection on the meaning of his ...
the meaning of all things"

"A remarkable book which defies characterisation. Ostensibly an account of the author's visit to the house on St Helena where Napoleon lived out the last six years of his life, it is also a meditation on history, biography and what it means to be a prisoner. Kauffmann, who was kept chained in a Beirut cellar for three years, only refers to his own experience of imprisonment once, and even then obliquely, yet this book remains most fascinating as an account of a profoundly intelligent man coming to terms with his past"   **TOM HOLLAND**, *New Statesman*

"The story of Napoleon's last years is beautifully interwoven with Kauffmann's attempt to understand how Napoleon felt in captivity . . . On these pages the very ghost of loneliness walks, vaporous, interminable"

SUSAN SALTER-REYNOLDS, *Los Angeles Times*

"Kauffmann's engagingly modest tone, his taste for following quirky avenues of reflection and his love of the trivia he collects along the route . . . are simply evidence that the best way to pursue his real purpose lies in obliquity and reticence. The result triumphantly justifies his decision, and gives the book resonance far beyond its nominal subject"   **IAN OUSBY**, *Financial Times*

JEAN-PAUL KAUFFMANN was born in 1944. He first worked as a journalist at *Le Matin de Paris* in 1977 and by 1984 was a reporter for *L'Événement du jeudi*. In May 1985 he was kidnapped in Beirut and was not released until May 1988. Kauffmann was editor-in-chief of *L'Amateur de bordeaux* and is currently the editor of *L'Amateur de cigare*. He is also the author of *L'Arche des Kerguelen: voyage aux îles de la Désolation* (1993).

The Dark Room at Longwood was the winner of six prizes on its publication in France including the Prix Fémina, the Grand *Lire* and the Prix Jules Verne.

PATRICIA CLANCY is a French translator living in Australia. Simon Leys' *The Death of Napoleon* (1991) in her translation won the *Independent* prize for fiction in translation. The English edition also won the first Victorian Premier's prize for literary translation.

Jean-Paul Kauffmann

THE DARK ROOM
AT LONGWOOD

A VOYAGE TO ST HELENA

*Translated from the French by
Patricia Clancy*

THE HARVILL PRESS
LONDON

First published by La Table Ronde in 1997 with the title
La chambre noire de Longwood: Le voyage à Sainte-Hélène

First published in Great Britain in 1999 by The Harvill Press

This paperback edition first published in 2000 by
The Harvill Press, 2 Aztec Row, Berners Road, London N1 0PW

www.harvill.com

1 3 5 7 9 8 6 4 2

A CIP catalogue record for this title is available from the British Library

This translation has been published with the financial support of NORLA

ISBN 1 86046 774 1

Designed and typeset in Bauer Bodoni at Libanus Press, Marlborough, Wiltshire

Printed and bound in Great Britain by Mackays of Chatham

For Odette and Marcel

It was like a tragic riddle . . .

Gaston Leroux, *The Mystery of the Yellow Room*

CONTENTS

Arrival at St Helena – The curator of the French properties – Devil's Island – The ultramarine blue of Jamestown – Atlantic melancholy – The typical St Helenian – The castle register – The climate, a thorny subject – Napoleon Street – The attendant at The Briars – Supremum vale – Napoleon's accent – "He was deathly pale" – The puzzle of his face – "Sire, we will live on the past" – The Emperor's companions – Saturn at The Exiles' Club – A crown of thorns – Discernment and the ability to discriminate – Napoleon plays the fool – The destruction wreaked by termites – The St Helena ordeal.

The last glass at the Consulate – Enter two English ladies – The four Evangelists – The Unnameable – The first sight of Longwood – A deceptive appearance – A haunted house – An impression of poison and stagnation – Marchand's watercolour – The Consul's worried forehead – "A cowshed" – Wuthering Heights – The smell of captivity – An atmosphere like a cellar – The prisoner's bath – "Theseus's ship" – The scratch on the globe – The Marengo cloak – The holes in the shutters – "A strange mildew".

The Dutchman's cannabis – Blücher the horse – Jacob's Ladder – Bernard Moitessier's paradise – Second meeting with the English ladies – The black DS' eagle – Michel Martineau's white trousers – Should we believe in ghosts? – "Either I give orders or I say nothing" – Napoleon's first interview with Hudson Lowe – The sudden appearance of Gilbert Martineau – Concerning the Dane's ghost – The dance of death – The wreath of everlastings – The castle in the mist.

The Fourth Day

Hudson Lowe's red hair – "The Emperor is sad" – A rainbow of smells – The court of King Pétaud – Sulking, a daily practice on St Helena – The mischievous sorcerer – The escapade of 3 January 1816 – The "flotsam from the wreck" – The Longwood Sheherazade – Pegasus and Medusa – The aperture in the camera *obscura – Bouvard et Pécuchet comes to mind – Finding the essence of the moment – Eylau, the censored battle – Rats in the shed – Michel Martineau, flower painter – The battle against the damp – The breath of solitude – Beating the thickets of time – The black snow in the cemetery – "I have lost a lot of people" – Medusa's head.*

The Fifth Day

The cemetery steps – Third meeting with the English ladies – "The wire bird" – The two riders – Napoleon's chastity – "You're just a puritan!" – Ali's bric-a-brac – Amy's crudity – Dialogues about Prince André – The teacher and Colonel Chabert – Karl Marx at Eylau – "The charge of the eighty squadrons" – The computer factory – Analogy between Eylau and Longwood – The invisible presence – Château Batailley 1986 – Discussion about Hudson Lowe – The misanthropist on his rock – The old man who does not want to die – The babies' toes.

The Sixth Day

The South African wine at Anne's Place – The Attorney-General's wife – Las Cases' "crime" – "Let us work on Waterloo" – "The Beans are good" – The 1817 earthquake – The Longwood biotope – About a bishop – The Jamestown sects – Who took the vases from the cemetery? – Meeting with the Governor of St Helena – His wife Delia – The Last Phase, the painting by James Sant – "Napoleon? He looks like a fat Spanish monk" – Plantation House, the antithesis of Longwood – The infernal gaze of the tortoises.

The Seventh Day   183

The Eighth Day   209

The Ninth Day   235

Epilogue   241

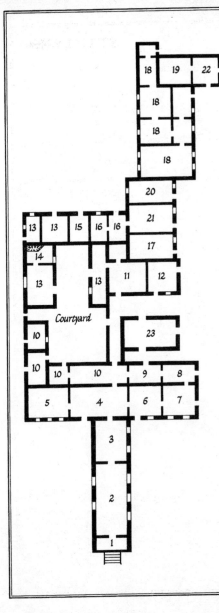

Longwood in Napoleon's time

1. Veranda
2. Parlour
3. Sitting room
4. Dining room
5. Library
6. Study
7. The Emperor's bedroom
8. Bathroom
9. Valet
10. Staff quarters
11. Kitchen
12. Linen room
13. Servants
14. Silverware
15. Pharmacy
16. Las Cases
17. Duty officers
18. Montholon family
19. O'Meara
20. Gourgaud
21. Dining room used by O'Meara and officers
22. Piontkowski
23. Servants' room

LIST OF ILLUSTRATIONS

View of Longwood, 1820 by Louis Marchand (p. 39). *Courtesy of Réunion des Musées Nationaux.*

The Emperor on St Helena Dictating his Memoirs to General Gourgaud (p. 82). A lithograph by Lanzedelly after a painting by Carl August von Steuben. *From the Collection Archiv für Kunst und Geschichte, Berlin (AKG, London).*

The Eylau Cemetery by Baron Gros (p. 102). *Courtesy of Photo RMN © /Daniel Arnaudet.*

The Last Phase by James Sant (p. 176). *Courtesy of Kelvingrove Art Gallery and Museum, Glasgow.*

Napoleon's Apotheosis by Horace Vernet (p. 233). *Reproduced by Permission of the Trustees of the Wallace Collection, London.*

All maps drawn by Reginald Piggott.

Foreword

I HAVE NEVER HAD ANY PARTICULAR LIKING FOR NAPOLEON. In fact I sometimes find the fascination he exerts over certain contemporaries of mine rather suspect. The triviality of the present makes them long desperately for the past and the Napoleonic epic. According to the historian Michelet, the Emperor was the idol of the uneducated.

I do admit to a weakness for Bonaparte. When I was a child, I used to imagine an incredible series of transformations all happening one after the other. How do you explain that in a single day – the Coronation – the gaunt young general of the Italian army could turn into a bald, plump god? As an adolescent, I couldn't have cared less when I learned that he would rule like a despot. But I was shocked: he had ceased to be the man he was at the beginning of his brilliant career – *l'homme du début* – the man Stendhal describes in *The Charterhouse of Parma*: "On 15 May 1796, General Bonaparte made his entry into Milan at the head of the young army that had just marched over the bridge at Lodi, and showed the world that after so many centuries, there was now a successor to Caesar and Alexander." And his arrival in Egypt was not without grandeur. After all, he disembarked at dawn in front of Pompey's column.

The Emperor's end has always fascinated me. I only like the beginnings and ends of biographies. The middle, which describes his glory, always bores me. All the eye-witnesses have commented that, after his death, Napoleon bore an uncanny likeness to the way he looked when he was First Consul. The death mask in the Army Museum at Les Invalides resurrects the features of the victor of Lodi, with his thin cheeks, prominent cheekbones and aquiline nose.

Like a lot of French people, for a long time I had no idea where to find the island of St Helena on the map. I didn't know then that the journey was so long and so complicated. The *RMS St Helena* is 500 metres long and has its home port in Wales. It's the only ship servicing the island, which doesn't have an airport. The crossing from Cardiff to St Helena takes a fortnight. You can shorten the voyage by catching the *St Helena* at Tenerife in the Canary Islands. I only spent one week in St Helena, the time it takes the ship to unload its cargo and make the sea link with another British possession, Ascension Island, 1,700 kilometres away.

While I was on the boat, I had time to read all the first-hand accounts of Napoleon's exile on the island. The more I read, the more I realized how difficult and incomprehensible the Emperor's last six years at Longwood had been. One vital clue was missing. I searched for a sign, a trace, an explanation, and I found them at Longwood. The sight of Napoleon's house had a profound effect on me. It's impossible to understand the very strange atmosphere of his captivity without breathing the smell of the place. I wouldn't be fatuous enough to claim that the sight of Longwood alone is the key to the mystery of that captivity. It does at least allow you to imagine its profound sadness. The real cause of his death was melancholy.

There is a puzzle about St Helena. Napoleon said everything about his past life, but didn't really reveal anything about his suffering as a prisoner. "He spent most of his day alone in his room, leafing through a few books or, more often than not, doing nothing [. . .] It was easy to see that he no longer had any preoccupation with the future, did not reflect on the past nor care for the present."

This type of remark, written by Las Cases in July 1816, is also found on nearly every page of the other companions in exile, Gourgaud, Bertrand and his doctor O'Meara.

What were the thoughts that troubled the Emperor in his small bedroom, which measured only seventeen square metres? I stayed for hours and even whole afternoons in this dark room at Longwood, listening to the wind shake the sash windows. I wrote this account to try and understand the reasons for the emotion, the uneasiness I felt there. It is not a historical work. It would be rather presumptuous to add yet another volume to the already abundant literature on St Helena. We know nearly all the fallen ruler's actions, from 15 October 1815 when he arrived on the island to 5 May 1821, the day he died. There is nothing missing. Except perhaps for one thing: the smell of Longwood.

This book began the very moment I entered that house. I only had to breathe the air, the odour of a damp cellar mixed with a strange tropical perfume – the heavy, rather peppery smell that fills your nostrils as soon as you open a cigar box – to become aware of the dimension of time on St Helena. It's of no real importance that the exotic smell comes from the African wood in the floorboards – the original parquet was destroyed by termites long ago. There's still a strong whiff of mildew, made a little less unpleasant by creosote, the sooty smell that comes from old fireplaces.

Captivity is first of all a smell. Napoleon had an extremely sensitive olfactory sense. "I have seen him move away from more than one servant, who was far from suspecting the secret aversion he had inspired," wrote Baron Fain, the Emperor's personal secretary from 1813.

Napoleon breathed the musty air and the damp exuded by the walls and fireplaces of Longwood. Nothing makes a stronger impression than this group of huts on a wind-swept plateau, high up on St Helena. It is the house of time remembered. The illusion of the past is so strong that you have the feeling the Emperor and his companions have just gone out for a moment, and that they will reappear around the corner of the veranda. Longwood is a haunted place. I know only one other house that makes you so strongly aware of the past: Hauteville House on Guernsey, also a disturbing place of exile and solitude. Rage and insanity still haunt its rooms and corridors. The presence of Victor Hugo is so intense that you have the impression of having suddenly entered the dark world of *The Contemplations*.

St Helena's isolation makes it easy to jump over the river of time to the other bank. The confining of Longwood has been its salvation, protecting it from becoming a shrine for worshippers. Longwood is an island within an island. In the heart of St Helena, the French enclave has its own life, its own inhabitants – there are only two of them, the French Consul and his father – and above all, its climate, which is very different from the rest of the island. You must be careful not to confuse St Helena with Longwood. As in the time of the Emperor's exile, they are two quite different and separate worlds.

"Napoleon exhausted the goodwill of the French, abused their sacrifices, covered Europe with graves, ashes and tears. Yet those he made suffer most, the soldiers, were the very ones who were most faithful to him, and even today, in spite of the time that has passed since then, in spite of different perceptions and new sorrows, crowds from all over the world pay homage to his memory and, standing next to his tomb, allow themselves to feel the thrill of greatness." This contradiction, expressed by General de Gaulle, is one I have probably not escaped.

On St Helena, the defeated, sick man inspires compassion, as all prisoners do. Napoleon battled against disintegration. His imagination crushed and pulverized the past. As the tropics rotted everything, he tried to pick up the pieces and put them together again.

Longwood is the story of a slow disintegration. Confinement itself is a kind of erosion. The prisoner wears himself out trying to understand why he has been abandoned. Oblivion, indifference and solitude sap his energy. In the end, these subversive activities destroy his will to live.

Captivity made Napoleon a naked, vulnerable man. He resisted it, relying on his former glory. He certainly found consolation in reliving his exploits as well as his disasters. An equal score. But he exhausted himself trying to rekindle the ashes of the past. For a prisoner, there is no worse suffering than remembering happier days . . .

THE DARK ROOM
AT LONGWOOD

Prologue

AT LES INVALIDES IN PARIS, NOT FAR FROM THE PORPHYRY
tomb where Napoleon lies, there is a room that visitors to the Army
Museum often don't bother to inspect. This alcove is an anomaly,
placed there in the middle of wax figures from the period of the
Restoration of the Bourbons (1830). It's hidden by a grey curtain
that you have to raise, like those you find in fairgrounds where
some monstrous figure is being exhibited in the gloom. But this
sight is not so much frightening as surprising and out-of-place. The
bedroom at Longwood in which the Emperor died has been carefully reconstructed, and with such accuracy that in the end the
tableau makes you feel slightly uneasy. This fidelity to the original,
frozen in a slightly improper, intimate scene, has something of the
waxwork tableaux of the Musée Grévin about it. Concern for detail
has not gone as far as exhibiting Napoleon's face in wax, but they
have had the indelicacy to display his intimate garments. On one of
the two camp beds you can see his underpants, his slippers and his
nightcap. Most striking of all is the pair of black stockings, carefully
displayed encasing two legs cut off at mid-thigh.

The fact that there are two beds is incomprehensible. Why two
beds? And why are they identical? They would look like two incredibly narrow children's bunks, or two pallets if they were not given
some height by a canopy. "Napoleon used two camp beds, and he

3

died in one of them," says a notice. Isn't it strange that he should refuse to choose? These debates about relics have always seemed ridiculous to me. The cult of Napoleon is partly built on quarrels about his hair, his hat and the inns where he slept.

For quite some time, Napoleon's life was summed up for me by beds. They were shown to me everywhere: in Champagne, Germany, Czechoslovakia, Russia. One could be forgiven for thinking that this hyperactive man spent most of his time sleeping. In a ruined house in Eylau, which is now in the Russian enclave of Kaliningrad, I came across a four-poster bed. My guide boldly assured me that the Emperor had slept there on the eve of the battle. I pointed out to him that Napoleon would have had to have lived for at least a hundred years to sleep in all the beds attributed to him. His bed is displayed in an alcove closed off by curtains on the island of Aix, in the sea off Rochefort, where the vanquished Emperor spent his last three days on French soil before surrendering to the English after the Battle of Waterloo. Why does the bed linen of famous people hold such fascination? No doubt because it reveals a vulnerable human being who suffers, who loves and who is like us. A man finally freed from the armour of legend.

The most moving object in the La Pagerie Museum at Les Trois-Îlets in Martinique, where Josephine was born, is a bedstead. The future Empress slept there as a girl. It's made of rare wood and is probably not the real one, but what does that matter? You can imagine the lovely Creole lying languidly on that bed. It's more effective than a picture in conjuring up the young girl they then called Yéyette and the woman Napoleon will later describe as "so graceful when she was getting ready for bed".

That is what drew me to Longwood: the revelation of the disarmed man in an unchanging setting. Longwood is a place that has a life of its own. The ghosts of Napoleon's exile come out of the walls and fill this maze of a house, full of passages and outbuildings.

Why does this strange neglected house seem so *true*, when the floor and the woodwork have been eaten by termites and replaced several times? Because it matches our idea of boredom, exile and death. The past has not been abolished from that house. You can feel it, with its obsessions and its habits. Madness lurks in this ridiculous setting. There is something frightening about the way past times suddenly come to life. History has settled like solid particles in suspension. This *precipitate* – a well-known chemical phenomenon – is visible in every room. There is a secret hidden in Longwood's damp, heavy atmosphere, like an insoluble body. The walls conceal the mystery of the connection that links us to the past.

I've touched that time, a time that had run its course and disappeared. It was not an illusion. In the uneasy atmosphere of the house, I've often had the sensation of coming into contact with another world. Not ghosts or shades; at the very most a vague, insidious, creeping presence, as in houses that forever carry the invisible but indelible stain of a murder. No murder was committed at Longwood, but the traces of that tragedy have not disappeared. Particles of the drama float in the air, especially in the prisoner's small bedroom. For some unknown reason, they suddenly join together like a flocculence of memory. Could they be trying to make contact with the world of the living?

There are two beds in the Emperor's bedroom on St Helena, identical to those in the Army Museum in Les Invalides. You will agree that some answers had to be found; even at the risk of succumbing in my turn to fetishism and the cult of the Great Man.

The First Day

I

I SOMETIMES PASS THROUGH ST HELENA, BUT I'VE NEVER stopped there. It's an empty place, silent and solitary. The houses sit on the grass as they do in Africa. Unlikely shops, a closed church, a deserted crossroads. Every time I pass, the place seems a little more deserted and sad. And yet I find an air of grandeur in that rather dismal severity. It's an unaffected, unfounded grandeur, I know. St Helena: a little village, not at all picturesque, in the middle of the Gironde forest in France. Yet the pompous, melancholy sound of the name impresses me every time I see the sign by the road at the entrance to the town.

On this November morning, it's my St Helena I'm thinking of – the village in the Médoc.

Standing on the foredeck, I'm watching for the moment when dawn lights up the island. Even though I'm prepared for it, the monumental citadel rising up from the sea is a frightening sight. "A catafalque of rock." Chateaubriand found just the right word for it, although he never set foot there. There is a threatening, gloomy atmosphere surrounding the 300 metre-high black cliffs that fall sheer into the ocean. It gives the impression of a ravaged fortress. St Helena lives up to its legend. Right from the outset, it bluntly states the fact that it is a maritime prison. 5.40 a.m. The ashen-coloured dawn hangs oppressively over the nearby land.

7

Daybreak holds no promise; on the contrary, it already suggests the fatigue of the day's end. Only one ray from the rising sun manages to pierce the clouds, falling on a corner of the coast with a dull light, as through a basement window. This slit in the sky gives the basalt towers and crumbling coastline of the island an outline of black shadows.

I look at the passengers' faces. Like me, they have all insisted on rising before dawn to get a view of the island. The Helenians, or the "Saints" as they are called, show no surprise on seeing their homeland again. After a fortnight at sea, their faces express relief, which changes to an almost blasé contentment as the ship approaches land. I note the stunned faces of the other passengers. The shock they feel on seeing the island for the first time expresses disbelief, fear and perhaps compassion. At this moment, I feel a mixture of all of them. The desolate rock seems to live up to its reputation almost too well, and yet I can hardly believe my eyes. The shore and the turrets are bristling with various pieces of artillery. There are walls and loopholes everywhere, as if you were meant to believe that nothing has changed since 14 October 1815.

On that day the *Northumberland*, with the deposed Emperor aboard, dropped anchor in Jamestown bay after seventy days at sea. "There was not a ridge on that sterile façade that did not have a canon hanging from it: they seemed to have wanted to receive the prisoner in a way that was appropriate to his genius," Chateaubriand also noted.

It looks massive and obstinate, hostile to anything coming from the sea. The ceiling of clouds that are always banked up over the island increases the impression of stillness, heaviness and dullness. The low, leaden sky hangs over the island fortress like an unhealthy vapour.

There is a disconcerting reaction from the defeated general of the

8

Battle of Waterloo when he first sees his prison, which will also be his tomb. Both the English and French on the bridge of the *Northumberland* are waiting for the moment when he will look at the coast through his telescope, then give his opinion. He takes in the escarpments, observes the defences of the formidable volcanic fortress ... and says nothing. No doubt the man famous for his ability to assess anything at a glance, the strategist whose quick eye had won him so many battles, the eagle who takes in the whole scene at once, has already understood the situation. He goes back to his cabin without saying a word.

It is not until the second day that General Gourgaud hears the first comment from the exile: "It's not a very appealing abode; I would have done better to stay in Egypt. By now I would be emperor of the entire Orient." This sentence is worth examining more closely. It's a sulky, almost childish remark; as if the empire he had founded counted for nought; as if the defeated Emperor now only wanted to remember a time before anything was fixed and defined; a pathetic remark which shows the extent of the tragedy the exile will live out on St Helena: rather than undertaking a critical examination of the past, he will keep going back over it.

The sight he saw from the *Northumberland* has probably changed very little: a few white houses, a square church tower, some trees. What still today saves Jamestown from being an ordinary little town is the fragility of its situation. Every traveller has been struck by the position of this village squeezed between two mountains. It seems like an open mouth about to bite through the long thread of a street with its few buildings clinging down each side.

Ships have to lie at anchor in the open sea, just as they did in 1815. Passengers and goods are brought ashore in open boats and rafts. St Helena still has no port. Everything comes from England: from marmalade to videos (which the Helenians are very fond of, as there is no television).

9

Michel Martineau, the French Consul to St Helena, is very obliging with the usual formalities. Our representative, a colossus of a man with a wide brow and piercing, deep-set eyes, remains very reserved for the time being. He took over from his father, Gilbert Martineau, in 1987. The two men live at Longwood which, together with the valley of the Tomb, makes up the French enclave. After long negotiations with the British cabinet, initiated by Napoleon III, the property was sold to France for the sum of 178,565 francs. Michel Martineau is both Honorary Consul and Curator of French Property on St Helena. We have exchanged numerous letters. His paper has the letterhead: MICHEL MARTINEAU, LONGWOOD HOUSE, ISLAND OF SAINT HELENA, SOUTH ATLANTIC. I'm very impressed by it, especially the "SOUTH ATLANTIC". This seventh continent, the limitless oceanic kingdom where he represents us and watches over our interests, inspires respect.

Today, as in Napoleon's time, you have to look sharp to catch hold of a rope to jump on to the jetty. Napoleon had written "St Helena, a little island . . ." on an exercise book when he was a lieutenant at Auxonne. His pen wrote nothing more on the subject. Many comments have been made about the ellipsis. It was added to indicate that the statement is interrupted. And yet, are there any more appropriate three little dots anywhere? "St Helena, a little island . . ." The phrase is still accurate. I'm struck by the extreme narrowness of Jamestown, a cramped, ill-formed, lilliputian village. St Helena . . . This grain of soil in the middle of the ocean is an accident, a scab on Neptune's skin. "The devil sh–t this island as he flew from one world to the other," General Bertrand's wife later said.

The waves of the Atlantic, which pound against the black stone of the Jamestown jetty, trace a long silvery strip that looks very like a shroud. But even though banishment, loneliness and decline take hold of one's imagination from the moment one arrives, there are also certain details that do their utmost to contradict this gloomy first impression. I have scarcely put my foot on the little flight of steps on the pier when something that looks like a little principality from an operetta comes into view.

Customs formalities take place in a mud brick shed: it's Africa without the chaos, a hybrid of the dignified courtesy of British officials and a very tropical sense of improvisation. The traveller is asked to open his bags and spread them out. That's all; they don't inspect any of it. Like Gibraltar or the Falkland Islands, St Helena belongs to the group of British dependencies. St Helena has only 6,000 inhabitants, but it has its own police, money, constitution and judicial system. And its own prison. After you enter the handsome town gate, that is all you see. Its well-kept ultramarine blue facade is quite elegant. The building was erected in 1827, six years after Napoleon's death.

There is a paradox in Napoleon's captivity: as a prisoner, the Emperor was never actually imprisoned. He stayed in a prison without walls, which measured 122 square kilometres, the area of the island. Beyond this space was the limitless horizon of the sea. St Helena, the jail on the heights, looks over vastness, emptiness, infinity. The prisoner has freedom of movement, it's true, but the size of the jail is not important when the warders never stop spying on him. It was Wellington, the victor of Waterloo, who chose St Helena. He had stayed there in 1805 on his way back from India.

The most perceptive work on the Emperor's exile, *Napoleon: The Last Phase*, was written by an Englishman – not just any Englishman, as this man, Lord Rosebery, was Prime Minister to Queen Victoria. "Was it necessary to send the defeated Emperor to St Helena?" he wonders. When Napoleon gave himself up to his enemies on 15 July 1815, he imagined that he would end his days in some English manor house. A fortnight later he learned that he was to be deported to the island of St Helena. The British note states that "The climate is healthy and its geographical situation will permit him to be treated with more leniency there than else-where." To which Napoleon protests that he had surrendered "of his own free will". They had deceived him. "They pretended to extend a hospitable hand to this enemy and, when he was handed over in good faith, they destroyed him," he complains. Lord Rosebery, a self-confessed "intelligent admirer" of the Emperor, examines the decision and Napoleon's hopes. Could he not have led the life of a "country gentleman" in England? "This we think, though we say so with regret, was impossible," he maintains, adding that the proxim-ity of such a man who had "a genius for upheaval" in Europe would have been too dangerous.

This surrender is still something of a mystery. When he retired to the Château de la Malmaison after Waterloo, Napoleon very clearly indicated his intention of taking refuge in the United States. He took many books on America with him. On the island of Aix, off Rochefort, he changes his mind and decides to give himself up to the English. The reasons he gave for this change of heart remain obscure. Perhaps he set too much store on the victors' generosity.

2

Napoleon and his entourage finally enter Jamestown on the evening of 17 October 1815. They have had to wait on the ship for three days; long enough for the English to find a house for the prisoner. Whites and blacks line up to look at the loser of Waterloo in silence. We can imagine their amazement. Had they not learned in quick succession that Napoleon had left Elba to reconquer France, that he suffered a crushing defeat at Waterloo, that he gave himself up to the English, that they had decided to deport him to their own little island, and that he was finally there in front of them, coming up towards the main street by lantern light?

At the entrance to the little town, he probably saw the castle on the left. The building was destroyed by termites and rebuilt in 1860. The citadel, which is now the administration building, must have seemed more forebidding then. It displays all the exterior signs of a fortress: ditches, bastion walls, loopholes. A joke of a fortress now: the mouths of the cannon contain only beer bottles.

Jamestown seems to have come right out of one of those American cartoons that feature naïve pictures of the police station, the church, the prison, the post office etc. What is more, the square is called the Grand Parade. It's neither grand nor particularly suitable for parades. The lack of space is explained once again by the looming mass of the mountains – two great millstones that crush the town. All that is left is the pulp: a main street. The Porteus house, where Napoleon spent his only night in Jamestown, used to be in that street but has since disappeared. In its place is a cinema, rarely frequented by the inhabitants these days. They prefer to watch films on video, available in all the Jamestown grocery shops.

White and ultramarine blue houses with iron posts and verandas: ultimately a more Portuguese than British look, with the Atlantic melancholy, the languidness and the emptiness that overwhelm countries at the outer confines of the world. *Confined*, is indeed the right word to describe the little capital of St Helena. It's as if life could scarcely change in this limited space. The cars and the few little shops show no sign of modernization; but there are no makeshift repairs, as you find in Africa. It's a kind of ambivalent inertia. A refusal to choose. The physical appearance of the inhabitants is itself almost impossible to define. Being a mixture of black slaves, Chinese coolies, Malays and Whites, the Saints have olive or coffee-coloured skin, green or almond eyes, and jet-black hair reminiscent of India.

Time has not stopped, it simply lags behind. It's visibly dawdling somewhere around the 1960s, judging by the models of the carefully repainted Fords and the shops with their wooden floors.

There is heaviness rather than slowness, which corrects the too generally accepted image of tropical indolence; a sluggishness created by this unusual union of disparate elements. It's old-fashioned but not worn out, outdated but not at all down-at-heel. There is a feeling of emptiness. The main street makes you think of "Potemkin villages": a decor on a canvas backdrop with nothing behind it.[1] The fronts of the buildings are like *trompe-l'œil* paintings. The two mountains prevent them from having any real existence.

Jamestown has all the attributes of a town: a public library, a municipal garden, two hotels, a restaurant, a market – but in an abridged form. Napoleon's captivity was also subject to the same obsession with the minute and the mean. On the subject of the Porteus house, the Emperor's valet, Marchand, complains that it is "uncomfortable because of its position and its cramped quarters". Even today, Jamestown cannot avoid a sense of oppression that crushes both buildings and open space. The tar-coloured basalt rock and the heavy sky tightly seal the little town like the hull of a boat. How could anyone escape?

Close by the prison, the eye is caught by a steeply rising line streaking the mountain wall. Jacob's Ladder cut into the rock is Jamestown's only curiosity. It's a staircase with 699 steps, so steep that a trick of perspective makes the handrail in the rock rising towards the summit look like a slack rope. This 270 metre-long sloping ascent was built in 1828 and used to haul stores and munitions to the citadel on the top.

"Be sure to inform the Governor of your arrival," the Consul advised.

"Is it important?"

"It's customary," Michel Martineau said. "It's the usual practice for visitors, especially if they're journalists, to sign the register at the

14

castle. You'll no doubt want to seek an audience with the Governor during your stay."

We enter the paved courtyard. The castle, which was built in 1710, now houses offices. It is also the seat of the island's Council. The Governor only has his offices there. Like Hudson Lowe, Napoleon's jailer, he lives in his official residence at Plantation House, three kilometres away.

With polished floors, pannelled walls in tropical wood, old prints, a cosy club atmosphere, the studied air of the place suggests respectability, and yet it can't dispel the impression of a certain lack of precision. The only thing that gives any firmness to the ensemble is the iron staircase that resounds when walked on. Perhaps it's because wood here has a precarious and uncertain existence, as it's always threatened by termites. I sign the parchment-bound register. My cramped French handwriting stands out in contrast with the rounded calligraphy of the English.

3

After his one night in Jamestown (to which he will never return), Napoleon is invited to visit Longwood. It has not yet been renovated.

On that morning of 18 October 1815, he does something strange. While the English are waiting to show him over the former farm, the Emperor goes off on his own. He mounts his horse and gallops full tilt up the main street, which ends in a "Y". He doesn't know which path to choose. The one he takes is now called Napoleon Street, the only allusion to the Emperor in present-day Jamestown. No doubt one should not attach too much importance to this caprice. The prisoner was not trying to escape; he simply wanted to annoy his jailers, to show them that he still has some leeway, that there is still a bit of slack. One should not overlook the fact that he has an almost childish love of playing tricks. He loves to tease, to provoke, to mystify. His tall stories make his adversaries reveal themselves.

The souvenir industry is non-existent. Not one shop selling knick-knacks. Not the slightest trace of a cult of Napoleon, apart from a map of the island with Longwood and the tomb printed on a rough square of cloth.

During the crossing, I noticed that the Helenians are not ashamed to mention the figure of the man who made their island famous; it's more a kind of shyness. On the boat, I took a perverse pleasure in noting several indications of a contradiction or at least a confusion. An English engraving of Napoleon on the bridge of the *Northumberland* hangs in one of the passageways of the RMS *St Helena*. The Emperor looks like a big, sulky baby. The members of his party have been drawn in a flattering pose with their legs elegantly placed: they look more like dandies than soldiers. A text at the bottom of the print recalls the fact that with the surrender "the Emperor had run his earthly course". The best place on the ship, however, is reserved for the famous *Coronation* by Jacques Louis David. A fairly good reproduction of it hangs in the lounge. The library on board has only a dozen works in French, all of them on the Napoleonic era, and all written by the former Consul to St Helena, Gilbert Martineau.

Napoleon Street, a steep alley of brightly-coloured houses, leads up to a very narrow road called The Sidepath. It is cut out of the mountainside and leads to Longwood. Even today there is room for only one lane of traffic. A car coming down must give way to one going up by pulling over into one of the lay-bys along the road. The tall stalks of aloes and the cacti scarcely brighten up the coal-black ground. There's a certain faded quality that spoils the Helenian landscape, dulling the brightness of the tropical vegetation. "A damned awful country," the Emperor announced as soon as he saw it. Neither he nor his retinue ever got used to the extreme changeability of the climate. Hence the many different landscapes, which could come from the Mediterranean, Scotland, or even the moon, judging by the ash-grey petrified mounds that can be seen from the boat this morning. The unpredictability of the climate and the difficulty in identifying uncertain natural surroundings quickly become trying. In one of his books Gilbert Martineau notes: "The climate of St Helena is a very thorny subject."[2]

4

Two kilometres from Jamestown, on the road leading to Longwood, the Consul draws my attention to a small valley framed by a grove of trees. The pleasantness of the place contrasts with the aridity of the surrounding countryside – a detail that did not escape the Emperor. He noticed this oasis with its Chinese pavilion. The Briars belonged to a man called Balcombe, a representative of the East India Company. On the way back from Longwood, at the end of the afternoon, Napoleon asks to stop at The Briars. He inspects the pavilion that is used as a playroom by the Balcombe children, and suggests to the English that he stay there while work is being completed at Longwood.

All that exists today is the little pavilion where the Emperor lived. At the entrance is a copper plaque stating that it was given to France as a gift by a woman descendant of the Balcombes. Another inscription in English points out that Wellington had stayed there earlier on his return from India. A small museum was opened in 1972. This little doll's house has just been saved thanks to Michel Martineau. The wood used in its construction had come from ships and was impregnated with salt. For a long time it resisted the termites, but eventually they got through the wood that had finally been softened by the weather.

A drizzle of rain envelops the valley, releasing that gamy smell mixed with cloves, sweetish and peppery at the same time, vaguely over-ripe, so characteristic of the tropics. A red brick path leads to the little pavilion. After the trauma of Waterloo and the distressing weeks that followed, it's here that the exile will enjoy the least bitter days of his exile. He is not too unhappy here, in fact he is even described as calm.

The attendant stares at me almost in disbelief: a tourist . . . You'd think I was the first person of the year to visit The Briars. I guess from his over-zealous attitude that he's going to relieve his boredom by watching me as I go round the museum. He scrutinizes my every gesture but doesn't actually supervise me. He has a benevolent expression on his face, in which I even detect something like gratitude. He moves away, allowing me to look at the Balcombe's cup and saucer used by the Emperor during his stay at The Briars.

A small piece of the carpet that covered the floor is displayed in a glass case. The design has faded and it's impossible to work out the central motif. I make myself examine this web of worn wool that the imperial foot probably trod, until I've looked at it more than enough. As I force myself to examine the dull colours, I wonder about the value of these time-worn pigments. I stare at them, trying to imagine a secret pattern: as I gaze at them, they become iridescent. But there's no past left to be reconstructed in this well-lit but depressing room with its smell of damp, fresh paint and rather sickly spice. Nothing to be gained from this house with its paltry memories, a house as sad as the drizzle that sends a strange gurgling sound like laughter through the guttering.

Napoleon first entered this room on 18 October 1815. He is 46. What were the thoughts and feelings that filled his mind on that day? None of the books written by eye-witnesses give any satisfactory answer – those men who never took their eyes off him but never really saw him. Those who followed him into exile, like his jailers, closely watched the least of his gestures, but never really looked at him. Perhaps his companions were too preoccupied with their subject, too keen to register for posterity the way he bent his head and shrugged his shoulders, or what his words meant. It's impossible to describe a man when one's eyes are riveted on him!

When all's said and done, Napoleon's entrance into the pavilion at The Briars is quite a banal moment in his captivity: it has no dramatic significance at all. The English behaved fairly decently towards their defeated enemy – Hudson Lowe has not yet arrived on the island. Nonetheless, from now on Napoleon will be a prisoner and will be given no higher title than "General Bonaparte". Five and a half years will pass before his death. Once he stepped over the threshold of this pavilion which, ironically he chose himself, he lost his freedom for ever. *Supremum vale.* Goodbye for the last time. Those are the words given by Ovid to Orpheus when he loses his Eurydice for the second time. Napoleon goes in . . . It's the end of everything. The room is so small! Hardly bigger than a hallway.

5

What was the timbre of his voice? I've spent some time searching for a clue in reports by his companions at arms, the barons Fain and Méneval, and his private secretaries. What was his accent like? It has often been noted that his voice could be tender, haughty or sarcastic in turn. There is no lack of information on that subject. But how did Napoleon pronounce his words? He left Corsica when he was nine, an age when a child is still malleable, when the accents of his island can still easily disappear. One imagines that at the head of an army, where not only a wide variety of French provincial dialects were spoken, but also German, Italian or Polish, the strategist had a duty to express himself clearly in French. A good number of his marshals (Kellermann, Ney, Oudinot, Lefebvre) were from eastern France. If he wanted to speak to both Masséna, originally from Nice, and Macdonald, born at Sedan, the head of the Grand Army would have to use unambiguous language.

However, according to the Minister for the Interior, Chaptal, "Napeoleon didn't speak any language well. His mother tongue was Corsican, which is a corrupt form of Italian, and when he spoke in French, it was easy to tell he was a foreigner." The same Chaptal also describes a scene with Lebrun, the Third Consul after the 18th Brumaire: "Bonaparte was criticizing the style of the translation of *Jerusalem Delivered*. Lebrun replied: 'You would do well to learn the French language before criticizing it'."

It is known that he confused words: *section* for *session*, *rentes voyagères* for *rentes viagères*, *armistice* for *amnistie*. "Napoleon had retained language faults that were incredible in a man of his high position," the architect Fontaine reports. "He said *meublier* for *mobilier* and *colidor* for *corridor*".[3] Mme de Rémusat notes in her *Memoirs*: "What detracted from Bonaparte . . . were his habitual mistakes of pronunciation . . . He read his words with an accent more strange than foreign, which had something unpleasant and vulgar about it." And she adds later in the book: "He never liked to surrender to anything, even to grammar."

We are not told if he rolled his *r*'s or spoke with a singing intonation in the Mediterranean way. At that time, it's true, the sound of regional accents was so familiar to the French that they paid no attention to it. Witnesses nonetheless stress the fact that the modulation of Napoleon's voice was "foreign" and not provincial.

The first recordings of French politicians have always struck me because of an accent that no longer exists today: a slightly peasant bluntness in pronunciation, something both rough and quavering in their articulation, which give their words a strangely gruff and unreal tone, as if their voices were coming from beyond the grave. One could put this peculiarity down to the bad quality of the recording; I'm inclined to believe that this reaction comes from a feeling of transgression, of having infiltrated a forbidden zone. Unlike a portrait, the reproduction of a dead voice gives one an uneasy feeling.

In any event, that voice had made an impression on the Balcombe's thirteen-year-old daughter. The Emperor was going to live for three months in this pavilion where she played with her dolls. Her meeting with "The Ogre" on the late afternoon of 18 October was to leave its mark on her life for ever. "He alighted at our house, and we were all moved to the entrance to receive him . . . He was deathly pale, and I thought his features, though cold and immovable, and somewhat stern, were exceedingly beautiful." She remarks that: "When once he began to speak, his fascinating smile and kind manner removed every vestige of the fear with which I had hitherto regarded him."

What then was the secret of that speech, with its power to calm a little girl's terror so quickly? With her child's candour, Betsy Balcombe was able to explain Napoleon's attraction better than anyone else: "During the conversation, I studied his face. I have never seen a more remarkable one. Many portraits give quite a good likeness of Napoleon, but what none of them has been able to reproduce is precisely his smile and the expression in his eyes. That is what made him so charming."

"When he smiled, his face had a most delightful expression," notes Captain Maitland, who received the prisoner on board the *Bellerophon* three months earlier. One of the sailors, midshipman George Home, who often saw Napoleon on deck, exclaims: "What indescribable beauty in that smile!" Méneval, his private secretary, stresses the fact that "a most amiable smile lit up his face". This was the feature that struck Chateaubriand so much when they first met in 1802: "He had a beautiful, tender smile."

That smile and that voice have always intrigued me. They say more about him than any description. Nevertheless, no one will ever be able to explain the mystery. I don't mind this even though it makes history seem like an ever-retreating, illusory spectacle. Nothing will ever penetrate that inexpressible part of the man, known only to his contemporaries. No one will ever be able to reproduce or imagine that smile. "It was tender and beautiful" – that's all we know. Napoleon's smile remains a well-guarded secret. Who can capture that laughing expression created by the imperceptible movement of the mouth and eyes, the glow that suddenly transfigures a face? That elusive part of Napoleon intrigued his contemporaries.

Actually, the face that has become familiar to us through the portraits of David, Gros or Gérard is never true to life. "None of the prints of him that I have seen is a perfect likeness; most of them are nothing like him," the German writer August von Kotzebue says when he meets him for the first time in 1804. "There is no absolutely faithful portrait of the great man," remarks his classmate and later his secretary, Bourrienne. On St Helena, Captain Basil Hall, who meets Napoleon in 1817, is surprised "to find such a great difference compared with existing portraits and busts of him".

Michelet, who saw the Emperor in 1815, is categorical. There are only two faithful portraits of Napoleon: the bust of 1800 by Jean-Antoine Houdon: "wild, obscure, saturnine, a sinister enigma"; and a painting by David, showing him full-length in his study "without eyelashes, without eyebrows; sparse hair of a doubtful chestnut brown . . . Grey eyes, like a pane of glass in which nothing can be seen".

This dissimilarity becomes more apparent in the last days of his reign. In fact the extraordinary difference between portraits is quite disconcerting. The secret of Napoleon's charm probably lies in that expression, which no artist could reproduce.

The mystery of the smile and the voice haunts The Briars, the first place where Napoleon reflects on the tyranny of time. It's in this house, the last haven of pleasure and peace, that the defeated Emperor will undertake the laborious journeys into the past that he had already begun with Las Cases on board the *Northumberland*. Yesterday and today, formerly and latterly, gone over again and again. The unrelenting time machine that transports him back into the past is set in motion. One day on board the boat going to St Helena, Napoleon asks Las Cases: "What can we do in that isolated place?"

"Sire, we shall live on the past."

At that moment, the prisoner probably has a flash of inspiration. The man who frantically threw himself into work in Finkenstein castle, where he had withdrawn after the butchery at Eylau and composed more than 300 letters, suddenly announces: "Yes, we must work. Work is also the scythe of time." Las Cases already has some idea of how he will profit from this recounting of Napoleon's memories. To avoid any jealousy, the Emperor will relate one episode of his life to each of his companions. He announces the fact to his entourage on 28 October: Bertrand will have Egypt; Gourgaud, the events of 1814 and the return from Elba; Las Cases the campaigns of the First Consul; Montholon, those of the Empire.

It is worth spending a moment on these men who followed the exile.

Count Emmanuel de Las Cases, 49, a former émigré who came back to France in 1802, was appointed Chamberlain in 1809, then a member of the State Council. At The Briars he became Napoleon's preferred companion and was chosen to live in the pavilion with him.

General Baron Gaspard Gourgaud, 32, was appointed the

Emperor's aide-de-camp in 1811, and is devoted to his master. He repeats to anyone who will listen that he saved Napoleon's life at Brienne in 1814. He hates Las Cases.

Count Henri-Gatien Bertrand, 42, Grand Marshall of the Palace, is a reserved man. His loyalty and sense of fidelity make him the noblest figure of the entourage. He was followed by his children and his wife Fanny, née Dillon, who came from a family related to the Empress Josephine. They are a very close couple. "La grande Fanny" has a capricious nature and a piquant charm. She's a very graceful woman. Bertrand played a decisive role at Wagram by building huge bridges on Lobau island. He is the only person who really knew the Emperor before his fall.

Charles Tristan de Montholon, 32, a diplomat and a rather dubious character, was accused of misappropriation of funds in 1814. He saw his career ruined by his marriage to Albine de Vassal, who came to St Helena with him. This ravishing woman, too free in her behaviour and already twice married, is three years older than Montholon.

The most attractive person among the servants allowed to follow the prisoner is the Emperor's first valet, Louis Marchand. His devotion and attentiveness to the fallen sovereign will help alleviate the sadness and the harshness of exile. He is assisted by Ali, also called "The Mameluke", although his real name is Louis-Étienne Saint-Denis. Ali will be the librarian at Longwood and scribe for all the witnesses of Napoleon's captivity, as he has an excellent memory and a reasonably good education. His *Memories* were published in 1926, but many papers remain unpublished. We think we know almost everything about the exile. But has the faithful Ali, with his prodigious visual memory, said his last word?

Why did these men agree to follow the fallen ruler? Greed, devotion, admiration partly explain their action. Napoleon does indeed have large sums of money at his disposal in Europe. The Montholons hope that the prisoner will express his gratitude in the appropriate manner. Las Cases is driven above all by literary motives. Disinterested though he is, Gourgaud is not unmindful of the fact that he could benefit from the Emperor's generosity. Honest Bertrand, however deeply he is attached to the Emperor's person, still expects to be rewarded for his devotion, although this motivation remains of secondary interest. The servants' attitudes seem to be most disinterested; Marchand and Ali, especially, are models of self-sacrifice.

None of these motives takes account of the most important aspect: the uncertain, risky aspect of a totally new situation. These Frenchmen, who have agreed to leave their homeland and follow an exile, have no idea what their own fates will be. Uncertainty overcomes the ambivalence of some and the ignorance of others, even if they all sense, in a more or less confused way, that they are part of a legend. But in 1815, the epic has not yet been magnified by the popular imagination. The man they are accompanying is the person responsible for the disaster of Waterloo. He is generally perceived as a sort of *condottiere* who cares only for his own glory.

6

The second room in The Briars contains a collection of engravings put together by Gilbert Martineau. They are lithographs and original drawings related to the exile on St Helena. Examining a contemporary print, I realize that The Briars has scarcely changed. Admittedly the Balcombe's house has disappeared, but the little valley is still almost intact. Today there are sheep grazing on it. Cables and wires with large coils have been unwound and left lying all over the ground. It looks like an abandoned worksite. The British telecommunications company Cable & Wireless, which took over from the Eastern Telegraph Company, had its storehouses in this part of the Balcombe's property. For a long time, the Emperor's pavilion housed the director of the company.

To help pass the time, the employees of the telephone company built a bar, The Exiles' Club, on the high land of The Briars. The Exiles' Club is closed at this time of day. I glance through the window: candles in bottles, a billiard table, a dartboard, skittles, a reproduction of a strange Renaissance engraving. It depicts an old man leaning on a scythe, eating a child. I suppose it's Saturn, figure of melancholy, the gloomy, solitary god driven from his throne and banished to the end of the earth . . . Whose idea was it to hang that engraving on the wall? Saturn is framed by two signs of the zodiac, Taurus and Capricorn. I would like to examine the scene more closely but the door is padlocked. The low moaning of the wind rises through the floor-boards of the veranda. Napoleon's little house seems pleasant by comparison.

You can smell melancholy at the Exiles' Club: it's something damp and languid, the heady odour of mildew, the acrid taste of dust, which indicate a fixation with the past, the monotony of memories, neglect, idleness. And death. Yet it's quite likely that people feel happy at The Exiles' Club. Doesn't the plainness of the decor show the power of the imagination? A nice beer and the enigmatic picture of Saturn on the wall is all you need to dream of the England you've left behind. Exile is a Helenian specialty. The island didn't wait for Napoleon to create this special form of the tyranny of distance. The identity of this rock, discovered by the Portuguese in 1502, is founded upon banishment and deportation.

Its first inhabitant was a renegade, Fernando Lopez, abandoned on the island in 1513. He came from Goa, where the governor had ordered his right hand and the thumb of his left to be cut off. Lopez had not only gone over to the service of a Muslim despot, he had also converted to Islam. For a long time the Portuguese deliberately gave false coordinates for St Helena on maps. The first acts surrounding the discovery and occupation of the island are marked by silence, desertion and deceit.

From the moment it was claimed, St Helena was declared an exclusion zone; it has been kept at a distance, *relegated*. This is exactly the word Las Cases uses when he is at The Briars: "By *relegating* us to the ends of the earth, amid privations, ill-treatment, needs of all kinds, they [the English ministers] wanted us to drain our cup to the dregs." And he adds: "St Helena is a veritable Siberia; the only difference is in heat and cold, and in its small size."

This comparison does not really help describe the deceptive climate of St Helena. La Cases understood its ambiguity well. With its mango trees and its cacti, the vegetation at The Briars presents the pleasantest face of St Helena and seems to conform to what one would expect of an island in the tropics.

Napoleon enjoys the coolness of the valley during the two months he spends with the Balcombes. He takes a walk there every day. He has no choice. The pavilion is so small that he has to wait outside while Marchand cleans the one room he occupies. It is bedroom, study and dining room all in one. While walking in the Balcombes' garden, Napoleon sometimes talks with the slave, Toby, a gardener, originally Malay but abducted and sold to St Helena by the crew of an English ship. "Poor Toby is a man who has been taken from his family, his native land and his own life," Napoleon remarks with indignation. He doesn't seem to remember that in 1802 he re-established slavery, which had been suppressed by the Convention. "It's an infamous act, bringing him here to die in slavery," he says, losing his temper.

Las Cases, who describes the scene, tells of Napoleon's strange reaction. "But I see in your eyes that you think he is not the only example of that kind on St Helena." The exile is annoyed to hear himself compared with a slave. He then declares: "My dear man, there can be no comparison here . . . We have not had to endure

27

physical suffering, and, had it been tried, we have a spirit that would foil our tyrants! . . . Our situation has some advantages. The whole world is watching us! We are martyrs of an immortal cause!"

On 31 July 1815, at the very moment when Napoleon heard of his deportation to St Helena, did he find consolation in anticipating the prestige he would gain from his misfortune? Later he will say: "My fame lacked only one thing – misfortune. I have worn the imperial crown of France, Italy's crown of iron; and now England has given me one that is greater and more glorious still – that worn by the Saviour of the world – a crown of thorns."

The recollections that Napoleon dictates relieve his boredom, but above all they construct the legend. Gourgaud works on the 18th Brumaire; Las Cases records the Italian campaign. The energy that produces this flow of words, this fixation with the past, fuels a mechanism that whirls round and round. At The Briars, the circular movement is already in place. Everyone has a turn at recording! Reading the accounts of these witnesses, you can see him day after day: the Emperor experiences dreadful times when he stops soliloquizing. He is the shaft. The axle that makes everything turn must never cease moving. He must speak, always be articulate. Words, monologues, expound, remember. Right to the end.

Las Cases had already observed this process of going over the same things when they were on board the *Northumberland*. Admittedly, Napoleon always had some difficulty beginning: "He seemed to doubt himself, saying that he would never manage it. Then he thought for a few minutes, got up, started to walk around and began to dictate. From that moment on, he was a different man: everything followed naturally, he spoke as though inspired; expressions, places, dates – nothing held him up!"

Ultimately, there are few images, colours or impressions in his accounts. His memories are monochrome, black and white. In these recollections, it's not the places that interest him but the time.

Repetition is an important element in Napoleon's intellectual ruminations. But first he has to go to the heart of the subject. That releases everything. Baron Fain has noted that "Once he had found the key concept, and every day had its own, he had a great flow of words."

Napoleon creates series as a painter repeats the same picture. "This idea was in all his letters and in all his conversations." Baron Fain had the impression of always hearing the same note. "Once the string was set vibrating again, it gave out the same sound with remarkable fidelity." When time and space happen to telescope in the course of this mining of the memory, astonishing visions arise, like the one of the dog on the eve of a battle during the Italian campaign:

"In the deep solitude of night, bathed in moonlight, a dog came out from beneath the clothes of a dead body. It rushed at us, then returned almost immediately to its shelter, howling with pain. It would lick its master's face and rush at us in turn, at the same time asking for help and seeking revenge." And then Napoleon makes this extraordinary remark: "Nothing has ever made such an impression on me on any of my battlefields."

One could compare the indifference of the war leader towards his men with this sentimentality for a dog wandering amid the casualties. We should also note that he speaks as though he owns them, unless he is speaking as the gardener of death: *my* battlefields, signifying that he really had the use, the disposal and enjoyment, in an exclusive and absolute way, of this land where battles are fought. He makes this surprising confession: "I had given orders for battles that would decide the army's fate; I had watched dry-eyed as movements were carried out leading to the loss of many of our number; and here I was moved, stirred by the cries and the pain of a dog." We should also note the "dry-eyed", a confession of indifference that doesn't even try to create an illusion.

29

Many of his feelings or thoughts are linked to sight, to looking. The dog is literally *vision* that has meaning. Everything he has ever experienced should have a meaning. The periods of melancholy and suffering will come from the difficulty, if not the impossibility, of giving a meaning to what has happened. He suffers when he dictates Waterloo to Gourgaud: he cannot understand the reasons for his defeat. He ceaselessly goes over the battle plan, looks for signs, indications, mistakes which always escape him. It makes one think of Koutsov in *War and Peace*, who had sworn never to abandon Moscow and one fine day finds himself far from the capital. How did it happen? Koutsov is obsessed by that question: "When was the decision taken to leave Moscow? The mistake that made that withdrawal inevitable; when did it happen? When could I have done that?" And he becomes aware that it happened naturally, imperceptibly. He who thought that he was in charge of events realizes that he was only the tool. Napoleon has not yet come to that understanding. The course of things, the way they develop, horrify him because they make no sense.

Between his surrender at sea off the island of Aix (15 July 1815) and the announcement of his deportation to St Helena (31 July), he sometimes makes incoherent statements, or acts in an inexplicable way. He is wavering, but not for long. The severity of the English decree that casts him away on a rock far out in the middle of the Atlantic brings clarity back to that legendary quick mind. Napoleon has great powers of discernment. Discernment, that ability to separate things, to distinguish true from false, the real from the imaginary, the particular from the general. He will shame his persecutors – without uttering a word of complaint. Protests and grievances are made to Bertrand and Montholon. The commander gives the orders and the soldiers carry them out. It is the responsibility of Bertrand and Montholon to explain his hardships to the English; of Las Cases to record them for posterity. At the Briars he announces in the lapidary style worthy of the Italian army communiqués: "I command or I remain silent!"

Enigmatic periods of depression are already becoming apparent: the Emperor is fighting himself. He stays in his room and will not see anyone (23 and 24 November 1815). None of the witnesses ever gives any explanation for these periods of depression. Las Cases certainly speaks of "lassitude", but he tries to reassure himself by putting it down to the prisoner's bad health. "He is far from having an iron constitution, as was generally believed; it is only his spirit that is made of iron." But on the subject of this spirit, the recorder of the Emperor's memoirs says nothing.

It's difficult to imagine that the god of battle, the thundering Jupiter, the terror of Europe, could play the fool to cheer up Betsy Balcombe and amuse himself by frightening her. He's not afraid to tousle his hair, make horrible faces and roar like a lion. He discusses subjects with her as equals, such as the plague victims in Jaffa or the occupation of Moscow. On the subject of that town, he says to her with a smile: "It was I who burned it down." The man of the pyramids finds it hilarious that the young English girl snatches his sabre and jabs him with it. She burns his fingers with hot wax, sings a ballad that laments the death of the Duke d'Enghien, and calls Napoleon a "frog-eater". He's happy, amused, touched. He plays blind man's buff with her, and never reacts when she shows him the malicious English caricatures of The Ogre.

Nonetheless, these amusements come to an end. Napoleon feels more and more cramped in his "nasty hut" at The Briars. He is impatient to move into Longwood.

Las Cases, who visited the Emperor's future residence, is filled with dismay. "Sire, here we are caged in – there, we will be penned in."

The attendant at The Briars insists on showing me a board eaten away by termites. On one side the wood seems to be intact. He gives it to me. It's like cork: the other side is so eaten away that the piece of wood crumbles into dust. The attendant tells me that two policemen were once conversing under a tree. One of them leaned against the trunk, which suddenly collapsed, felling the tree that had been pulverized from inside by termites.

Could time, eating away slowly in the dark, be St Helena's own form of torture? It quietly gnaws at the still surface of things, wearing away rock, vegetation and the human will.

I know that rumbling sound. You could mistake it for the ocean's roll, but that vague menacing presence is nothing but the buzzing of time, the fermentation of memory. It is a low, disturbing sound that unsettles the imagination. Hermits and island dwellers have always known this wandering of the mind and its secret song. Clouds rush by, the sea rolls like thunder, the lament murmuring in their ears never ceases. In the end, reason becomes clouded by obsessively trying to escape that haunting, monotonous chant.

1. Prince Potemkin was a field marshal, administrator, politician and favourite of Catherine II of Russia. In 1787 he organized a triumphal tour of the Crimea and the new Russian territories, setting up model villages for the occasion along Catherine's route. (Tr.)
2. *Napoléon à Sainte-Hélène*, (Tallandier).
3. Quoted in the *Journal intime* of Cuvillier-Fleury, (Plon).

The Second Day

I

MY FIRST NIGHT ON ST HELENA ... I'M STAYING IN A LITTLE house the Consul found for me high up in Market Street, the continuation of the main road in Jamestown. The street, which is on a slope, is made up of several buildings used for religious services by Baptists, Adventists and Anglicans. It's one of those dead, empty avenues you find in the tropics, languishing before its time because of the sun and the imperturbable inhabitants. There's nothing sordid; on the contrary, it's very clean and tidy. Hence the arid dreariness that doesn't inspire any feeling in particular, apart from a vague sense of boredom.

In the middle of the roundabout, two banyan trees with winding aerial roots are scarred with incisions. They are marks left by nails that were hammered into the trunk at slave auctions.

I occupy a room at the bottom of a little closed garden. The few tourists who disembark from the RMS *St Helena* usually stay at The Wellington or at The Consulate in the main street of Jamestown. The Consulate is a Georgian-style building with a veranda eaten by termites long ago and now supported by railway tracks.

The bar at The Consulate is the only lively place on the island. Last night I couldn't resist going there for a drink. When the barman heard that I was French, he insisted on introducing me to the manager.

33

"Why is your hotel called The Consulate? Is it an allusion to Napoleon?"

"Napoleon! . . . What do you mean?"

"Perhaps you wanted to recall the period of Napoleon's Consulate."

"The Consulate! I don't understand. Napoleon was an emperor, not a diplomat. Besides, I didn't name the hotel."

He had obviously never heard of the First Consul.[1] I didn't bother explaining to him that on St Helena the English didn't recognize the prisoner's title of Emperor, and called him Bonaparte. Could the name of the hotels be a relic of the final humiliation inflicted on the loser of the Battle of Waterloo? I imagine that every French citizen visiting St Helena is on the lookout for the slightest sign of British pettiness, but not without a certain amusement. In this game played by our rules, we are the victim but we think we come off best.

The hotel owner has suddenly begun to scowl. Perhaps he thought that I was suffering from a persecution complex, like all French pilgrims here. Luckily an elderly Englishwoman, whose acquaintance I had already made, arrived on the scene and created a diversion. She had caught my attention on board ship, because of her high-handed manner and her wheedling smile. I had also noticed her companion, the type of unassuming but humorous old maid you find in Jane Austen novels. They had amused themselves during the journey by commenting on all the passengers on the ship, drinking heavily and laughing out loud like schoolgirls.

"What a frightful hole this is, don't you think? We had a better time on the boat!"

Contrary to their fellow countrymen, who are mad about social games, they didn't go in for Scrabble or bingo. On the other hand, they were the first to order when the bar opened. Now that all the passengers have dispersed for their port of call at St Helena, the ladies are bored.

"How far have you got with your Napoleon?"

I replied that my investigations were only at the beginning stage and that the serious business would begin tomorrow, with the visit to Longwood. She had tried to tease me about Napoleon when we were on the boat. I lent her the French translation of Lord Rosebery's book *Napoleon: The Last Phase*. I had praised the insight of the work, even though the author had not known about the accounts written by Ali and Marchand. She had read it very carefully, judging by the flood of questions she directed at me. Her companion had also seen it, but didn't say anything about it. The topic that interested my despotic friend most was Napoleon's love life on St Helena. I repeated that, according to the first-hand accounts, the Emperor had remained chaste, even though there is a lingering doubt about his relationship with Mme de Montholon. Besides, she might have noticed that Lord Rosebery had had the good taste not to bother with the subject.

"But this question has nothing to do with good or bad taste!" she exclaimed.

"You know, Napoleon himself confessed that he wasn't a great lover."

"How do you know that?"

Why had I felt obliged to produce some evidence for her? I gave her a quotation from Gourgaud, to which Napoleon had replied with a sigh: "Bah! Women . . . When you don't think of them, you don't need them." That wasn't enough for her. I had to produced other evidence. I'd become caught in the game. I'd also had the weakness to think that this research would allow me to test my dexterity at finding my way in the Helenian "jungle".

The historian Jean Tulard claims that the cult of Napoleon has its four gospels: Las Cases, Gourgaud, Montholon, and Bertrand.

There are other recollections written by the doctors (O'Meara, Antommarchi) or the servants (Marchand, Ali), not to mention a good many pieces by English officials or visitors to the island.

One would think that, 180 years after the events, all the first-hand accounts would now be known. Not so! The period can still produce many surprises, as shown by the publication in 1969 of the journal written by Hudson Lowe's aide-de-camp, Major Gorrequer. His notes throw much more light on the personality of Napoleon's lugubrious jailer. The publication of Grand Marshal Bertrand's *Notebooks* in 1949 had already caused a sensation. People were astounded when they were able to read the shorthand written in secret by this close companion of the Emperor. From 1816 onwards, Bertrand had described the captive's life day by day, using a complicated system of signs and abbreviations that were practically indecipherable. With a great deal of patience and ingenuity, a scholar named Paul Fleuriot de Langle had nonetheless managed to crack the code. The Longwood witnesses described their hero, but, as Marie Bonaparte remarked, "the man was missing". This psychoanalyst and friend of Freud fully recognized the cruel veracity of these *Notebooks*.

In this journal, in which everything has been noted down – from the monthly consumption of Bordeaux wine to the great man's bowel movements – I'd found the remark Napoleon made about his elder brother that had disturbed my English lady: "I was saying to Joseph, 'You spend your time enjoying everything; I spend mine in thought and never in enjoyment . . . You love women. I scarcely think of them.'"

Had I convinced her? And of what? Is there anything significant or even decisive in the account of those five years? An abundance of minor facts and anecdotes, and indeed some spicy details. Some people may dismiss them, but I couldn't resist making an inventory of a certain number, especially from Bertrand. He quite fearlessly records in his journal the advances the prisoner made to his own wife (29 September 1819: "The Emperor makes a scene with Mme Bertrand, who leaves the room in tears"). Nothing is ever clearly stated. The self-control, the silences, the mysteries are the most fascinating part of these accounts. Will things left obscure and unnamed deny us access to Longwood's secret doors and dark corridors forever?

"Perhaps we could go to Longwood together?" the elderly English lady had suggested, with her wheedling but insistent smile. "It would be frightfully exciting to see that house with you!"

How could I let her know that I had no desire to have her breathing down my neck on my first visit? Luckily her companion intervened.

"Mr Kauffmann is working . . . We're just tourists. Don't you see that you've already taken up too much of his time with your silly questions about Boney?"

I'd protested weakly. We promised to exchange impressions here, at The Consulate. The companion, with her self-effacing air, had mentioned the hated name, "Boney". It was night when I'd returned to my house in Market Street, feeling vaguely elated, but also a little perplexed. What would I feel when I saw Longwood? The hollow tone of the word itself had always resounded in my ears like the tolling of a bell.

2

"We left The Briars at last and started out for Longwood. The Emperor mounted the horse that had been brought over for him from the Cape," Las Cases wrote on 10 December 1815. The tone that the author of the *Memoirs of St Helena* uses in his account of that strange day is almost cheerful. Reading it, one feels that

Napoleon was delighted to be doing something new, and relieved to be leaving The Briars. Las Cases goes so far as to record: "On that day he was particularly charming and looked particularly well."

To get to Longwood from The Briars, Napoleon and his retinue had to go back to Jamestown. His final place of captivity was six kilometres from the capital. The winding road, cut into the basalt, first goes across vegetation consisting of cacti, bougainvillaea and aloes, with long bare stalks that fall awkwardly to the scoria-covered ground. Then the bush seems softer as it changes to pines and agaves. At Button Corner, halfway between Jamestown and Longwood, the traveller has to button up his jacket. The landscape suddenly becomes harsher and barer. Then you come out on to a plateau of sparse yellow grass. Around the grounds are a few houses, a picnic and games area, and a stone wall. And at the far end, Longwood . . .

There is something inexplicable about the site and above all about the house, something that does not correspond to one's idea of a prison or even of a dwelling. I had already seen numerous engravings and photos of Longwood, and yet none of them could account for what I see at this moment. I'm dumbfounded. Is it a house, a prison? It's more like a ghost, a weird illusion. I've rarely seen a more oppressive place. Not that it's gloomy – gloominess comes from a constant and incurable sadness. But the beauty and luxuriance of the gardens are in stark contrast with the dwelling, which is like nothing on earth: the very model of a haunted house. The setting is orderly, but the soul is unhinged. Some people will maintain that this sensation is inevitably induced by the memories that linger in a place like this. Imagination has transformed it into the embodiment of exile and misfortune.

If you discount history and fable, would Longwood be just an ordinary property in the tropics? The look of the plateau at an altitude of 500 metres is nothing like the landscapes of the rest of the island. It's far from Jamestown here and even farther from The Briars with its mellow climate reminiscent of the Canary Islands. Longwood is a kind of Ouessant in the South Atlantic.[2] The sky and the trees are never still there, and the pines, twisted by the constant south-east wind, are all bent in the same direction. The trade wind has paralyzed the branches, leaving its mark in shapes that look like the lines comic strip artists use to imitate a missile trajectory.

Two men are busy in the garden: one near a bed of cinerarias and the other on a border. It inevitably makes you think of the watercolour that Marchand painted in 1819. It's the most accurate depiction of Longwood during the exile. The same two gardeners appear in the painting by Napoleon's valet. Nothing has changed and yet everything is different. With time and devotion, the place

seems to have filled out. There was not so much vegetation in Napoleon's time. The moment he saw it, he complained of the lack of shade.

"Well now! Come down to earth again!"

Standing there stunned, I hadn't seen Michel Martineau approaching. The French Consul's voice is somewhat ironic. My amazement, which must seem ridiculous, is partly emotion, but much more the strange feeling of having secretly crossed over to a forbidden shore where time is no longer chronological. It's bizarre and yet so easy, like moving from one time zone to another.

I've never taken seriously the adventure of two English women visiting Versailles in 1901, who claimed that they were transported back to the year 1789.[3] And yet, at this moment I think I'm having a hallucination. A vague sensation of the past suddenly crystalizes in a perfectly clear vision, as if an inconceivable phenomenon had just occurred: time going backwards. It has flowed in the other direction.

The look on Michel Martineau's face indicates that he seems to have observed the same confusion in other visitors. He looks amused. At Jamestown when the boat arrived he had been reserved, almost suspicious, whereas here I find him relaxed, even jolly, perhaps because he is simply at home as master of the place. From his considerable height, he dominates and oversees all he surveys. With an air of authority, he pulls out a weed as he speaks, or removes a useless bud. Then there are furrows on his brow and an impassive look on his face.

Tucked away in its greenery, the French domain of St Helena is a closed world. It really is an enclave. The tricolor flag floats in the centre of the gardens, flanked by two cannon. If I'm not mistaken, aren't they pointing towards Jamestown? But then, I usually think the worst. As a territory of the French Republic, Longwood somewhat provocatively flaunts its uniqueness in the middle of the

English world. The surrounds of the sanctuary may well be invaded by corrugated iron huts, a grocery store and petrol pump; these prosaic signs of modern life only highlight all the more the intimacy of the enclosure and its complete incompatibility with the rest of the world on St Helena.

"We were finally in our new dwelling at about four o'clock," Las Cases reports. As they arrive at Longwood, Napoleon's horse rears and stubbornly refuses to go through the entrance. The dominant mood of that day, 10 December, when the captive sees the gate of hell swing open, is nonetheless good-humoured. The British admiral directing the building of the extensions to the former farm looks relieved. "One had the impression that he dreaded being met with bad humour and disdain; but instead the Emperor was kindness itself," Las Cases points out once more. They all put up a good show, although it did not take long for the memorialist to realize that Longwood is an impossible place: "It is nothing but continual wind, cloud and dampness. The temperature is always monotonously temperate, which is perhaps more boring than unhealthy."

Boredom. Gourgaud uses the word all the time in his journal. According to Las Cases, there is a mysterious scourge that consumes the desolate plateau and the labyrinthine house. The violence of the elements seems strangely powerless in the face of that languor and emptiness. Perhaps the secret of Longwood lies in the relationship between that infinite sadness and the disturbing power of the site.

The Consul bends down to break up a clump of earth near the cinerarias. This plant with its ashen leaves suits Longwood – a funereal flower, but a living flower all the same. The Consul straightens up and comes back towards the path. It's so built up at the sides that it seems like a trench.

"Napoleon had it excavated to get out of sight of his jailers when he was walking," Michel Martineau comments.

"And the cinerarias? Were there any then?"

"The borders and beds are the same as in Napoleon's time."

"Yet when he arrived, Las Cases complained that the place was bare."

"These gardens were designed after he left. In 1819 Napoleon comes out of a long period of prostration. He suddenly discovers a vocation as a landscape architect. He then engages all those around him in gardening work and gives a plot to each of his three servants, Marchand, Ali and Noverraz."

"If I understand correctly, the garden so lovingly designed by the vanquished general was intended to make him forget the house imposed on him by the victor."

"Admittedly the house is bizarre. I've lived in it for six years now. You just don't know how to deal with it."

The Consul tells me that almost from the beginning the English had no other choice but Longwood. When their prisoner disembarked at Jamestown, they still didn't know where they were going to confine him. Plantation House could have been suitable, but this pleasant place was the Governor's residence. They had to find an acceptable house that was very large and above all easy to keep watch over. As Longwood and its bare plateau were surrounded by impassable chasms with an opening on only one side, accessible by a narrow road, they were easy to spy on. It's true that the sea is not far away, but on this part of the island, the sheer drop of the cliffs makes the coast inaccessible.

"Longwood itself," Lord Rosebery concluded, "was a collection of huts that had been constructed as a cattle-shed." Montholon calls it more precisely "a cowshed". Indeed the last dwelling occupied by the master of The Tuileries was originally nothing more than a barn built 60 years earlier by the lieutenant-governor of the island

42

to store grain. After that it was made into a stable. The house still bears traces of its humble origins today. You can make out the hastily constructed shed that was later reinforced.

In 1787 the Governor of the island conceived the plan of transforming the former farm into a summer residence. At that stage it consisted of a series of four rooms leading into each other with a fifth on the side at right angles. This is what the house was like when Napoleon arrived at St Helena. Once the English had chosen Longwood to confine their prisoner, some renovations were made while Napoleon waited at The Briars. An extra room was built, which would be the parlour. The whole thing was now "T"-shaped.

Why does this house give such a strong impression of torment? Grief would probably be more exact. What kind of burden could weigh upon it so heavily? It's obviously *tortured*, and it's not only the presence of the ghost that haunts it. Although the building is admirably maintained, down to the last detail, there is a feeling of deep unhappiness hovering over it. Is it the absolute isolation of the house that has such an effect on you? Is it the blood-red colour of the walls that gives it that solitary, suffering look? The line of the buildings is a puzzle in itself – something like a badly-aligned series of bungalows, a mixture of sheds and outhouses. And yet these words, which are normally applied to seaside holiday houses, cannot convey the dignified melancholy of the old house. It's a jerry-built place, but somehow imposing. Wuthering Heights in the tropics!

Longwood's deceptive appearance had not escaped Las Cases: "In short, Longwood could only look pleasant to a traveller tired by a long sea voyage, for whom any kind of land is appealing. If he finds himself there on a fine day and is struck by the strange objects he sees, he may well exclaim: 'How beautiful!' But that man is only there for a moment; and what suffering his mistaken admiration brings to the prisoners condemned to stay there for ever."

"If you like," Michel Martineau suggests, "we can enter Longwood just as the Emperor and his companions did on 10 December 1815." At that moment he has the serious but jubilant look of a magician who is master of his tricks.

After going up the five steps, we stand for a moment on the top of the stairs. It's the same veranda with its wooden lattice-work that you see in Marchand's watercolour. Napoleon, dressed in his white trousers and green coat, is on the second last step. This "dance hall arbour", as Gilbert Martineau describes it, may well be modest, but it has become the main characteristic of Longwood, making it instantly recognizable in engravings and photos.

Michel Martineau opens the door. The first room I enter is the parlour, hastily built to enlarge the prisoner's accommodation. What surprises me at first glance is not the billiard table, which takes up almost the entire room, but the smell. It's unique! You could mistake it for mildew, but there are other more pervasive and complex strands in it: scents of exotic woods, something like sandalwood and cedar. It makes you think of the stale iodine smell that pervades seaside villas in the off-season, plus overtones of resin.

The most lingering of all is the odour of boredom. The incense of melancholy and the musk of depression permeate the inside of the house. You don't need to know who lived there. I've already experienced this storage-room smell, the olfactory sign of neglect. But where? At Guernsey, in Victor Hugo's house. Hauteville House smells of regret, the wild delusions of isolation, the madness suffered by the poet's daughter Adèle. Exile has a particular kind of atmosphere. All prisons are the same in that. They are permeated by a strange aroma that is stale, rancid and sweaty. Longwood's effluents are different, subtler, more exotic, and not disagreeable. Seeing me sniff the air, Michel Martineau looks a little worried.

"You're the victim of what we call 'Longwood Weather'. Napoleon suffered from it for the whole of his captivity. You are in the dampest, windiest, in short the worst spot on the island."

"That smell . . . I find it quite tragic . . ."

"Tragic!"

He looks perplexed at first, then replies with amused solemnity.

"The smell of tragedy. Why not?"

He is silent for a moment, then continues.

"The dampness here is terrible. Napoleon had fires lit, but it made absolutely no difference. Tons of wood were burned in the fireplaces. The atmosphere was still like a cellar, because they didn't know at the time that the relative degree of humidity rose with the temperature."

"In his book, your father notes the astonishment of the inhabitants of St Helena when they learned that Longwood had been chosen as Napoleon's residence: its situation was so unappealing that no family had ever thought of living there permanently.[4] By the way, when shall I have the pleasure of meeting your father?"

"Later," he says vaguely.

I had been warned before I left. Gilbert Martineau is a man who likes solitude and avoids mixing with people. Both father and son live at the other end of the house, in the part Montholon had once occupied.

I wanted to make a quick inspection of all the rooms. There was a great temptation to linger in the parlour, the dining room and, above all, in the prisoner's small bedroom. I wanted to let myself be strongly influenced by my first impressions. Hidden truths can only be revealed at the beginning. But what is Longwood's truth? And does what is hidden there still have any meaning?

Our footsteps make the floor vibrate. Whenever we stop, all that can be heard is the rattling of the sash windows and the moaning of the wind. Michel Martineau was going to light the lamps, but I asked him to leave the rooms in the half-light. This must have

45

been what the inside of the house was like in full daylight: a meagre light, a gloomy twilight. I can imagine the men with their boots stamping over the floor of the cardboard house. In this very ordinary home, etiquette was the same as at The Tuileries: Bertrand, Motholon and Gourgaud in full uniform and the servants in livery. It's likely that everyone was in a bath of perspiration. The prisoner, who was very particular about protocol, would not allow a person to be seated unless he gave permission, nor speak to him first, except when the conversation had already begun.

<h1 style="text-align:center">3</h1>

The smell of Longwood . . . It was an obsession of the Emperor's. He had had to prolong his stay at The Briars because of the fresh paint. He couldn't stand the slightest whiff of it. He had therefore sent Bertrand and Gourgaud to smell the air in the house. Las Cases notes that "he had an extremely acute sense of smell. On board the *Northumberland*, the ship's paint was enough to make him sick."

It's rare in that period for anyone to mention smell, as this sense was taboo, harking back to our animal nature. Does Napoleon's aversion come from a psychological or physical reaction? Constant, who was his valet in the glory days before Marchand, notices that "in his bedroom, aloe wood, or sugar or vinegar was burned in little silver-gilt bowls". Constant also tells the story of the young girl from Madrid whom Napoleon had noticed and had brought to him. The Emperor's attraction turned to aversion because of the way she smelled, which irritated him to such an extent that he curtly sent her away. It has been explained that allergies were the cause of his acute sense of smell. For Napoleon, the ideal woman was one that gave off no smell at all.

This man who normally showed great self-control and could always feign anger when he chose, was furious over the paint incident. After Bertrand and Gourgaud have visited, he sends Motholon to Longwood to see if the smell is still there. He flares up, for the two reports are contradictory, and decides to send Las Cases to have another opinion. Did this man, Napoleon, who showered himself with eau de Cologne after bathing, know about the process of osmosis? He claimed he could recognize Corsica with his eyes closed by smell alone!

The bathroom is a dark gallery lit by a window facing west. The bathtub is probably the most fascinating object at Longwood. I share this thought with Michel Martineau who bursts out laughing.

"Be careful! You won't be popular with all those who worship Napoleon. They don't much care for these prosaic details."

"There's nothing prosaic really about the way one uses a bathtub. It's an art that requires skill and discipline. It appears that Napoleon was an expert at it."

"You forget that great men can't have a private bathroom."

The Consul gives a slightly mocking smile. The place entrusted to him makes him generally deferential, but he is not averse to giving the legend an ironic twist from time to time. I look closely at the bath, set in a wooden box. There's verdigris on the dented copper. The metal is black, as though burned by time, and tiny craters make the pitted surface uneven.

I mention that Las Cases, who usually avoids trivial detail, describes Napoleon's baths in the *Memoirs*. He even says that the first thing Napoleon does on that 10 December 1815 is have a bath prepared for him.

"That's true. He hadn't had a bath since he left Malmaison. Marchand tells how he got into it "with childlike joy". The first bathtub had been made by English carpenters. Now it's in the west garden. I'll show it to you."

Many of Napoleon's important decisions were made in his tub. Baron Fain notes that he took too many baths. "They were too frequent and too hot." The Emperor thought that they relieved his dysuria. Since the siege of Toulon, Napoleon had been suffering from chronic pruriginous dermatitis which made him scratch until he bled. Many witnesses like Marchand comment on the fact. Those moments of relaxation were a wonderful aid to reflection. While he was taking his last bath at the Élysée Palace he summoned Lazare Carnot, who advised him to seek refuge in America. Immediately after this meeting, the defeated general of Waterloo decided to leave the Élysée Palace.

Napoleon always sought physical contact. He loved to touch, to stroke, to feel. To show he was pleased, he would pinch or tweak an ear or cheek. Nevertheless, in all his gestures there is a hint of apprehension, of some hidden aversion. Skin smells, sweats and secretes.

Where did the habit of rubbing his body with eau de Cologne come from? From a distaste for odours *sui generis*? Marchand and Ali had managed to slip a few bottles into the luggage, but it didn't take long for the Emperor to run out of his favourite lotion. More could not be ordered from Europe, as the shipping time was too long.

Napoleon then called on his companions to try and remember how it was made. With the help of treatises in the library at Longwood, Ali finally managed to produce a home-made eau de Cologne. The recipe, which was found among his papers, enabled Jean-Charles Kerleo, perfumer in the firm of Jean Patou, to reconstitute the St Helena eau de Cologne.[5]

I couldn't resist the temptation of procuring a bottle of it. It's in my luggage. I propose to take it to Longwood and open "the only true remaining olfactory memory of the Emperor" in the prisoner's bathroom.[6]

Las Cases insists on the fact that Napoleon was fat, with relatively hairless white skin. He makes the following strange comment: "The Emperor showed a certain plumpness that was not typical of our sex, which he occasionally remarked upon quite happily."

The house has obviously undergone a number of repairs since Napoleon's death, but it is still intact. Fortunately it has escaped the fate that awaited it: namely to be turned into a museum. There are objects on display, but they have been relegated to the area outside the "sacred perimeter". They are grouped in the library or in the little antechamber next to the bathroom. Longwood has escaped preservation and display, the last unfortunate aspects of modernity. The parts built from wood – framework, doors, windows – were attacked by termites and have doubtless been replaced several times since 1860.

The paradox of "Theseus's ship", which poses the problem of conservation and restoration, has always fascinated me. The ship in which Theseus, slayer of the Minotaur, returned home from Crete was kept like a sacred relic by the Athenians for centuries. Over the years the old pieces of wood had to be changed to save the vessel from the ravages of time, to such an extent that after so many replacements and substitutions, it could quite legitimately be claimed that the original ship no longer existed. For the Greeks it was always Theseus's ship, with the same shape, the same history and the same symbolism.

How long will it take for this house to actually be a different one? For two hundred years, Longwood has had the same existence as an ordinary house: it has been abandoned, used as a barn again, damaged, almost demolished, patched up, done up, and finally restored to life. If it had been in France, it would immediately have become a place of worship, a jewel of the nation's patrimony, one of those glazed relics of our national heritage industry. Because it is isolated and beyond the mainstream, it has escaped a very French obsession with fossilizing a living building so that it can be protected and preserved by the devotions of the faithful.

Here the "cake of impressions" described by Jacques Rivière is intact and almost delectable. Longwood still has its flesh, thin and miserable though it may be. You can see that the life of the sad house hangs by a thread. Still, it has always been like that, from the moment the captive entered these walls. Chateaubriand was the first to recognize what an inferior house it is. He hastened to add the rather perfidious remark: "Those who were in The Temple tower and the keep at Vincennes were housed in even worse conditions; admittedly, those in power were thoughtful enough to shorten their stay."[7]

4

Michel Martineau's words come into my mind again: "You just don't know how to deal with it." It's one of those badly planned houses that have more hallways than rooms. I retrace my steps to examine the parlour, hastily built by carpenters from the *Northumberland*. The walls are painted green. The most intriguing thing, however, is the huge billiard table with five pockets, which takes up the whole room. The baize has faded and the cushions have softened. I pick up the old ivory balls that the captive liked to squeeze in his hand and make them cannon into each other. He didn't play billiards. The vast table-top was used for spreading out the maps and books he referred to while he stood there dictating. Time has ground the balls down. They are no longer completely round. The slightly flattened sphere has marks that have eaten into the ivory and put it out of shape. The captive's palms massaged these balls every day. Was this the automatic action of someone absent-minded or dreamy? He touches them, but only to help him focus on something else.

He's not in a dream, as you might think. On the contrary, his mind is intensely concentrated. The failed miracle-worker still likes to touch people and things.

A pencil of light comes through a slit in the shutter, suddenly bringing to life the miniatures on the walls of Napoleon's son, the King of Rome, and an engraving: *The Farewells at Fontainebleau*. The room lights up then fades and dies a moment later. The engravings are in the dark again, leaving a black screen with a few silvery glints across them.

"You can understand why the exiles liked to be in this room," Michel Martineau remarks. "It's the pleasantest part of the house. The least dark and damp, as the foundations don't sit directly on the ground. In Napoleon's time, the walls were not very thick. They were made of wooden boards, which let in the summer heat and the winter cold."

Like the rest of the house, the billiard room tries to make a noble impression. It's the biggest room in Longwood (43 square metres) and the highest. The space is less cramped than elsewhere, but two globes mounted on tripods show up the pretence of the decor. One represents the terrestrial globe, and the other the celestial. The surface of our planet is much more worn than the realm of the stars; one may conclude from this that the captive liked to turn the first more than the second. Does that mean that the former demi-god cared little for the starry dome, seat of divine power? Did he stay invincibly attached to the temporal domain that he had brought under his authority? On this stylized sphere, Europe is an indistinct, almost microscopic spot. The globe with the cross that emperors held in the palm of their left hand on their coronation day, at Longwood is nothing more than a big empty ball that is turned at random, as in a lottery. "I have carried the world on my shoulders," Napoleon confides to Las Cases. Now he plays with it like a child. Luck has turned. The lucky name *Bonaparte*, the good part, the first prize, which according to Michelet explains his fabulous destiny, has changed course.

You can wager that the ball always stopped turning at the same place. A finger has rubbed a certain spot so often that it has almost disappeared. The scratching has spread, making a swelling on the cardboard skin of the globe. You can guess that it was St Helena. The island itself has been eliminated! Now it's nothing more than a smudge, a blot in the middle of the South Atlantic.

These two globes had ended up in the Jamestown citadel after Napoleon's death. They were identified by Octave Aubry when he visited St Helena in 1932. No one knew where they came from until the historian formally identified them from Ali's description in his *Memories*.

Longwood's renaissance owes much to objects like these recovered after investigations and cross-checks worthy of a detective story. In 1965, Gilbert Martineau retrieved a large mahogany wardrobe with copper handles from somewhere on the island. It had been used to house the First Consul's uniform and the cloak worn at Marengo.

The captive was not totally destitute in exile. He had been able to bring with him the silverware and Sèvres china used at The Tuileries, not to mention a number of precious objects like the splendid washstand made by Biennais and Genu, and a considerable sum of money. The members of his retinue had been able to hide it from the English when the *Bellerophon* was searched.[8]

We sit down near the terrestrial globe, at a chess table. The round top of the chessboard is inlaid. The great strategist of Austerlitz and Friedland, who saw the battlefield as a chessboard, was a mediocre chess player. He naïvely rushed at his adversary and was easily captured, which didn't stop him cheating shamelessly.

"Shall we have a game?"

The question just popped into my mind. I realize immediately how incongruous my suggestion is. Have I committed sacrilege? The Consul is tactful enough not to show any surprise.

"There are pieces missing," he replies. "And besides, I play very badly."

Longwood is intimidating, and yet I feel there is something familiar in these rooms.

"It's a small house that was supposed to function like a palace. But, if I may say so, it wasn't capable of it. History and some construction work have thickened its walls and given it some strength. In Napoleon's time, with its tarred canvas roof, it undeniably had a cheap and rubbishy side."

I tell the Consul that I'm surprised to see holes cut in the shutters.

"Napoleon had thought of this ruse so that he could observe the comings and goings in the garden. He was short-sighted. He placed his spyglass in the opening and could see who was arriving at his house."

"But who put the holes in these shutters? I don't suppose they are the originals."

"I have to admit that it's a reconstruction – one of the rare ones at Longwood. In this case we conformed to this tendency, but it does help to understand the atmosphere of Napoleon's captivity better."

The billiard table, the two globes, the holes in the shutters, and the lonely wind whispering around the window frames. Poor Longwood, where absence reigns supreme! Imagination – that burning mirror which distorts and inflames the figures of the past – has played havoc in this place. Imagination . . . It's obvious from the accounts of Napoleon's companions, that they were desperately trying to put together again something that had been dismantled for ever. One really has to fight against annihilation in this atmosphere of tropical decay. The damp attacks leathers and weapons, rots books and playing cards (they were put in the oven before a game), saps energy and weakens memory. "Every evening, when I leave my little room with its fire and go into my bedroom, I feel as though I were entering a dank cellar," Napoleon confides to his doctor, O'Meara.

The dampness that saturates the air oozes out everywhere. It fogs up the window panes. But most of all it blots out reality. The mind gives up trying to grasp the subtleties and contrasts of the climate at Longwood. Heat and cold, drought and rain, storm and fair weather follow each other without the slightest transition. At the height of summer, as soon as the sun sets behind the mountain, a sudden coolness drives away the midsummer heat and rushes down to the plateau. The thermometer can drop ten degrees in a few minutes. According to Lord Rosebery, this weather was a real trial to the exiles: "There seems to have been something in the air of St Helena that blighted exact truth." Then he adds, rather mysteriously: "There is a strange mildew that rests on them all [the various accounts], as on the books and boots in the island."

Mildew, with its beautiful velvety spots and delicate silky threads. Everything spoils, everything deteriorates here. Everything changes into something else. If St Helena has a secret, is there anywhere better to look for it than in this stagnation and decay?

1. Before being a hotel and bar, the house had been the offices of a firm called Solomon. At the end of the nineteenth century the head of the firm had been honorary consul of a dozen or so countries, including France. Hence the name The Consulate.
2. Ouessant is an island off the Brittany coast. [Tr.]
3. This affair intrigued quite a few people, including Jean Cocteau who states: "Their adventure is doubtless the greatest of all time." After examining the

54

facts, he concluded that they are evidence of "an invisible presence that has nothing to do with ghosts". See *Les Fantômes de Trianon* by C. A. E. Moberly and E. F. Jourdain (Le Rocher).

4. *Napoléon à Sainte-Hélène*, op. cit.

5. See the booklet *L'Eau de Cologne de l'Empereur à Sainte-Hélène* by Maître André Damien.

6. Ibid.

7. *Mémoires d'outre-tombe* [*Memoirs from Beyond the Grave*].

8. 250,000 francs, or approximately 5 million francs in 1997. The Emperor has numerous deposits with the banker Laffitte, Prince Eugène and his brother Joseph.

The Third Day

"NO ONE ESCAPES FROM ST HELENA. I DON'T THINK THE IDEA ever crossed your emperor's mind."

I note the fact that the chief of police uses the slightly deprecatory term "your emperor". He pronounced these two words with a distinct pause. Is he expressing some reserve or quibbling over the title? For Hudson Lowe and the British Government, Napoleon was simply "General Bonaparte". Is that also the policeman's opinion? I notice that I'm pleased whenever I happen to uncover evidence of English perfidy on this subject. It's reassuring to imagine that national characters haven't changed, and to put on a show of indignation regarding Joan of Arc, St Helena and Fachoda. To tell the truth, this type of amusement interests hardly anyone now. The chief of police on St Helena obviously prefers the present. He dismisses the past with a wave of his hand: "Napoleon represents scarcely six years in the history of St Helena." What interests him is the number of prisoners behind bars at the moment. There are seven of them. Actually, the term "behind bars" is incorrect.

"Strictly speaking, they're not locked up – at least, not always. In fact they have a lot of freedom. St Helena's isolation is the best jailer of all. You can't escape from a prison with no walls. So, we're considerate towards them."

"But that's terrible! What can a prisoner long for, if it's not to

57

escape? If you take all hope of escape from your detainees, you'll drive them to despair. I imagine that their sentences are shorter."

"That's true. Their months are counted as only 28 days. But they have to show good behaviour. You can meet them if you like."

"Outside the prison?"

"Of course. For example, when they go swimming in the ocean or when they go fishing."

My surprise fills the policeman with delight. He proudly puts up seven fingers.

"Seven." I confirm the number. "Is that a high figure for the island?"

"Not at all. It's very low. The people here are very law-abiding. St Helena has one of the lowest crime-rates in the world."

As if to qualify this idyllic picture that somewhat devalues his role, he adds in a quiet voice:

"We had a case here . . . in 1984. A crime of passion."

"Our only problem," he assured me in a very professional tone of voice, "is people getting drunk on Saturday night. They're letting off steam. It's an offence we treat leniently."

"What misdemeanours have the present prisoners committed?"

"What! You don't know?"

My ignorance seems to sadden him. He suggests I look at the wall on the left. The front page of a newspaper with the headline: "THE MOST IMPORTANT EVENT ON ST HELENA SINCE NAPOLEON." Good Lord! It's the seizure of five tons of cannabis resin hidden in the hold of a ship in 1990.

"It was a matter of some importance. A judge had to come out here from Great Britain. The captain, who was a Dutchman, received the heaviest sentence. He won't be out until after the year 2000. You can see him if you like. He spends his time painting, and he's very talented. Look, I'll call the prison. You only have to cross the square."

I had noticed the prison when we disembarked. It's behind St James' Church. It was built on the site of a chapel in 1774, during the Portuguese occupation.

You can just walk in. The warder is reading a newspaper.

"Just a moment! I'm not sure whether the prisoners are there."

He opens a door behind him. The only noteworthy thing about it is the large bolt, which he hadn't even bothered to close. I can see a long room with three cells on one side; each one has four bunk beds.

"I told you so. They're outside."

"It doesn't seem to worry you."

"Why should it? It's their football day."

Walking down Market Street, I make the acquaintance of a jovial fellow called Nick Thorpe. He's a member of one of the oldest white families on the island. He proudly informs me that the business Thorpe & Sons was founded in 1860. Nick invites me for a cup of coffee in the firm's office. There is an engraving on the wall of a horse called Blücher – the victor of Waterloo.

"Oh! Don't take any notice of that! It was a damn good horse . . . I don't know who had the bad taste to call it that . . . Sorry," he says jokingly.

"You're forgiven . . . By the way, Napoleon . . . What do the Helenians think of him today?"

"Frankly, not much . . ."

He thinks for a moment.

"You see, he was a prisoner . . . Well! I don't think the Saints feel very honoured. They think it belittles them. Between ourselves, Napoleon isn't a very thrilling topic of conversation here."

"What do people talk about on St Helena, then?"

"The airport. That's about all, the airport. Should we or shouldn't we build one? That's the only thing people are interested in. But I don't think the debate will lead very far."

"Why? Won't there ever be an airport?"

"That's not what I meant . . . But you've seen for yourself! Have you taken a good look?"

"At what?" I replied, somewhat surprised at his question.

"Why, St Helena . . . What is St Helena after all? A museum, a representation of the good old days when we had an Empire. It's very reassuring, don't you know. But this fantasy costs the British dearly. St Helena lives totally on State aid. The government employs 80 per cent of the population. It's an island of civil servants . . ."

He bursts out laughing.

"We're so dependent that we can't even complain," he jokes. "To think that we've lost the chance of being the Hong Kong of the South Atlantic!"

"What happened?"

"The Hong Kong Chinese wanted to invest here. But nothing came of it. The Saints were afraid of losing something."

"Of losing what?"

"They still don't really know. The Saints have a very particular view of the world. On their pebble of an island, they feel that the world is still vast, while everywhere else it has shrunk. That's typical of islands: their perspective is often wrong. Essentially, St Helena's problem is one of scale."

His words are truer than he thinks. It's remarkable that the prison looks out on Jacob's Ladder, the stairs that scale the mountain and give access to the surveillance point, Ladder Hill. The black buildings of this observation post overlook Jamestown Bay. Why did they call this ramp Jacob's Ladder? The name is an allusion to one of the most mysterious events in Genesis. Jacob, the son of Isaac, has a dream. He sees "a ladder raised from the earth whose top touches the sky; the angels of the Lord were going up and coming down". When he awoke, Jacob was terrified by the memory of that dream and cried: "This is a frightful place!"

St Helena's form of terror begins to strike you as you near the top of the stairs. I climb the 699 steps one by one, sometimes leaning on the guardrail. On the 450th step I meet a young boy. He looks at me with astonishment. It's obviously madness to walk up Jacob's Ladder.

The misshapen layout of Jamestown is even more striking from the summit: the town is garrotted by the two mountains. They strangle it, leaving it no chance to breathe. Squeezed into this funnel-shaped valley, the little town tries to stretch out its length over the thin strip of earth. The most surprising sight on the heights of Ladder Hill, however, is still the line of gun batteries pointed out to sea. The guns are set on enormous cement constructions, now abandoned. These long cannon were brought here between the wars, but were never fired. It's one more hoax the island plays on you! If a cannon has sometimes rumbled in St Helena since 1673, the year the English took the island back from the Dutch, it has only been to give a certain rhythm to the days and to mark an exceptional event. Nothing is real in this show of strength.

What did the captive think of it, he who once maintained to Las Cases that "there is only one secret to being a leader, and that is to be strong, because in strength there is no error and no illusion; it is the naked truth"? Here truth cannot be contrasted with illusion or even with error. I'm beginning to realize that on St Helena it's an infinite variety of states that change and metamorphose without ever reaching stability – just like the microscopic sailboats I can see at anchor in Jamestown Bay. The way they bob about makes them seem somehow indecisive.

For navigators, St Helena remains "the Atlantic Ocean inn", the salutary stop between Africa and South America. I'm thinking of the solo yachtsman Bernard Moitessier, who put into port at Jamestown for several weeks in 1957. He refused to see the gloomy side of St Helena, the Longwood side. He praised the gentle nature of the inhabitants and the healthy climate. "We had landed in a little paradise," he writes. And yet, a strange incident occurs during his stay. Moitessier notices that there is rot in the hull of his boat and the planking is as weak as cardboard. He has to repair and caulk the boat. Cardboard, disintegration.

Thanks to the kindness of the Helenians, he will get out of his difficulties. One rainy day he hears a passing sailor accuse the English of having murdered Napoleon by imprisoning him "in this infernal drizzle and rain". This remark annoys him. He finds it unjust and exclaims: "No! Napoleon wasn't murdered. At least not by St Helena's climate."

Oh, the climate! . . . It's an endless subject of dispute that makes Napoleon's captivity seem like a drama that is always topical. "St Helena is an enchanting place if you have a return ticket in your pocket," the late Paul Ganière used to say.[1] The uncertainty of St Helena's weather reflects the elusive atmosphere surrounding the Emperor's last years.

The climate at Longwood owes a lot to that kind of weather, which makes people emotional, anxious and irritable. On this subject, the historian Frédéric Masson even talked of "colonial passion", claiming that "everything is incomprehensible if that element is not taken into account."[2]

It's certain that the actors in the tragedy are perpetually on edge. "People become warped: from being normal in Europe, they become abnormal on the equator." Strangely enough, one man escapes this general nervousness: Napoleon. He goes through periods of high energy that don't last, especially in the beginning. Then bouts of lethargy and depression become more and more frequent, especially in the last months of 1816.

I wander round Jamestown, but I can't get Longwood out of my mind. Michel Martineau expects me there in the early afternoon.

"Well now, did you like Longwood?"

Lost in contemplation of the bay, I hadn't heard the old English-woman and her companion come up behind me. They suddenly appear, whispering and giggling like schoolgirls who have played a trick on someone. They have come up to Ladder Hill in an old open car that had already attracted my attention in the main street of Jamestown. It's an old jalopy that is both weird yet ingenious, ludicrous yet comfortable. I imagine it was an estate car that has been transformed into a roomy convertible in a way that is typically English. The "charabanc", as they call it here, is used to transport the few tourists who come to St Helena.

"Like it? Not exactly, but disturbed by it, yes."

"Disturbed! What's disturbing in that awful shanty?"

"Is that the only effect it had on you?"

"The house is of no importance. On the other hand, the garden is superb."

"I don't agree. Longwood is important. It's ordinary, mediocre and cramped if you like, but it's also full of meaning. You under-stand everything when you see that house."

"Understand what? Like all Frenchmen, you're playing with words. Forget the legend, there's nothing much left of that ... dump."

She has a peculiarly vulgar way of speaking our language, with an intonation both mocking and childish that softens her rather despotic manner.

"I don't agree with you. There are ghosts in that place. It's a house of suffering and death. You can feel it as soon as you go inside."

She interrupts me sternly: "You have too much imagination. 'Suffering', 'death'! There's a frightful smell of mildew. Yes indeed!"

She likes to punctuate her statements with a "yes indeed!" [*ah oui*!], rounding her lips in a comical manner. Her silent companion looks at her sharply.

"You didn't understand a thing at Longwood. You did nothing but complain the whole time you were there. Why on earth do you insist on going to museums? You hate them. What's more, you've no feeling for history. I found that house quite moving."

"You're probably right. It's true, I'm only interested in the living. I caught sight of the Consul in the garden. He's so young! Fancy shutting oneself away from the world at his age! He must be terribly bored."

"I don't think so. He's not alone. His father lives with him at Longwood. They come back to France every year to avoid August and September, which are the worst months here."

I actually know very little about these two ladies.

They got on the boat at Tenerife. Why did they choose to come to St Helena? Because of Napoleon? That's not very likely. They are obviously trying to kill time before RMS *St Helena* gets under-way again. The companion intrigues me. She certainly accompanies the other woman, but she is not a lady's companion. She uncomplainingly accepts her abrupt manner, but on occasions can put her in her place with a certain detachment and a kind of suppressed mirth. She always looks secretly amused. She seems to see an incurably comic side to people and things – except where Napoleon is concerned. It's impossible to know what she really thinks about that subject. She must hide a romantic nature under that seemingly cold exterior.

We wander round the houses. They seem run down. Even the villas in course of construction already look like ruins. Is it the climate that damages everything in this way? I come across a black DS19 in a garden overgrown with weeds. The car is still in quite good condition although the vegetation has started to wind itself around the bodywork. The sight of the radiator cap stops me in my tracks: it's a silver eagle. Is it an imperial eagle or an American eagle? I want to find out who owns it. My two friends go up to the house and knock on the door. There's a refrigerator lying on the ground, which is littered with old beer bottles. Not a soul . . . [3]

2

I have the same feeling of unreality when I glimpse Marchand's watercolour once again: the two gardeners, Ali's flower bed covered by an archway, the grotto, the Chinese pavilion . . .

Michel Martineau is waiting for me on the steps of the veranda. On the same spot as the Emperor, and he's wearing white trousers as the Emperor was in the painting. I must point out that he's not wearing a green jacket, but a sky blue shirt.

At the time I suspect he might have deliberately set up that scene, thought to have taken place in 1819. The magician's look he sometimes likes to affect makes me think that he's quite capable of playing a trick like that. From the look of him at the moment however, his thoughts seem to be elsewhere.

He holds out the key, as though about to give it to me, but in fact he's indicating that I'm free to wander round the rooms at Longwood as I like. He opens the door and puts the key back in his pocket.

"I can't come with you this time. Do as you wish. I have an electrical problem in the Gourgaud quarters to attend to. You see, I'm a jack of all trades here: woodcutter, gardener, plumber, painter, electrician, not to mention my administrative duties. Off you go. I'm sure you don't mind inspecting the haunted house on your own."

He said "the haunted house" in a slightly ironic tone of voice, his way perhaps of letting me know that he guessed what I felt on my first visit and feels he can trust me.

"Do you believe in ghosts?" I ask.

"I don't know. I suppose that certain tragic events that happen are powerful enough for images to leave their mark on the place and leave traces there. But I believe especially in the magnetic power of memory, in the strength of the imagination. That's what brings places back to life again."

"Anyway, all places are haunted. Think of all the people who have died one after the other in the same house."

"Oh! You believe that their souls wander about tormenting the living?"

"I've no idea . . . You know, I often think of hotel rooms and all those bodies that have slept there piled up on the same bed. Perhaps that explains all the strange noises you hear there – knocking pipes, creaking floorboards . . ."

"It sounds like something out of *The Night of the Living-Dead*. In the beginning, it's true, I used to have the feeling of living with ghosts. I never think of it now. Longwood is the place where I work. Does that disappoint you?"

"No, but it's difficult to forget the past: for example, the electricity failure in the quarters formerly occupied by Gourgaud. And then there's the Montholon wing where you live . . ."

"And my studio in the room where they used to keep the silverware . . ."

"Your studio"

"Yes, I paint. But only flowers."

"The flowers here at Longwood?"

"Agapanthus, irises. I'll show them to you. But I must go."

The billiard table is covered with a sheet. The balls are imprisoned in a triangle. Actually, the smell of Longwood isn't really unpleasant. Perhaps I've just become used to it. The house smells of mildew, but also of humus, of something earthy and herbaceous, like moss under trees. There is also a more subtle spicy perfume that still manages to come through these stronger odours. This is what makes the famous dank cellar smell that Napoleon complained of quite pleasant.

The billiard room is in darkness. As the Consul has given me permission to open the windows, I set about raising them one by one, then opening the shutters. Shafts of light suddenly penetrate the room, bringing pictures and objects to life.

It's into this antechamber-cum-parlour and waiting room that Hudson Lowe is ushered for the first time on 16 April 1816. The jailer has just arrived on St Helena and wants to see his prisoner. The former monarch, however, does not take kindly to the fact that the time of the audience has been imposed on him. He sends the message that he is indisposed. He has actually been secretly watching the scene from the beginning, behind a shutter in his bedroom. Hudson Lowe will have to return the next day.

Lying in wait, watching in the shadows, is a position Napoleon is quite familiar with. Moreover, he has a spy on St Helena: Cipriani, the Corsican butler, whose family has served the Bonaparte clan for ages. This disturbing person knows everything that happens in the island, ship movements, Jamestown rumours . . .

Did the prisoner's "police minister", this poor man's Fouché, already know Hudson Lowe? The two men probably rubbed shoulders at the siege of Capri in 1806. Gourgaud complains that "His Majesty would give us all up for Cipriani". Hungry for information and fond of gossip, the captive spends long periods of time questioning his butler. Was Cipriani devoted to Bonaparte? It's not beyond the realms of possibility that he was a double agent.

The enclosed world of Longwood is shrouded in an atmosphere of cheating and duplicity. The rooms that lead into each other, the dark corridors, this complex domain with its sheds, outhouses and store-rooms lend themselves to intrigue, whispered asides and secret meetings. Several aspects of the Empire left their mark on

Longwood: its police and roughneck soldiers, its spying, its brusque manners like those of troops on campaign, its disdain for comfort and love of secrecy.

Napoleon acts in the wings while Bertrand and Montholon have the task of officially responding to the English. The convict may well be in the prompter's box, but he's nonetheless the director. "Either I give the orders or I say nothing." In actual fact he does both. The role he has given himself must be a silent one, but the ex-"Jupiter-Scapin" directs the gestures, the attitudes and even the facial expressions of his little company.[4]

There is something of the actor in Napoleon's behaviour when he faces Hudson Lowe at their first meeting. It's obvious that the prisoner wants to impress his keeper. When the Governor is introduced, Napoleon says nothing. A disconcerted Hudson Lowe ventures to begin the conversation himself. The two men speak in Italian, which makes the meeting seem even stranger.

Hudson Lowe knows Corsica well. He fought the French there and even lived for a while in a house owned by Letizia Bonaparte, which had been requisitioned by the English. In 1799 he went to Minorca in the Balearic Islands to instruct Corsican refugees hostile to the French. These recruits formed the Royal Corsican Rangers whom he took with him to Egypt. After the Capri affair, when he was duped by the French, he thought of leaving the Army, but in the end decided to take part in the conquest of the islands of Ischia and Provida. After the abdication, he is the one chosen to take the news to London. At the beginning of the Hundred Days, he is one of the Duke of Wellington's staff officers. He does not take part in the battle of Waterloo and has to be satisfied with entering Marseilles as administrator. It's here that he learns he has been appointed Governor of St Helena and Napoleon's jailer.

The two men are face-to-face. There are no witnesses. As usual, Napoleon tries to find out the lie of the land, changing from one subject to another, asking apparently incongruous questions. He wants to know whom he is dealing with. He asks the former chief of the Corsican Rangers what he thinks of the inhabitants of his island. Is he married? What is his service record? And what about Egypt? Always that tension, that feverish mind searching for a clue. Get to know your opponent from a look, a comment, perhaps even a smell – smells can be revealing. Did he sense something suspect about Hudson Lowe? Napoleon, who usually penetrates the surface and quickly sees the true nature of people, has difficulty in measuring the man's "draught" – a nautical expression he often uses. The first of the modern leaders, he needs to quantify, size up, take people's measure. After Hudson Lowe leaves, he merely states: "This new Governor says very little, but he seems polite."

<h1 style="text-align:center">3</h1>

I inspect the fireplace where the captive used to stand when he received visitors. A black marble mantelpiece, the empty grate carefully polished: no fire has been lit there for ages. Besides, it would do no good in such a damp atmosphere. Nonetheless, the fireplace is not completely dead. Air drawn in from outside makes it hum. I bend down to look at the flue. A sulphur yellow light appears at the top, which has wire netting across it.

"So, you think that the chimneys at Longwood are pure decoration?"

A man is standing in front of me in the doorway that leads to the dining room. I don't really know whether he's making a face or joking. His half smile – if it is a smile – is accentuated by the cigar in his mouth. He stands there with his hands in his pockets, staring at the fireplace. His cold expression is at odds with his ironic attitude. The smoke, which makes him screw up his eyes, gives him the look of an inquisitor.

"Are you interested in chimneys? No doubt you know that a good or an evil spirit inhabits each chimney. It all depends. Did you realize that some smoked for no apparent reason?"

"It's probably because of the goblin," I reply facetiously.

"You don't believe those stories, do you?

"Yes I do. I imagine that's why you have wire mesh over the top of the chimney!"

"There's wire over the flues because of the mynah birds. They are the second plague on the island after the termites. In Napoleon's time the chimneys smoked atrociously. There was never enough wood or coal. You know of course that the Emperor couldn't stand the smell of coal."

"I didn't know that . . . So, do you think that spirits still haunt Longwood?"

"Don't you know about the Dane's ghost?"

"The Dane's ghost? I've never heard of it!"

"My dear sir," he mutters, "you must read the *Memories* of Mme de Montholon."

That's a bad mark against me! I've read most of the first-hand accounts, but not Albine de Montholon's. I try to find out more about her ghost. The man in the doorway pretends not to hear. He has lost interest in me. He hasn't smiled once.

A smile would obviously indicate a willingness to make contact, and he doesn't want that. There is something enigmatic in his nonchalant manner, at odds with his abrupt tone of voice and tense gestures. He is nearly always tight-lipped, even when he speaks.

"You must be Gilbert Martineau."

He agrees coldly. My question seems to have made him even gloomier. As I ask him a question about the white marble bust of Napoleon in front of me, he interrupts.

"Please. Don't ask me anything. I no longer have any official function here. You should ask my son. I don't exist any more."

"But I'm not after an interview. Is it such an imposition to ask you for a piece of information?"

"Don't insist."

He turns his back on me.

The Longwood bear lives up to his reputation. His publisher in Paris had warned me: "He's difficult to approach, you'll see."[5] I had questioned him about his author. He could not understand why he had withdrawn from the world: "To tell the truth, I know very little about him. Perhaps he wanted to live out the end of the epic in the original setting. He's the shyest author imaginable. He couldn't care less about the print runs of his books or whether they're successful or not. His biography of Pauline de Bonaparte sold well. He's not at all jealous of the success enjoyed by comparable historians like André Castelot or Alain Decaux."

His books on Napoleon's family do not present any new revelations, but the account is well written and the characters vividly portrayed. But there's another Martineau, more scholarly and also more subtle: he is the chronicler of St Helena, who has succeeded in describing the drama of Napoleon's captivity from the inside. A third Martineau is hidden behind the biography of Byron. *La Malédiction du génie* is a lofty, sombre book.[6] You feel the fascination of the author for the man who was the dark angel of English poetry. "His great strength was not to believe in happiness," he writes.

Martineau left Paris for good in 1956 to take up residence with his parents on St Helena. He arrived at just the right moment. The buildings at Longwood had only just been restored. When George VI had visited St Helena, a British possession, he was disturbed by the dilapidated state of the property, which had been ravaged by termites. A French consular clerk had acted as caretaker, but he had left the island. A retired British army officer had then been put in charge of looking after the house. Cut to the quick, our country suddenly realized that this enclave was French and moreover that it would be humiliating to leave the matter in the hands of the Emperor's former executioners. It was important to appoint a person who was acceptable to the British authorities – the French enclave comes under our Consulate General in London. Gilbert Martineau, an ex-naval officer, was chosen through the intervention of President Vincent Auriol and the support of Prince Philip, Duke of Edinburgh. Martineau had known the Queen's future husband when he was studying Latin and Greek at Eton. "His perfect command of English and British society, which had led to his appointment, greatly facilitated the taking up of his post, and for the first time perhaps since the terrible exile, the French and English lived together in harmony."[7]

Martineau has lived in this mysterious domain for forty years. What has he seen? What has he heard? The wind that makes the loose windows of his deep cello voice gently vibrate must tell strange things.

This house holds a secret . . . It seems to float in a state that is neither the present nor the past. It's a suspension. At Longwood time seems to stop for a moment, as if it wanted to make a pause in its course. I sense movements of energy, as if spreading out from an unknown source. At times I feel caught in a trap. The light, the sounds and the smells of Longwood have a quality that becomes more and more insidious.

Gilbert Martineau has disappeared down the end of a corridor. I can hear the creaking of the floor and the squeaking of new leather that the man leaves behind him.

The pictures in the drawing room are lit by a strange light. The glass in the frames begins to shine. On the walls, the soldiers of the Italian army and the Marie-Louises whom Napoleon passes in review at Montereau come to life. The blaze of light sweeps through the drawing room. History floods into the room. The people in the pictures come down from their frames; the cortège of soldiers grows bigger as they emerge from the shadows. The wind chants the death march with a chorus of moans. A shadow moves across the light, then everything goes dark. The rusty marks made by the damp are back where they were on the pictures. All that remains is the dark, heavy smell of stagnant water and tuberose, which goes to your head and has an intoxicating effect in the suffocating afternoon heat.

The historian Octave Aubry was not a particularly impressionable person. When he visited Longwood in the 1930s, the pilgrimage affected him so profoundly that he made this unusual confession in the first pages of his book: "I saw his ghost. I saw him rise up behind those flat doors, in those cramped rooms . . . I heard him speak, talking about his life to those very few, last faithful followers."[8] Was it the literary device of a historian in the grip of a powerful emotion? We can't know. Nevertheless, Octave Aubry describes a phenomenon that I have just experienced: the sensation of time not regained, but reversed, *going backwards*. Yesterday I had rather naïvely evoked a return to the past. And it was indeed a reversal: I discover an unknown facet of time, a rerouting, a kind of change in destination. This new orientation reveals not the opposite side of time, but its reverse side, like the wrong side of a material that is less bright than the right side.

4

Napoleon died on 5 May 1821 in this room where I met Gilbert Martineau. What a contrast between the doll's-house drawing room and Chateaubriand's famous comment: "He gave up to God the most powerful breath of life that ever animated human clay." At sunset, in the presence of his last faithful followers, he breathes his last in the camp bed he had at Austerlitz, mumbling these words: "Army, head of the army . . . Josephine." He is 51. At that precise moment, his valet Marchand stops the clock in the drawing room. It shows 5.49. When his life was drawing to a close, the sick man had been carried into this room, which was bigger and more airy than the small bedroom.

There is a copper plaque screwed to the floor between the two windows where the bed had been placed: *The Emperor died here on 5 May 1821*. A wreath of dried flowers lies on the ground. They are immortelles, everlastings. The flower that symbolized Napoleon's captivity is still there all around Longwood. It's the flower of mercy, symbol of generosity and sensitivity. An admirer of Napoleon, Lady Holland, had some English seedlings sent to him to make his captivity a little easier and remind him of his native Corsica.

The space is roped off to keep people out. It's the only shrine in the house. A reproduction of the death mask made by Antommarchi, the last doctor to care for the Emperor, is displayed in the middle of the area. On this bronze cast, the face is black with the bridge of the nose slightly curved. The emaciated features remind one of Pascal's mask. He looks like a Saint-Sulpician holy picture with an effusive, almost obscene expression of suffering and a hint of mawkishness.[9] It's nonetheless the same moulding as the one in the Musée de l'Armée in Paris, but the colour changes everything. The dark brown metal makes the face look as though it's grimacing and gives the features such an other-worldly expression that it becomes almost comical. Those who were there assert that after Napoleon died his face looked younger. "The slightly contracted mouth gave his face a contented look. He seemed no more than thirty," writes Marchand.

On the wall between the two windows hangs Steuben's engraving describing the death scene itself in minute detail. Telescoping time in that disturbing Longwood way, it joins past and present in a perfect illusion.

I can't take my eyes off the death mask. The muscles of the mouth still seem distorted. The grimacing smile makes one think of the cold shiver on the faces of the dying in German Renaissance art. And then there's the head, set on the bronze cushion with its folds and the tassel, which is intended to give the whole thing an air of nobility.

Sometimes the bronze shines, reflecting the changing light from outside. Then the features of the face quiver, the head seems to awaken, the forehead and the cheeks gleam as if sweat were running down them.

The pressure of the clouds has been released at last. Great drops of rain as dense as hailstones hit the ground, spreading a light puff of steam. The gardeners have taken shelter under the veranda. Mist has crept over the garden. Everything perspires: grasses, plants, objects and humans. The rain and the scorching heat send into the air a pungent smell of mud and rotting vegetation mixed with a slightly medicinal hothouse perfume.

The atmosphere is too oppressive inside the house. I cross the drawing room, nearly knocking over the two globes in the billiard room. The gardeners who were looking pensively at the falling rain suddenly move away. The water has blackened the cinerarias in the garden.

The two men have put jute sacks on their heads like hoods. Leaning on their picks, they look like two soldier monks guarding the front of a castle in the mist.

1. Author of the brilliant *Napoléon à Sainte-Hélène* (Libraire académique Perrin).

2. *Autour de Sainte-Hélène* (Ollendorff).

3. A pilgrim to St Helena managed to buy the eagle after I left the island.

4. Abbé de Pradt.

5. Yvon Chotard, former managing director of Éditions France-Empire.

6. *La Malédiction du génie* [*The Curse of Genius*] (Tallendier).

7. Jacques Jourquin in *Le Souvenir napoléonien*, no. 403.

8. *Sainte-Hélène*, vol. 1: *La Captivité de Napoléon*.

9. A reference to the highly coloured, idealized holy pictures sold in the religious art shops in the district around the church of Saint-Sulpice in Paris. [Tr.]

The Fourth Day

I

ON 30 APRIL, HUDSON LOWE IS USHERED INTO NAPOLEON'S
house for the second time. The Emperor has a cold and receives him
in his bedroom. Unshaven and wearing a dressing gown, the captive
looks disgruntled. The new jailer gets on his nerves. Hasn't he
laid down new rules, imposed extra restrictions? He has insisted on
Napoleon's companions and servants making a written undertaking:
they must accept the same living conditions as their master or leave
Longwood. "Everything here exudes deadly boredom. The location
is unpleasant and unhealthy; there is no water and this part of the
island is deserted," the prisoner complains.

As usual he chooses to attack so that he can measure the famous
"draught" of the man he is speaking to. Lowe quibbles, avoiding
controversial discussion. Napoleon takes this cautious refusal to
engage in combat as a sign. Consequently he knows from the
beginning what kind of a man he is dealing with. After that second
meeting, everything has been said. "What an ignoble, sinister face
the Governor has. I have never met anything like it in the whole
of my life. Being left alone in the company of a man like that would
be enough to put one off one's cup of coffee," he confides to Las
Cases. The look of the man obviously does not appeal to him. All
those who were there were struck by the strange features of this
Cerberus with his pointed, freckle-covered face, his large forehead,

long nose, thin lips and red hair. As his temperament is stubborn, his personality indecisive and his character authoritarian, he is a mass of contradictions and never gives a clear answer to anything. The Emperor is somewhat frustrated. He would have liked to catch the expression on the person's face the moment he attacked him, but night had just fallen and it was no longer possible to make out anything in the room. "And so, when I tried to study the expressions on his face to find out what impression I was making at that moment," he confides to Las Cases, "it was quite useless."

Hudson Lowe, who has already talked to Montholon and Las Cases, is so insincere that he even praises the beauty of the site. The two men protest indignantly: the climate is frightfully hot and there are no trees to give shade. "'We shall plant some,' he told us. What a dreadful thing to say!" Las Cases complains. This way of seeing the future, as if the prisoner was going to spend the rest of his life on St Helena, seems to have depressed Napoleon. He still has wild hopes of the great powers changing their attitude to him, of returning to Europe perhaps . . . The captive shows that the blow has struck home. He stays shut up in his bedroom, as he always does when he is in the doldrums. He does not like people to see him unhappy.

As he did yesterday, Michel Martineau has allowed me to walk around Longwood as I please. I'm sitting in Napoleon's small bedroom, where he stayed for days or even weeks on end when he felt depressed. I try to work out the dimensions of the cell: not more than 16 square metres. I think I have a better understanding now of the prisoner's sadness and loneliness. In everything there is a feeling of being cramped, of lamely trying to keep up rank and appearances, even to the point of near destitution.

A tropical dullness added to this shabbiness gives the whole place a dismal air, an oppressive, grey chill. "One needs to go to sleep and not wake up for a year or two," he declares to Gourgaud. The impatient demi-god, who in times gone by warned him, "I am ready to give you anything but time", is now bowed down by the accumulation of days. "The only thing we have too much of here is time," he sighs.

The eternity of the moment . . . Every prisoner in the world fights against the way time stretches out endlessly. The dry dusty smell of this slow disintegration still lingers in the bedroom. Every room in Longwood has its particular smell. Where does it come from? The wood in the floor can't explain it all. One is not always aware of these changes. Sometimes a rainbow of odours suddenly spreads out like some meteorological phenomenon. Could it be the iridescence of memory or the refraction of the past? These scents are so intoxicating that it takes hours for them to disappear from one's nostrils.

All exiles are the same. Far from palaces and the bright show of power, the retreats of the great seem eternally dark, bitter, uncomfortable places. I found the same gloomy dignity at La Boisserie, an austere and badly laid-out house. In the lonely Champagne countryside, I felt the same sadness and the same dull pain of waiting. General de Gaulle playing patience and talking at length is a Longwoodian figure.

"Our days were characterless and colourless, and the memories they left are equally vague," Las Cases writes on 25 February 1816. "He was out of sorts and retired early", he notes on 28 March. "At dinner the Emperor was sad and silent: he was out of sorts" (14 April). "He said he had felt languid, heavy and sick at heart all day" (1 September). When it is filled with lassitude and melancholy, Longwood is like the court of King Pétaud, a house in which everyone wants to give orders and speak at the same time.[1] When that happens, the downcast monarch can no longer manage to keep control over his squabbling little band.

The most insufferable of them all is without any doubt Gaspard Gourgaud. This artilleryman and graduate of the École

Polytechnique had been raised to the title of baron in 1812 for being the first person in the Kremlin to discover the mine intended to blow up the staff headquarters of the Grand Army. He was promoted *in extremis* to brigade general after Waterloo. It was only at the last moment that he wrested permission from the authorities to follow Napoleon to St Helena. He idolizes the great man, but his jealousy poisons the atmosphere during Napoleon's captivity. Although he is very punctilious about etiquette and the way he should be addressed, the Emperor tolerates this companion's extravagant behaviour with an indulgence that is difficult to explain. The impulsive, argumentative Gourgaud seems to tyrannize the object of his veneration.

He comes out in his journal as being a fairly straightforward person. Gourgaud is the opposite of Las Cases. He describes his hero as he is and not the way the legend dictates: a man who is both egotistical and patient, sometimes overtaken by events, often helpless before the impertinence of his former senior aide-de-camp. Gourgaud enjoys rebuffing and contradicting the Emperor. The relationship between them is a series of quarrels and reconciliations. "His Majesty is angry. So am I. He is calming down. I am not speaking" (23 January 1816). On St Helena, not speaking is the daily practice of bored people. One day Gourgaud takes the liberty of questioning one of Napoleon's assertions. The Emperor maintains that he could have reversed the situation if he had remained at the head of the army in Russia.

"Pardon me, Sire, it was too late."

"Do you think that *I* could not have held out at Vilna?"

"No, Sire."

On another occasion Gourgaud rebukes the Emperor, who is dictating the Italian campaign. Quite out of the blue, he points out that Napoleon is repeating himself too much (2 June). It sometimes happens that when Napoleon wants to make peace, Gourgaud continues to sulk.

"Are you still suffering from diarrhoea?"

"No, Sire" (19 July).

Quick-tempered and touchy as he is, Gourgaud detests Las Cases, but loathes the Montholon couple even more. He is a man continually frustrated. He would like to have been the prisoner's sole confidant. One day Napoleon exclaims in exasperation: "You thought that by coming here you would be my friend. I am friend to no one." Making his meaning quite plain, the former Caesar adds: "I have to be the centre" (25 December 1816). It's a pathetic admission, coming from a king without a crown wanting to reign alone on his wretched little farm over two soldiers and their wives, a maladjusted bachelor and a smooth-mannered former émigré.

2

Gourgaud and Napoleon are there in front of me. The Emperor, who looks untidy, has a red madras handkerchief tied round his head. His right hand is unceremoniously placed inside the front flap of his trousers while the left is holding a page. The Emperor is thoughtful, his eyes are a little sad, his lips pursed and he has a growth of beard on his chin. Napoleon is about to speak. He is concentrating, about to defy time and revive former glory. Nonetheless there is a hint of melancholy in that look. Gourgaud is waiting, pen poised, ready to record the imperial words. The expression on his face is assiduous and a bit conceited. He is alone with his master! How happy he is, and how important!

This scene, painted by Steuben, hangs on the wall between the two windows. Once again I recognized the subtle hand of the magician at work. Longwood is full of these tricks. A facetious sorcerer devotes himself to producing these effects of bringing the past

and present face-to-face. The engraving is placed on the wall that is portrayed . . . in the engraving.

Also placed opposite each other are the busts of Marie-Louise – on the fireplace – and Josephine. The two wives look at each other like china dogs in their husband's tiny bedroom. Josephine seems a little mischievous as she stares at her rival. This impression is probably due to that impish nose, which gives her face a piquant look. The Hapsburg woman's face is expressionless. The protruding eyes make her look slightly stupid.

Napoleon takes his breakfast on the little table and washes in front of the window. The sofa is placed perpendicular to the fireplace, as it used to be. The captive likes to lie down there to read. He seems to be free, master in his own house. Contrary to ordinary prisoners, he can organize his days as the mood takes him. Is Longwood really a prison? Approximately a thousand soldiers are permanently stationed in the vicinity at Deadwood to keep watch over the house. Napoleon can go where he wishes, within a perimeter of about seven kilometres, but at sunset sentries surround the buildings until dawn. They never take their eyes off Longwood, standing under the windows at intervals of 15 metres. Another limit, with a circumference of about 20 kilometres, encircles the first area. The Emperor can move freely within it, but may encounter patrols with orders to keep watch over him. A British aide-de-camp who lives permanently at Longwood must personally check twice a day that Bonaparte is present.

However, on 3 January 1816, he leaves the regulation area to visit Sandy Bay on the south of the island. It is one of his only excursions outside the perimeter of Longwood. Three days later, giving the English aide-de-camp the slip, he goes with Gourgaud as far as Rock Rose Hill, a point about a mile from the sea. This little escape on 6 January is still something of a mystery. Did Napoleon want to put the English surveillance system to the test? It's probably a unique moment in his captivity: the two men are alone, and at that moment the panic-stricken English have no idea where Bonaparte is. The sea is close by; no sign of a sentry or battery of artillery. The prisoner pensively scans the horizon. The coast of Africa is 2,000 kilometres away and America 3,000. Perhaps at that moment he felt even more confined than at Longwood. Facing the limitless ocean he suddenly realizes the nature of the prison where he is confined, not by a lack of space but by an excess of it. "You don't try to escape from a prison without walls," the island's chief of police had told me.

Napoleon gives a sign to return to Longwood. The English will never forgive him for that moment. He has crossed a forbidden line. He has been at an interface, on the surface that separates two states of being, neither really free nor truly set free. There is no doubt that much of the harassment he encountered later originated from this break out.

Did the prisoner ever have any plans to escape? This is a question about Napoleon's captivity that still has not been satisfactorily explained. In any case, although his supporters in America were not idle, they had not managed to coordinate their efforts and act as one.

In 1816 there are 2,784 men in the St Helena garrison. Hudson Lowe has at his command a squadron of three frigates, two armed ships and six brigs continuously cruising around the island. Any ship approaching St Helena is immediately located and can only come into shore after receiving permission from the authorities. The prisoner cannot receive visitors without an authorization from the Governor, nor send or receive letters that have not been censored by the English. They deny him his title of Emperor. On St Helena, he is simply General Bonaparte.

One day when Hudson Lowe sends him a letter under that name, the Emperor returns it to him with this comment: "I have had no further news of this general since the Battle of the Pyramids." This is how Las Cases sums up the situation in 1816: "The Emperor keeps everyone and everything around him in order, and assumes the attitude of dignity oppressed by force; he occupies the moral high ground."

The prisoner has decided once and for all to shut himself in his prison. He even goes so far as to confess to Gourgaud that if they gave him the whole island, he would have no desire to go any further. "After a time everyone would have seen me, and that would not have as great an effect as staying here, as I do now." He has no wish to mollify Hudson Lowe. "There can be no social contact between a jailer and his prisoner," he confides to Bertrand.

The striking thing in this room, as in the rest of the house, is the lack of *grandeur*. It's the dwelling of a petty bourgeois, living from hand to mouth. He tries to create the illusion of it with his few remaining possessions, remains of past splendour ("the salvage from the wreck of his family and his empire," as Lord Rosebery puts it). There's an element of a student's study in the basic decor which the servants have tried to transform with whatever is at hand. Even the Emperor sometimes turns his hand to making something. One day he cuts out illustrations of birds from a big book. "He had them put on the pelmet over the curtain in his study. He also detached a large eagle from the same volume, but did not cut it out. He had that put over his desk," Ali reports. The fallen monarch is thus reduced to tearing the imperial bird out of an album. Longwood sullies every gesture and turns the free flow of memory into a meaningless mire.

There are, of course, Napoleon's dictations. But this pilgrimage into the past is nearly always disillusioned and painful. One only has to read the accounts of Las Cases or Gourgaud to realize that this exercise is the manifestation of an anguish that seeks relief in a profusion of detail. Napoleon devotes himself to re-establishing, repairing and restoring. There's a Sheherazade side to him. He has to relate and bring to life the thousand and one nights of his reign in order to delay the fatal denouement. Otherwise he will perish.

Prisoners have to tell themselves stories if they are not to give way to despair. Napoleon has scarcely any close relationship with the living now and the only one he wishes to establish is with his memories. It's Jacob's Ladder reaching not to the heavens but to the depths. The Grand Empire, Europe united under his sceptre, his brothers and sisters made kings and queens, all these successes are nothing but promises of future disaster, just so many steps leading down into the abyss. It is the opposite of Jacob's dream, which promised a long posterity, giving birth to a people and ultimately a nation.

Napoleon, who likes to comment on the slightest episode in his life, only twice mentions his dreams. The first he tells only to his valet Marchand. Strangely enough, what he saw concerns his descendants. One night he dreamed of Marie-Louise and his son, whom she was holding by the hand. "She looked young, as she was when I saw her at Compiègne. I took her in my arms, but try as I might to hold her fast, I felt her slipping away from me, and when I tried to embrace her again, everything had disappeared and I awoke."

"I felt her slipping away from me": the fear of desertion, of downfall! On St Helena there is only one thing he fears: that his companions might leave him. On 15 July 1816, Gourgaud writes in his usual forthright style: "If we all left, His Majesty would have to kill himself." It's Gourgaud who mentions the other dream told by the Emperor in which "he killed an English hussar who charged at him".

Napoleon always was a fatalist. On 2 September 1816, when recalling the height of his reign, he confesses to Las Cases: "I saw the fatal hour coming quite clearly. My star was waning, I could feel the reins slipping from my grasp, and there was nothing I could do about it." It was a foresight of disaster, which contrasts with the admirable phrase from the early years when he was general of the army in Italy at 25: "I could already see the world receding beneath me, as if I was being carried aloft in the air" (a confidence, once again, to Gourgaud, 1817). This snapshot image has an almost Stendhalian quality about it: the fusion of lucidity and dream leaves such a luminous impression in one's mind. It flashes across the dismal days and suddenly lights up the dull, heavy atmosphere of

Longwood. Everything is contained in that vision. The willingness to take risks, limitless happiness spread out before him, adventure's great ride. Pegasus takes flight, the bit is between his teeth, and fate bolts into the future . . . "I felt the reins slip from my grasp, and there was nothing I could do about it." Hadn't he one day said to Las Cases "One can give an initial impetus to events, but later they drag you in their wake"?

Pegasus, born from the blood of Medusa, whose gaze always haunts the dark room. Pegasus-Medusa, the beginning and the end, inspiration and expiration.

In these moments of sincerity, he no longer plays hide-and-seek with his memory. Nevertheless, he rarely says *mea culpa*. If truth conflicts with his glory, he chooses glory. When he recalls his failures, he engages not in self-criticism, but in a strange game of finding the error. He looks for the missing piece, the detail that put him in a difficult position. On the subject of Waterloo, for example, he says: "Everything failed me only after everything had succeeded." But where did he fail? The real question that should be asked is "Why am I here?"

This is the room where he tried to work out the puzzle. He devoted himself to letting the light of memory into this dark room, this *camera obscura*. The shutters are lowered and the curtains drawn. One single band of light cuts across the darkened wall. The sharp, brilliant ray through the lens hole enters the chamber and forms an image, a mysterious shadow that grows bigger as the object moves away from the opening. Is it a cloud, a tree in the garden, the silhouette of a man, a bird? The shimmering point of light is turned on to the black grate in the fireplace.

"He was in his bedroom. The wood fire gave his face the strangest and most melancholy expression," writes O'Meara, his doctor. The word "melancholy" is used relatively rarely by those who wrote memoirs of St Helena. Gourgaud uses it occasionally: "Boredom, melancholy" (11 July 1816). Is there a hint of romanticism in this comment? Napoleon was a great admirer of the poems of Ossian, those Celtic ballads full of mists and howling winds. Here on the Longwood plateau, he himself faced nature's fury. The captive who hated the fog and the trade wind that constantly battered his prison, found himself in the heart of a countryside that bore some resemblance to the wild, craggy images of the romantic imagination. But neither that kind of melancholy nor the gothic novel atmosphere of the desolate house was of any interest to the prisoner. The melancholy Napoleon experienced hides a much earlier sorrow. "Surrounded by men but always alone, I leave them to come and dream alone and give myself up to the intensity of my melancholy. What direction has it taken today? It has turned towards death." These lines were written in 1786, when he was still a lieutenant.

On St Helena, periods of euphoria are followed by periods of depression. The smallest thing is often enough to revive his spirits. On a fine day he once suddenly said to Gourgaud, beaming with joy: "Could that be a sign that happiness is returning?" Happiness appears only fleetingly in his practice of recalling the past. The building of the legend forbade it. Bonaparte never sought happiness; he was intent on glory. Aristotle affirms that "all exceptional beings are melancholy". Napoleon is doubly so on St Helena because he has lost everything and he keeps recalling the past. He is dispossessed, but of what? Of power, honours? That would be too simple an answer. He suffers from something vague and unnameable, a call, a mystery that he can never identify. This inability to come close to the secret is evident in the dictations and the interminable evenings at Longwood. What is he afraid of? Probably disintegration. He is obsessed by it. He prowls around it, fearful that he might slowly dwindle away and be destroyed from within. The struggle against fragmentation is the battle all prisoners fight. Weary of resisting, the prisoner of Longwood will finally capitulate little by little, wishing for death in a way that is very like suicide.

Napoleon incessantly proclaims that he is the only one really suffering. He is fond of pointing out to Bertrand, Las Cases, Montholon and Gourgaud that they are not really prisoners. All of these people have sentenced themselves to exile, but they had a choice, they know why they are there. He alone is a victim. He only uses the word "we" derisively to exclude himself. When his companions complain, he exclaims: "We are very happy here: we can ride, we eat well, we may leave whenever we wish, we are well received everywhere and covered in glory." He is quite clearly accusing his companions of depriving him of his suffering. "I am the only unhappy one, firstly for having fallen from such heights, and then for not being able to go about as you do without an escort."

The fact that they have come with him to be able to tell the world later of his decline and fall has not escaped him. In the evening after dinner they listen to him prophesying and declaiming Voltaire's tragedy, *Zaïre*. This is such a tiresome exercise that one day Gourgaud and Mme de Montholon decide to hide the book. There is only one thing they are really eager to do: get back to their rooms to write down what they have heard. They don't want to miss a scrap. "His Majesty says that we cannot talk any more because we are keeping journals about everything," Gourgaud remarks. The great man who thinks and dreams out loud says one thing and also its opposite. St Helena is a story of different points of view. The perspective often changes and the viewpoint is transformed. The four evangelists religiously record all the nonsense they hear. They are soldiers after all, and not men of letters.

There are few references to the *Bouvard et Pécuchet* aspect of this forced retirement.[2] The little group spends its time at Longwood doing experiments. The former demi-god and his companions are fascinated for weeks by an ice-cream-making machine sent from England. Then they tire of it and take up another occupation. The

Emperor and Gourgaud amuse themselves for several weeks trying to work out the rate of flow of the Nile. On another occasion they make estimates of the use of fire pumps in the defence of fortified towns. They love calculations. Napoleon becomes enthusiastic about botany and gardening. However the periods of excitement do not last long. He is a soldier who loves to inspect, *to review*. He needs to examine things in succession and then turn his back on them, as during the time of the Grand Empire, when he inspected the troops. It's also his way of *cutting things short*.

In the evenings at Longwood, they solemnly converse on such subjects as love, God, matter, the French language, fate . . . The eyewitnesses dig each other in the ribs to stop bursting out laughing. "I sat through the *Dialogues of the Dead*," Albine de Montholon says in jest.[3] Napoleon quite seriously asks Gourgaud to reorganize the French artillery. One day the captive with nothing to do takes it into his head to reform the infantry. He planned down to the smallest detail, for example allocating pieces of iron to each company so that they could cook wheat pancakes. But the Emperor and Gourgaud quibble about a detail and the reform of the infantry stays on the drawing-board.

These fanciful projects are part of a game played by the strategist and his companions. A remark made by Grand Marshal Bertrand is a case in point: "The Emperor dictates a plan to organize the Army to General Gourgaud, who is to give it to the Grand Marshal. Gourgaud laughs as he says to Mme Bertrand: 'I didn't know that we were beginning a campaign. We are organizing the Army'."

Action is the only thing that eases his anguish. However, useless missions, incursions into science, which are nothing more than lost expeditions, metaphysics or the art of warfare, have nothing to do with action. They are nothing but abortive raids, battles with no fighting, a way of passing the time. They all know it, beginning with the main person concerned.

Napoleon has this attractive quality: he is never fooled. He always goes straight to the point, and bluntly. Even though he is sometimes a victim of self-deception, his clear-mindedness always wins through in the end. Longwood is the wrong side of the tapestry. Nonetheless, the side that shows the weave and the frame also helps us to understand the central motif. At Longwood the artist has nothing more to lose; he explains his technique and his framework. The colours of the part he shows are brilliant and just as good as the right side. On the subject of his past power, doesn't he maintain that "a throne is only a board lined with velvet"? He often repeats that "a general should be a trickster". The fact that he has no illusions makes these outpourings rather sad. There are days when Napoleon doesn't seem able to put his thoughts together. He keeps trotting out the remark, "I should have died at the Moskowa." The famous molten flow of thought and action that used to set all in its path ablaze is now directed towards domestic matters. The monotonous, repetitive words hang in the air above the ravages of memory. It is then that recollection loses its harmony, disintegrating into a hubbub that the scribes later try to put into some kind of order. They manage to do it, but at the cost of truth. In the last years of Napoleon's captivity, however, Bertrand seems to faithfully record Napoleon's erratic, disorganized discourse.

How does one recapture the quintessence of a particular moment? "Now at this moment, while I'm speaking to you, I'm casting my mind back to the Tuileries. I can see it; I can see Paris," he explains to Gourgaud. All things considered, it's not happiness that he feels nostalgia for, but exceptional moments, perfect moments. He concentrates above all on time in its pure state, on the unique instant, on intermittence. He is not really sure when he was happy. He racks his brains . . . "When do you think?" he asks his entourage. This rather mocking way of making others assess his past happiness is

amusing. Gourgaud replies: " Your marriage to Marie-Louise." Mme
de Montholon: "When you were First Consul." Bertrand: "The birth
of the King of Rome." And his own opinion? "Perhaps it's at Tilsit.
I had just been through trials and tribulations, at Eylau, among
others, and I was now victorious, dictating laws, with emperors and
kings paying court to me" (May 1817).

Eylau: the name Napoleon does not want to speak. It's a forbidden subject, a censored battle, probably because that carnage spells
the "beginning of the end". During one of the evening conversations when they rewrite history, Bertrand maintains that "what
had impressed him most in the Emperor's life was the time at
Eylau, when alone with a few of his staff officers he found himself
almost struck by a column of four to five thousand Russians." In
fact, Napoleon came very close to being captured. "It was more
than time, the Emperor had not moved, everything around him had
trembled," Bertrand relates.

Usually a word or an allusion is enough to start an almost unstoppable flow of memories – he is quite capable of talking for three
or four hours at a stretch. But curiously enough, this reminder of
Eylau falls completely flat. Las Cases mentions it without any
commentary: "The Emperor had listened to this story without
making any comment."

That silence is revealing. Eylau is the premonitory battle. The
course of its development anticipates the disaster of Waterloo. In
an act unprecedented in the history of the Empire, Napoleon
remains on the battlefield for a week, as if to show the world that
he has now established this bloody victory as his.

Eylau is the beginning of the enigma, the origin of his failure.
Is that why he is reluctant to speak of it? Although he is verbose
about his reign, his loves, the conduct of his battles, Napoleon
particularly evades the great confrontation of 8 February 1807. He
hardly mentions Friedland, the battle that followed three months

later, which nonetheless gloriously avenged the bloody engagement at Eylau. They are too closely linked.

The exposés on St Helena are also useful for what they leave out, for what they don't say. Napoleon is always interrupting the chronology of events. He has always had a liking for abrupt changes of subject and a talent for compressed turns of phrase. He has little appreciation of transitions or intermediary ideas, hence his jerky speech and fragmented images. This way of tuning in, of zapping from one memory to another, sometimes gives his dictations a disjointed style that is very modern. It's an interrupted flow that is echoed in the movement of Las Cases's *Memoirs of St Helena*. In his memoirs, past and present become confused (as they do in Chateaubriand's *Memoirs from Beyond the Grave*). This feeling for condensation, for the moment that starts off the treasure hunt, is quite fascinating. It's a puzzle that the defeated emperor tries to solve through memory. The resonance of a series of images, words or dates evokes a hidden content that he must discover. Hudson Lowe's vexations are linked to the evacuation of Moscow. Longwood's climate triggers an image: the sky of his native Corsica, which in turn leads to a detail about Pascal Paoli, the independence hero, then a digression about the family. Finally, power . . . Like Chateaubriand, Napoleon can well exclaim: "Oh memories! You pierce the heart like a sword!" Napoleon's dictations progress through bouts of reverie, soul stirring, regret, and ecstasy. There lies within him a painter who can never again hold a brush, a sculptor who has lost his clay. "I love power, but I love it as an artist."

This heartrending cry rings through the tomb that is Longwood. Damp trickles down the walls. Rats scratch about everywhere over his head. Buried under the weight of past deeds, he shouts himself hoarse in his hut in the tropics: "It's not weakness but strength that is suffocating me. It's life that is killing me!"

3

The rain dripping off the roof gently hits the ground in the garden. An endless, monotonous whispering sound spreads gloomily through the small bedroom. A soft, enervating drizzle has settled over Longwood. It's neither rain nor mist but a kind of sticky floating wall that moves sluggishly in whitish banks. The water vapour is so dense that the saturated air seems to have liquified.

The English had chosen the place well. Longwood is a prison of clouds, a cell in the air. In this jail, the prisoner enjoys all the outward signs of freedom: the limitless ocean on the horizon, the open plateau, a view up towards the highest point on the island, Diana's Peak. Nevertheless, the air and sky isolate and confine as surely as a cell. "I hate this Longwood, this *vento agro*," grumbles the Emperor. Strangely enough, when he complains of the climate he uses his native language – his doctor O'Meara's memoirs are full of Italian words. He calls St Helena the *isola maladetta*.

Michel Martineau, who was working with the gardeners, suddenly appears in Napoleon's bedroom, secateurs in hand. I really like this familiarity of the past with the present. The Martineaus make the dwelling a mellower place. In the case of the present consul, the gardens are his life's work. He draws his artist's inspiration there.

"Tropical flowers are brilliant, but they have no perfume. The roses are wonderful here, but there's no perfume. The only things that have a strong scent are the Persian lilacs and the ginger plants. It's the flowers at Longwood that made me want to paint."

"Who taught you?"

"No one. In the beginning there was a lot of trial and error."

"You'd never held a brush before coming to St Helena?"

"Never. Perhaps it's the fear of boredom that forced me to paint. After living at Longwood for two years, I told myself that I had to find an occupation. It's through working in the gardens that I had the idea of depicting the flowers growing in them. Without my painting, I couldn't have stood it."

"Why? Is living here so awful?" I say to him, rather hypocritically.

The expression on his face indicates that I have just crossed into territory that is, if not forbidden, at least private, and does not concern an intruder such as myself. He exclaims with a certain stiffness and a hint of irony in his voice: "What do you think? Who can consider themselves immune to boredom, at Longwood or anywhere else?" I seem to hear his father speaking . . .

He continues, this time with a smile:

"But why should one try to guard against it? I need a bit of boredom to make myself take up my paint brushes. If I wait too long, boredom overcomes me and I can't do a thing."

"And Napoleon's boredom? How would you describe it?"

"Ah, Napoleonic boredom! I think he came from a life that was too regimented, too routine, also too cloistered. The dictations, the outings at four in the afternoon, dinner always at eight, the evenings in the drawing room . . . It's in November 1816, that everything begins to founder. Slowly but surely lassitude and lethargy will overcome this man who had always been on the move. This is a point that can never be overemphasized. 1816 sees the arrival of Hudson Lowe, the persecution and departure of Las Cases in November. It certainly had a big effect on the Emperor."

Las Cases was a former émigré who had come back to France in 1802, and before 1815 he had never been in close contact with Napoleon. As the chamberlain and *rapporteur* of the Council of State, he was one of the many anonymous faces in the imperial administration. After Waterloo, when he comes to the Élysée Palace to serve him, Napoleon does not take long to judge the man. It's true that "Ecstasy" (as Gourgaud called him) is a flatterer, but he has finesse and judgment. On board the *Northumberland* and at The Briars, he often found himself alone in an informal atmosphere with the fallen monarch; to the great displeasure of the other members of the entourage, who call him "The Jesuit" or "The Cockroach".

According to the *Mémorial*, Napoleon acts the great charmer with Las Cases. Gourgaud's jealousy unmasks the behaviour of the Emperor who, in his words, "plays the saint" with "little Las Cases". The man who used to terrorize the Council of State declares ingratiatingly to his confidant: "Why did you not come to see me? . . . That was very wrong of you." During his time as an émigré, Las Cases had written a *Historical Atlas*, which had been very well received at the time. So Napoleon exclaims: "Why did you not let me know of it? But it should be said, my dear man, a little intrigue is indispensable to sovereigns."

This need to explain, to sometimes throw off the mask, is quite captivating. He may be an actor, but he is not an affected man. As a moralist concerned with power, he must forget other considerations and concentrate on discovering its secrets. "To me you were one of the crowd; I became aware of you in a very ordinary way. You approached me and did not know how to take advantage of the situation . . . To me you were unremarkable." He then adds bluntly: "The way I made appointments to certain positions was something of a lottery." This refusal to harbour illusions, this often lively forthrightness, sometimes flashes like lightning in the midst of the obsessive litanies of the past. The eagle with the infallible eye is only interested in situations, not in human beings. He tells Las Cases quite plainly: "A man destined for public life and authority does not see people. He only sees things, their importance and their consequences!" Napoleon is a man who likes to strike, he needs to land blows: with a whip to demythologize oneself, with a hatchet when it comes to judging others.

Las Cases objects that on one occasion, after a mission to

Holland, the sovereign could have taken the opportunity to make contact with his councillor. This gives rise to one of those recollections from the deposits left by certain images, so typical of Napoleon's thought processes. A vague memory begins to stir and grow in that prodigious memory: "Yes, I remember it well. I seem to recall now . . . I was struck by your idea." Las Cases thinks: "He's going to make amends." Not at all! It was because Las Cases had not put himself forward: "You did not understand my questions, or your replies were not noteworthy, not positive . . . And so I passed on to the person next to you. I repeat, that is the way I always acted, but I had no time to do otherwise."

"I had no time to do otherwise." That's him exactly. No regrets, the open acknowledgment of the absurdity of power, the inevitability of events, which has to be taken into account. A somewhat cruel admission in the present circumstances. The enemy he has fought most constantly from one end of Europe to the other is none other than time. The trouble with Spain and the Russian campaign are the reactions of a man for whom "time is short", "time is getting on".

On St Helena he has all the time in the world. What he lacked before he now has in abundance. In this bedroom, to the left of the doorway, one can see the object that best illustrates the punishment time can inflict. Could I have forgotten that I undertook the voyage to St Helena because of a bed I had noticed in the Army Museum in Paris? There it is, in front of me, the narrow bed with the white canopy.

"This bed is a copy," Michel Martineau admits apologetically.

"A copy! In this bedroom, it couldn't look more authentic. This is the real bed. The one in the Army Museum is an imitation reality."

He rolls his eyes.

"The true is false and the false is true. You can play this game forever, you know. It's the same with relics, a question of faith or confidence. Well, this bed is only a copy. Are you disappointed?"

"Yes, but I'd like to work out the reason for this disappointment. I've often wondered why one needs to believe in the authenticity of an object or a place. Perhaps because it declares that its origins are genuine; reality in a material form, which also has something to do with touch. There's something of the talisman or the amulet in museum objects. What's your opinion of the rather superstitious idea that contact with a famous person endows the object with an absolute, almost magic power?"

"Don't you think that believing it is enough? Then the imagination takes over."

"Yes, it's quite a mystery. I remember visiting the museum at Chantilly, which houses the famous miniatures of the *Très Belles Heures du duc de Berry*. The visitors were in ecstasies as they looked at the colours of the fifteenth-century illuminated manuscripts. They must naturally have been the originals, since they were exhibited in a glass case. Then something extraordinary happened. The guide mentioned in passing that they were copies. Well! Everyone immediately lost interest. The guide pointed out to them that the copies showed the original brilliance of the blues better than the real manuscripts, but to no avail. The spell had been broken."

The Consul, who had still been keeping an eye on the garden, leaves the room for a moment. I take advantage of his absence to sit down on the bed. It's not permitted, I know. I feel as though I'm betraying Michel Martineau's trust. Ever since I arrived he has allowed me to wander wherever I please in Longwood. Too bad! I must know what that bed feels like. It's not the real one after all. As I sit down, I have the feeling that the base is folding in two. It's just like a child's bed! There's no thickness in the mattress . . . and then there are the legs on castors. It looks like a spare bed with a foldaway mattress. The canopy may be intended to counteract the instability of the imperial couch, but it also highlights the lilliputian appearance of the room. Napoleon has always used what is officially called the "small model" camp bed. He slept in the same bunk at Austerlitz. The steel frame bears the stamp of the locksmith Desouches, by appointment to the Emperor and the imperial household. Two camp beds of the same model were brought to St Helena. When he could not sleep in his bedroom, the prisoner went and lay down on the other bed set up in the adjoining study.

Michel Martineau comes back into the room. I was nearly caught out. His eyes narrow, the bridge of his nose creases. I feel he is on his guard. But no, he smiles at me.

"As you see, I get caught up in my role as Guardian of the Temple. The gardens, the house . . . It's an endless battle against the invasion of the tropics. Longwood has to fight . . . against damp, against the wind. Just two years without any upkeep and everything is in ruins."

"And what about the battle against time?"

"That's the most insidious one of all. I have the feeling that at Longwood time hasn't the same consistency as elsewhere."

"And what about the men who live there . . . what threatens them?"

"Oh! You and your tricky questions!" he says with a laugh.

"Tricky? I think they're fairly direct."

"All right then. If you like, we'll talk about just that with my father."

"With your father?"

"Yes, if you would like to come to dinner. Tomorrow, if that suits you? I'm sure you'll enjoy yourself. The meal will be served in the O'Meara quarters."

"But I thought that your father was not fond of socializing."

"Socializing! I wouldn't call it that. We're happy to have you."

The fireplace in the bedroom registers the slightest change of wind. Just when the murmur is about to die down, a strong gust bursts

99

down the chimney and howls round the hearth. The hoots increase in number *recto tono* like a Gregorian chant, die down, then suddenly rise again before expiring with a sound like the growling of a cat. The sound is unbearable yet fascinating, like the moaning of an invisible presence in the room. Gilbert Martineau was right: spirits do live in chimneys.

I hear the voice forever weeping. Prisoners are the only ones who can hear that lament. It's the pain of endlessly going over everything again and again that rises in whispers from small, barred windows and cries behind the iron doors of prison cells. It's like the monotonous song that can be heard humming in empty sheds after the irregular gong of the galvanized iron has disturbed its sad harmony. The call sometimes rises an octave, then there is a bellow from the chorus. Something like falsetto voices make up the recitative. But this poor aria cannot ever express the feeling of abandonment, the indifference of the world outside and the desolation of endless days.

Loneliness too has a smell and it hits me in the face. It's not really a bad smell – like faded cloth, dry, slightly musky, a bit sour, like the staleness you become aware of as soon as you enter an empty cinema.

The chanting of the shrill voices still wavers, as if they could not hold such a high register for much longer.

The glazed expression on my face alarms the Consul.

"You look as though something is wrong. What's the matter?"

"It's nothing. The wind in the chimney . . . What a strange moaning sound, don't you think so?"

He listens and shakes his head.

"I can't hear anything. The wind is such a natural presence here . . . Its whistling in my ears is so familiar that I hardly hear it."

Napoleon is getting ready to dictate. Gourgaud picks up his pen. He sits there waiting in a flattering pose. What vanity it shows! Napoleon is feeling low. He has probably noticed the self-satisfied air of his scribe. He becomes withdrawn and stoical. The life force seems to be wavering but his energy overcomes it. He will go hunting again with his groom Gourgaud. Before they even start, he's tired of pursuing memories to be captured or killed. Fortunately he will do quite a bit of poaching as he beats the thickets of time. Cheating is part of the game . . . "A forgery factory" is what the historian Jacques Bainville thinks of Longwood.

The Steuben engraving is obviously at odds with the wall on which Martineau has hung it. He has made a good choice of where to put it, but it won't stay still. On that spot, the scene and the people in it have no choice but to move about. The master of Longwood has so cleverly imprisoned them in their decor! Nailed to the wall behind a representation of themselves, they are subjected to the most refined torture possible: perpetual static reproduction. Napoleon and Gourgaud in their poses slide down the forbidden slope without ever falling. It's a set of scenes within scenes that makes you dizzy. He's about to start dictating . . . Looking self-important, Gourgaud has dipped his pen in the ink . . . Quickly, on to what comes next!

Nothing will ever come next.

That picture of confinement is in front of me now. It repeatedly foreshadows the completion of a task that never ends. Napoleon's face has the same intensely vacant expression as in *The Eylau Cemetery*, the first depiction of Napoleonic melancholy, which Baron Gros captured in such depth. The eyes roll upwards in a very strange way, with the whites of the eyeballs emphasizing the vacant stare. Delacroix claims that "It is the most magnificent and most certainly the most true to life portrait that has been done of him." In any case, it's the most disturbing. Gros only reveals a part of the secret. He gives us some indications of the Emperor's sadness, but in veiled terms. The mystery of Saturn on horseback. Napoleon extends his gloved hand over the battlefield, while in the distance fire consumes Eylau. The sky is dark, swirling clouds of smoke rise from the burnt-out plain. With artists, light is always the signature of a painting. In this picture everything is black. The snow looks like soot, the Emperor's pale face is half hidden by a dark growth of beard. The face seems burned from the inside.

The king who worked miracles is now incapable of producing one. His gesture is dull, tired, and above all quite senseless. The victor, who looks like a ghost, doesn't know what to do. Here too, he is waiting for what comes next. The great strategist never quite manages to make the gesture of blessing. The most extraordinary thing is that he refuses to look at the battlefield; his moist, almost fearful eyes are gazing at the sky. His gestures mean nothing, or rather the Emperor is raising his arm as if to say: "Listen, I don't understand", or even "I have nothing to do with it."

Twenty-seven painters had taken part in a competition on this subject set by Napoleon and commissioned by Vivant Denon, the director of the Imperial Museums. Encouraged to enter by Denon, Gros was the last to apply. It's interesting, this obsession of the monarch's with wanting to immortalize the first great slaughter of his reign.

He inspects the fatal plain, faced with death and the inexpressible on all sides. The surgeon Percy comments that: "Never had so many bodies covered such a small space". Percy is the only civilian in the painting that Gros has chosen to depict in the midst of all those uniforms – he is on the left, with a scarf on his shoulder.

"My dear, a great battle took place yesterday. Victory was mine, but I have lost a lot of people," wrote Napoleon to Empress Josephine the day after the battle. *I have lost a lot of people*. He talks about his dead soldiers like a rich bourgeois who has made a bad gambling bet – still, one can't always maintain a noble style.

Those words are moving, nonetheless. He is genuinely taken aback by the result of the uncertain battle. He shows himself as he really is at these times. The prosaic suits him quite well. These letters written in the bivouac soon after the event have the ring of truth: "I am rather weary. I have been wet twice or three times in the course of the day." He jots down these words for Empress Marie-Louise after the Battle of Bautzen.

He knows that the plump Austrian is only interested in down-to-earth details. This man always knows the right words to use for the person he is addressing, be it to flatter or to hurt.

He has lost a lot of people . . . At St Helena, does he consider that the people of the world have lost a lot in him? And yet he always seems to say: "I have lost, but I remain faithful to this loss, to this ruination. I am the loyal supporter of my misfortune. My downfall is my faith."

The leaden sky at Eylau is similar to the sky at Longwood. Eddies rises up from the blood-soaked plain; they merge into the muddy snow. The same ones float above the plateau. The great man's melancholy gaze is already directed towards St Helena. The dirty melting snow at Eylau and the rot of the tropics are two sides of the same destiny. The weariness of the great Russian plain meets the desolation of St Helena. The disturbing element present in Gros's picture is omnipresent at Longwood, but there it is like a nightmare.

Napoleon had ardently desired that art competition. He wanted to create the image of the conqueror full of pity. Of the illustrations required, the most essential one was mercy: the Emperor had to be shown in a compassionate attitude. It was not enough to reproduce the carnage; the artist had to go beyond the vision of horror through commiseration, comfort, indulgence. The victor sends help to the vanquished. To this effect, Gros shows a young Lithuanian, his right arm swathed in bandages, gratefully leaning towards the conqueror. It would not be fitting for him to touch the monarch, so he strokes the neck of his horse.

Gros has included many details, like the bayonet dripping with bloody frost crystals. The painter asked Murat to make a sketch on the back of the preparatory drawing. He even went as far as asking Empress Josephine the favour of examining the hat and fur-trimmed coat Napoleon had worn during the battle. "He may keep them as long as he likes," the Emperor replied. Gros kept them until the day he died. The painter could not take his eyes off the inside edge of the black felt tricorn hat. The silk still bore traces of the Emperor's sweat. It's true that he had felt hot. The thrust of 4,000 Russian grenadiers towards the observation post where he was stationed had taken him by surprise. He owed his rescue to General Dorsenne's grenadiers. These hardy soldiers had charged the

Russians head on with fixed bayonets. It was a slaughter. Caught both from the side and from behind, the assailants were massacred.

With the unlikely success at Eylau vindicated four months later by the exploit at Friedland and the triumph at Tilsit, 1807 marks the zenith of Napoleon's reign – rather than the birth of the King of Rome in 1811. There is, however, an uneasy feeling casting its shadow over this high point in his career. Like a premonition of what is to come, the future prisoner at Longwood is already beginning to experience that link with misfortune that will be his lot eight years later. Nevertheless, like all pariahs, it is not compassion he will demand on St Helena, but justice and the recognition of his rights, which Hudson Lowe and the English will dispute more and more fiercely.

Everything is a portent in *The Eylau Cemetery*: resignation in the face of the fatal hour, hostile nature, the glaciation of memory, not to mention the comic note that inevitably accompanies the horror. In the centre of the massacre is Murat, got up like an oriental prince, his leg showing to advantage, astride a bay horse bedecked with jewels. It's an astounding, over-the-top image. Gros is apparently respecting the conventions of hagiography. The subjects' gestures and the general impression of the battle conform to ideological necessities. Yet every detail works against the official propaganda. Gros tries to lessen the cruelty of the carnage by accentuating Murat's self-conceit.

He was no doubt unaware of the caricature. Once he had finished the work, the artist had dreadful misgivings: had he given too much importance to Murat to the detriment of the Emperor? Gros was a very vulnerable man. In despair over the failure of his *Hercules and Diomedes*, he committed suicide in 1835.

Of course Napoleon, the sagacious leader of men, had understood it all. The mass grave, the fundamental melancholy of the scene, his look of exhaustion. What extraordinary expectancy, what uncertainty at that moment when Gros presents his painting and when the monarch sees his double with the mad, staring eyes for the first time! What will the icon say? In the midst of his happiness, this *other* that he glimpses, his own image, which he doesn't recognize but which is still himself, is the *Mene, Thekel, Phares* of his reign, the mysterious hand that heralds the end. From that moment on, time will be *counted*, Eylau *weighs heavily* on him, the Empire will be *divided*.

What reaction will the new Belshazzar, also a usurper, have to this fatal warning?

He takes his own decoration of the Legion of Honour from his jacket and pins it on the painter's chest. This gesture says much about the monarch's inexplicable indulgence or daring. How could he have accepted such a picture? Everything points to his guilt: the frozen faces, the mutilations, the mass grave. Gros even took impropriety to the point of painting a dead body under the Emperor's horse. Admittedly, you can hardly see the head that the animal's hoof is about to crush, but the desire to distort the official line is obvious. This weakness from a monarch as coldly self-interested and quick to work out everything at first glance is incomprehensible. Unless one must accept another, simpler explanation: the memory of Eylau has traumatized him forever.

Curiously enough, this calculating man has a trait that belies his egotism: the capacity to become enamoured of things that are unfavourable or hostile to him. He will always have a weakness for people who have the power to harm him: Fouché, Talleyrand, not to mention the English. He is captivated by his enemies. Hudson Lowe is the only one that he will never try to charm.

With his impassive face, staring eyes and frozen gesture, Napoleon is paralyzed, as though he had seen Medusa. Medusa, one of the powers of darkness, the face of horror. He has seen something. But what? His own image, his double? Medusa's head still haunts the tiny bedroom at Longwood. Remember O'Meara's disquiet when he surprised him alone one evening in front of the fireplace looking at the wood fire. The doctor had been particularly stuck by the captive's "melancholy expression". One often has the impression that, since Waterloo, he has been in a dream from which he cannot awake. He is like a watchman of ruins asleep on his feet, who suddenly opens his eyes and then drowses again. This lethargy is also a means by which the prisoner can try to cheat time. His valet, Ali, notes that "He often treats night as day or day as night. In a word, he acted like someone overcome by boredom who uses every means possible to make time pass more quickly."

Eylau is the first shock. The waves made by the impact will reach the shore at St Helena. The black star, like the star of the Three Wise Men, has stopped above the house at Longwood. It indicates the man whose life is wasting away from boredom and who will die of melancholy.

The disaster happens at 10.30 in the morning. Napoleon gives orders for Augereau's corps, deployed to the south of the cemetery, to relieve Davout. At that moment, a sudden snowstorm strikes the plain. Augerau's soldiers are blinded by snowflakes that the east wind lashes into their faces. Having strayed from their path, the mass of foot soldiers find themselves in front of the Russian artillery. The 6,500 French are hit at point blank range by the hail of fire of 72 enemy guns. An enormous breach is opened up in their defences . . .

At the time of the 1940 débâcle, all the paintings in the Louvre were evacuated. The convoys were sometimes stopped in the flood of refugees. *The Eylau Cemetery* frightened people. The huge canvas had been rolled up and stuck out of a truck like a long tube. People thought that it was the barrel of an anti-aircraft gun used to return German air fire.[4] They saw it as a threat.

1. The expression "it's the court of King Pétaud" is a reference to a time when beggars used to choose a chief they jokingly called King Pétaud. He had no authority and hence his court is a place where everyone wants to give orders. [Tr.]

2. An unfinished satirical novel by Gustave Flaubert about two mediocre men who dabble unsuccessfully in science. [Tr.]

3. A satirical dialogue by Lucian of Samosata (AD 125 – c. 190) on the vanities of human life by those who have died and know what comes after. [Tr.]

4. *Le Front de l'art*, Rose Valland.

The Fifth Day

I

IS IT AN AMPHITHEATRE, A GIANT STAIRCASE PERHAPS?
What is this construction built into the side of the hill way out here
in the countryside? Cows graze in the hollow of the valley. The
neo-gothic chapel hidden in the trees looks as though it's no longer
used as a church. Standing on tiptoe I can see an altar, a cross and
a wooden bench through the church window. A faded bouquet
makes me think that services may sometimes be celebrated there.
Strange long-legged birds take flight as I pass.

There's something besides the rustling of the tall trees that disturbs the silence in the valley. It's an almost still hum that emanates
from the calm of the place – a solemn, continuous sound like a
soundtrack that hasn't recorded anything and can therefore only
amplify a vague, gentle hiss.

I go up to the terraces on which several rectangles have been
marked out – about ten rising gradually. They're covered with black
gravel and surrounded with a white-painted cement border. On
each rectangle is a number . . .

Below stand two marble columns ending in a pyramid point.
About a hundred Dutch-sounding names are inscribed on the
sides of each. I'm in a South African cemetery. The rectangles of
black stones on each terrace are actually graves. The numbers
have also been put on the columns with the corresponding name.

What an awful resting-place these dead men have been given. They're nothing more than numbers.

I go up several levels and stop at random in front of a grave. It carries the number 34. Why should I suddenly want to know the identity of number 34? I feel as though I'm trespassing, at least breaking the rule of silence that has been imposed on this valley. "Number 34, Boshoff . . ."

There's the sound of a car engine, someone slamming the doors. Voices come nearer . . . I think I recognize one of them from its abrupt tone and cajoling modulations. It's my two English ladies. You'd think they were following me.

"You see, we're always at the same place together," whispers the domineering lady with the wheedling smile. "But tell me, my dear, aren't you being unfaithful to your Bonaparte? Have you finished with Longwood?"

"No, no. I'm going back there at midday. I'm not only interested in Longwood you know."

Once again her companion looks annoyed. She obviously does not appreciate her friend's irrepressible love of provocation. I don't mind it. I like her rather direct style, which she softens by her elegant deportment and her subtlety of tone. She must have been a very beautiful woman. When she gets carried away, the irises of her green eyes glimmer with gold. Her shoulders may be more rounded now, but she holds herself straight and her gestures are still amazingly supple and smooth. Perhaps she was a dancer . . .

The companion is not as free in her manner, but her eyes have a look that is both bright and knowing. She lectures her friend in a way that could be either joking or preaching – it's hard to say which. They seem to understand each other extremely well. But I have the impression that they've been walking aimlessly round and round this tiny island. It's only in the late afternoon in The Consulate bar with a scotch in their hands that they are their usual cheerful selves again.

"Well now. What do you think of this cemetery? Revolting, isn't it? They're Boer prisoners' graves. There were up to 6,000 prisoners here during the Transvaal war. Among them were 13 Frenchmen who had fought on the side of the Boers. I read about it in my guide book."

"Who herded them in here on St Helena?"

"You know that very well. Us of course, the English . . . We were at war with these people."

"And these graves?"

"They were prisoners. They died in an epidemic of typhoid fever. They were herded in, as you put it, on Deadwood Plain, near Longwood. The sanitary conditions were frightful . . . 180 prisoners died."

It's my turn to get at her.

"You English have a real knack of being mean to your prisoners. After Napoleon, the Boers . . . And the graves are numbered, as in a concentration camp. That shows a certain lack of generosity."

"You're exaggerating . . . What can I do about it?" she mumbles.

"You can't do anything about it, it's true. These events took place early in the century. But there must be a curse on this island."

"A curse! Do you believe such nonsense?" she interjects disapprovingly.

"Everyone who visits it speaks of its tragic side."

"St Helena isn't a cheerful place, it's true. We can't wait for the boat to get underway again. But we've found some spots that are really paradise on earth, you know."

"Paradise on earth, here?"

"Yes indeed . . . They're mainly on the western side of the island. I don't think your Emperor ever saw these places. He refused to visit them. He was a strange prisoner all right! He shut himself away in his shack of a house out of pride."

She's obviously looking for an argument, but I have neither the inclination nor the energy to open hostilities with her. What's more, she'll want to be right all of the time. Instead of annoying her, my silence makes her face light up. She thinks I've given in.

"Shall we look around the cemetery together?" I say after a moment.

"Oh yes!" she simpers, tugging her companion's arm.

She suggests reading us some of the information in her guide book.

Here, even more strongly than at Longwood, I can smell the stagnant odour of oblivion. The captive's house has slyly managed to disguise the poisonous scents of memory with its luxuriant gardens and tortuous passageways, while this dead hill exudes a lifeless air and listless vibrations: it breathes defeat and exile. The losers always end up on St Helena. Why did the victors choose such a narrow space for their captives? To humiliate them? In a remarkable *tour de force*, they've managed to miniaturize a grandiose site. One would think that these excessively cramped tombs could only contain homunculi. Time has worn the wreathes right down to the woven-wire framework. With their badly aligned white surrounds, the tombs look like open skylights on roofs.

My energetic friend reads us the story of General Cronje, a figure in the resistance to the British invaders. He was captured, brought to St Helena and housed in Kent Cottage at the foot of the former High Knoll fort. Unlike Napoleon who refused to have any escort, General Cronje insisted on being accompanied on his outings by horse guards.

Let's hope she's not going to start a discussion on Napoleon's pride again . . . No, not at all. She keeps on reading aloud. When the peace treaty was signed in 1902, the prisoners went back home. The two obelisks were built in 1912. She informs me that before the Boers, the British deported a Zulu chief called Dinizulu to St Helena. In 1915, it was the Sultan of Zanzibar's turn. He was interned with his family in a house on the outskirts of Jamestown. The last prisoners to be sent to St Helena were three men who had tried to assassinate the ruler of Bahrain in 1957.

"Look at the wire birds!" she exclaims.

"Wire birds?"

Highly excited, she points to the long-footed birds I saw a while ago.

"They're a very rare species," she continues enthusiastically. "It only exists on St Helena. It's called the wire bird because of its feet."

Two people on horseback suddenly appear from the valley below. That's what made the wire birds fly away. One of the men is wearing white trousers and a red riding cap. He urges on his companion, who is having trouble keeping up. They gallop past us. The latecomer is a woman . . . We have a brief glimpse of a face with gentle features but a passionate expression. The man greets us ceremoniously. He looks rather uncertainly at his woman companion. He has the same sorrowful, vacant look as Napoleon in the painting by Gros.

"Did you see the woman's face? . . . Her flushed cheeks! Don't you think she has the look of someone who's been caught out?" whispers the other English lady.

"What story are you making up now? An adulterous affair? But you're dreadfully behind the times. That hasn't been considered anything shameful for ages!

They left, no doubt arguing for another good half-hour. Lost in thought, I watch the two people on horseback disappear into the distance behind Brown's Hill. A dog follows them, running round the horses and frightening them with its bark.

2

During the preparation for the Russian invasion in 1812, Napoleon is on his horse on the banks of the Niemen, gazing at the water. In a few moments the die will be cast. A hare suddenly appears and runs between the horse's legs. When the frightened mount shies, the Emperor falls to the ground. An ill omen which eye-witnesses don't fail to notice.

At the beginning of his captivity, Napoleon goes riding almost every morning. Gourgaud, who has been appointed head equerry, is in charge of the stables and accompanies Napoleon on these outings. But the twelve-mile limit quickly irks the prisoner, who feels as though "he is on a merry-go-round". From 1816 on, he gives up that exercise and only goes about in a barouche. He has it harnessed and ready at four o'clock in the afternoon. Mme Bertrand and Albine de Montholon take their places beside him. The Archambault brothers – two of the twelve servants accompanying the fallen Emperor – crack the whip. The six horses gallop off around the park. The road is bumpy but Napoleon insists that the barouche be driven at full tilt. Occasionally the wheels nearly leave the track, greatly alarming the ladies who are thrown this way and that. They are so shaken that they are almost choking as they get out of the carriage. The whole outing scarcely lasts more than half an hour. Napoleon is delighted and seems to be amused by his passengers' haggard faces. It must be said that distractions at Longwood are few and far between. The year 1816 is notable for its many vexations.

The third interview with Hudson Lowe takes place on 16 May. Napoleon indulges in his usual long silences, staring at his jailer for two or three minutes.

"If Lord Castlereagh has ordered you to poison us or kill us all, do it as soon as possible!" the captive exclaims.

"Sir," replies Lowe, "I have not come here to be insulted." As he is leaving, the Governor meets Grand Marshal Bertrand. He relates the difficult conversation he has had with "the General". For once, he makes a fairly pertinent remark: "He wants things to happen just the way he wants. He created a make-believe Spain, and a make-believe Poland. Now he wants a make-believe St Helena."

The conventions signed by the Allies in 1815 had made provision for representatives of each of the powers to be sent to St Helena. The English had certainly been given the responsibility of guarding the prisoner, but these representatives were charged with "verifying Bonaparte's presence". They disembark on 17 and 18 June. Count Balmain had been appointed by Russia, Baron Stürmer by Austria and the Marquis de Montchenu by France. Prussia had sent no one. "St Helena is the most miserable, inaccessible, difficult to attack, unsociable, poorest, dearest place in the world, and above all the most appropriate for the use to which it is now put," the Russian delegate writes to his minister on his arrival. The Frenchman considers it "hideous".

The three representatives have an unenviable stay on the island. Left to their own devices and persecuted by Hudson Lowe, who thinks that the men are only there to make his task more difficult, they are never allowed to see the prisoner. Napoleon lets them know on one occasion, with more than a hint of irony, "that he could offer them some books from his library, if reading was a way of relieving their boredom".

After a purely formal meeting on 20 June, Hudson Lowe comes to Longwood again on 16 July for the fifth time. "Ten minutes passed before the Emperor said a word." Then, all of a sudden, he bursts out with a series of "bitter reproaches". Out it all comes: "the henchman's" little humiliations, his mean tricks.

"I cannot invite anyone to dinner, and if I had a girl or a mistress, I could not have her brought here."

"You haven't any," quibbles Lowe.

"But I could have."

"You haven't any!" exclaims the jailer, apparently sure of the fact. He is obviously kept well informed about his prisoner's private life. But by whom? Probably by certain servants. In October 1816, Longwood has 32 servants of whom twelve are French, assisted by eight inhabitants of the island, ten soldiers and two Chinese. There are no secrets at Longwood. The little French colony lives in such close proximity that a love affair would be known immediately. Gourgaud does not hesitate to spread hints, leading others to think that Mme de Montholon is Napoleon's mistress. This causes considerable annoyance to the man in question, who one day exclaims in Bertrand's presence: "It's not true. She's too ugly!" Then he adds: "That could be put in the gazettes and do some damage." He is very concerned with his image and does not want Europe to laugh some passing fancy to scorn. Moreover he is still Marie-Louise's husband, although he knows everything about her liaison with Neipperg. Perhaps he wants to feel invulnerable as far as the Austrian court is concerned. His father-in-law, who belongs to the victors' camp, has it within his power to change his situation. The captive has not given up hope of one day returning to Europe.

3

"Tell me, did Napoleon remain chaste on St Helena?"

My English lady has come back to the attack. It's bizarre. You would think she could read my thoughts.

"You have a one-track mind."

"Oh! Don't be such a hypocrite. That question fascinates everyone, beginning with those who claim that it's only *la petite histoire*, as you say in French.[1] Napoleon's melancholy and all the other things you've been telling me, that's all well and good! But if he was sad, it's simply because he didn't have a woman."

"That's a rather hasty explanation, don't you think? I've already told you everything about that."

"Everything?" she retorts indignantly. "But how can one know everything about that question?"

She gives the word "everything" a comic emphasis. She's a tough old lady, that one. Her companion tugs her arm, trying to divert her attention. She pushes her away almost roughly.

"You're . . . You're just a puritan!" she splutters.

I try to explain to her that Napoleon had become rather disenchanted on that subject and that it seemed to have killed all desire in him. She sniggers.

"'Killed all desire in him' . . . You have such a way of speaking about things like that . . . He didn't want to fuck, that's all. That's the word Frenchmen use among themselves, isn't it?"

"That's right. Personally, I rarely use it. I'm a puritan . . ."

She bursts out laughing and plies me with questions.

"Did he talk about his past loves when he was at Longwood? And what about Albine de Montholon? It seems Josephine was an expert at it . . ."

I quote her some of the captive's confidences, in particular the one he made to Gourgaud: "I've never been really in love, except perhaps with Josephine, a little, and then because I was 27 when I met her."

"But you know, love was still the main topic at Longwood," I tell her.

"Ah! There you are . . . I knew you were hiding things from me," she complains.

"Not at all. It's not what you think. Bachelors like Gourgaud pined for it. Marchand, the Emperor's valet, pursued one of the

Montholons' maids and had a child by her. Ali ran after the native women, tried to win another of the Montholons' maids, then fell in love with the governess to the Bertrands' children. Napoleon wanted to hear all these stories, reprimanded this one and that, and wanted to act as arbiter. He certainly had a voyeuristic side. He was very displeased with Gourgaud, who brought women up to his room at Longwood from time to time, and would lecture him: 'Ah! Love is a strange thing. We become like animals'."

"You mean that he too was ultimately a puritan," the English lady remarks thoughtfully.

From the beginning I've been very careful not to tell her about a strange discovery I made when going through Ali's notes.[2] The Emperor's librarian, who was an indefatigable polygraph, filled hundreds of sheets of paper about St Helena with his fine handwriting. These pages, stuffed with repetitions, parentheses, additions and refutations are a jumble that would need classifying chronologically if they were to be published. Let me point out again that Ali is the eye or the photographic memory, if you will, of Napoleon's exile on St Helena. These observations were written a long time after his return to France. He will remember the smallest detail. He will spend his time carefully going over the accounts of Las Cases and of O'Meara, which appeared a few years after Napoleon's death. His method is quite simple: it consists of correcting an anecdote that he finds inaccurate and then relating it in detail. He weaves his own memories around this event. It's a prodigious work of memory that sometimes makes one almost dizzy. The endless detail, which never seems to stop, becomes a kind of hypertrophy. Yet this excess is what makes Ali irreplaceable.

It's precisely during the meanders of a long description that the detail, the gesture, the incident that reveals a whole hidden facet of Napoleon's captivity suddenly appears. Ali's annotations indicate, as if it were necessary to do so, that the official eye-witnesses assumed to have recorded the prisoner's slightest gesture have not said everything. So what does Ali reveal among the interminable details on the habits of the Chinese on St Helena? A trifle, buried under all the bric-à-brac, but it's puzzling!

"One evening, contrary to the usual practice, a light meal was prepared consisting of a certain number of rather delicate and intricate small dishes, accompanied by a nice little dessert. These unaccustomed preparations made me ask M. why they were being done. I did not receive a reply, but later I learned that they had been done to entertain a woman or a girl, and that this woman had come, but the Emperor, finding her too young, and respecting her youth and innocence, had instructed that she be paid a certain sum of money and had sent her away as she had come."

Some might call it a piece of trivia. The poor prisoner surely has the right to some consolation! The most surprising thing about it is that none of the other companions makes the slightest allusion to this visit. One has grounds for supposing that it was not the first nor the last. Of course one may argue that this type of anecdote would scarcely enthral the Emperor's entourage. What fascinates the prisoner's companions is the question of which woman is the favourite, and not some girl who has been brought there from the town.

Nonetheless, this argument does not seem convincing. If it's an unimportant matter, why doesn't Ali mention the name of the person he asks about it – in all probability Montholon? "I did not receive a reply," he writes. This sentence implies that it is important to observe the greatest discretion on the subject of these romantic affairs.

The strangest thing about it is that this is not the first time Napoleon has sent away a girl who is too young. His valet, Constant, describes how, when he was at Schönbrunn in 1805, a meeting was arranged between the Emperor and "a charming young girl", but that Napoleon "respected the girl's innocence and had her taken back to her parents".

4

"Yes, yes. You've told me that Napoleon didn't have 'a voluptuous nature'. You have a priceless way of talking about those things! I want details," she demanded with her overbearing smile.

"Where will that get you?"

"But my dear, that's the only thing that matters. It seems that as a lover he was impatient and quick," she chuckles, greedy for more. "So, he wasn't 'a good lay'?"

Where does she get this forthright language from? She systematically uses our crudest expressions as though it were a game. Yet everything in her comportment, her clothes, the way she expresses herself in our language is full of elegance and natural ease. The aquiline nose and the strong jaw give an impression of domination. Her nostrils quiver with an intensity of expression that makes her green eyes iridescent and highlights the gold of her pupils. Her companion has the same style, though her manner is less flamboyant.

"Come now, answer me!" she orders.

"Well! I think it's a myth. The actress Mademoiselle George said that he was a lover 'whose love had no roughness or haste'. He was very tender and modest. Besides, he had to maintain his rank. You know that in a country like ours, it's a monarch's duty to have mistresses. He had to bow to custom."

She seemed satisfied with my explanations. I think of Ali's story with some trepidation. If she ever heard about it . . . Sending the girl away is basically a logical attitude. He wants it to be known that he is still the sovereign. Appearances are the only things that count: he sends her away . . .

Strangely enough, on that subject the great man is quite boastful. Caulaincourt, who spent long periods alone with him after returning from Russia in 1812, notes that: "He liked to talk about his success with women. All in all, if there was a weak side to the gifts of this great and wonderful man, it was vanity about the past." At St Helena it's not delicacy that chokes him when he confides to Bertrand that "Josephine had the prettiest little c—— in the world". He dwells on the subject by comparing it to the Trois-Îlets in Martinique. Once again to Bertrand, he prides himself on having initiated Marie-Louise to physical love: "The first night she asked for more."

He loved gossip, salacious details. Caulaincourt stresses: "He was often indiscreet." Another witness, Pons de l'Hérault, who was close to him on the island of Elba, notes: "Napoleon had too great a liking for finding out the vulgar details of married lives."

"He could be amused by a trifle," Albine de Montholon notes. On St Helena the great man often becomes bogged down in inessentials. Being both a stickler for detail and indiscreet, he wants to know everything about everybody. It was because he was able to deal with the smallest details without ever being submerged by them that he came to power and dominated Europe. At Longwood his analytical mind has only small things to exercise it. Well may he say to Las Cases: "The details of St Helena are not important. Being here is the most important matter," his captivity is nothing but a series of unimportant events that finally exhaust his intelligence. Has he any other choice? To give in over a detail is to capitulate. On this point, he proves to be as intransigent with his jailers as he is with those around him. At Longwood, etiquette requires that one should stand in his presence during conversations. He is well aware that Bertrand is dead tired and that Gourgaud keeps awake by leaning on the mantelpiece. He pays no attention to that. He must be the "centre", to use his own expression.

In private, he's rather an accommodating man. He has always been kindly to his close relations, good-natured with the servants and indulgent with his own family. "People have often praised my strength of character; I've been as weak as water, especially with my own family, and they know it," he admits to Las Cases. After a disagreement with a very good friend, he insists on making it up. He could never bear going to bed without making his peace. Once again it's Pons de l'Hérault who notes: "Quarrels oppressed him like nightmares." This trait is also present in his dealings with Gourgaud. His aide-de-camp is often in the wrong. He's insolent, sarcastic, sometimes rude, yet after a petty quarrel he will leave Napoleon to make the first move. "Gorgo, Gorgotto, my boy Gorgo!" he exclaims in almost paternal tones. He feels affection for the impudent young man and lets him get away with everything.

This easy-going, even weak behaviour highlights the sentimental side of his personality. But he quite cheerfully forgets it when his rank or reputation are involved. Protocol is essential to survival at Longwood. These are the only times when he loses his temper. Ali, who never misses any of these occurrences, even if the story is against himself, tells of one imperial outburst of temper: "When I used the word 'you', instead of the commonly used expression, 'Your Majesty', he gave me a kick to punish me for my impertinence and lack of respect, berating me with the harshest and most humiliating terms his strong displeasure could summon."

I like this imperial kick aimed at the good Ali. The former uncouth artillery lieutenant, the boor, always lurks somewhere in Bonaparte. He has always been fairly uninhibited. He is rarely deceived about himself or others. Remember what he whispered to his brother at the coronation: "Joseph, if our father could only see us now." And at Eylau, when the Emperor was in the bivouac stuffing himself with potatoes as his soldiers of the old guard looked on . . .

5

"What are you thinking about?" the English lady asks.

"Nothing. Well, not entirely. I was thinking about Napoleon, about his lack of affectation in certain circumstances."

"Oh! Tell me about it," she asks with childlike eagerness.

"There's nothing to tell."

"Why? Am I too stupid to understand? I'm not interested in your Napoleon anyway," she retorts, turning her back on me.

"I'm delighted. We can talk about something else for a change. About you, for example."

"Me? I have nothing to tell," she says, quite indignant. "My life is unremarkable."

Suddenly changing her tone of voice, she whispers: "Now explain to me why you're so keen on this character. You're really obsessed by Napoleon. You're tracking him."

"Not at all. It happened by chance. Admittedly I've sometimes given chance a helping hand. But when you travel in Europe, you meet Napoleon everywhere. Wherever you go, you come across a battlefield, an inn or a castle where Napoleon stayed at some time."

"Have you been as far as Russia?"

"I've seen Borodino, but because of Prince André."

"Prince André!"

"Yes. The hero of *War and Peace*."

"*War and Peace*! Why, I know the book by heart," she confesses with a passion that I would never have expected of her.

"By heart! The book must be over a thousand pages long."

"But isn't that what you say in your language when you really love a book? It becomes part of you. The heart is the seat of passion, isn't it? I love *War and Peace* with all my heart."

"So do I . . . Well, we can agree at last."

"But we understand each other very well! It's your *idée fixe* that stops us from being on good terms."

"Really, you go too far Amy," says her companion breaking into the conversation. "*Idée fixe*! You're very thoughtless! This gentleman is not at your beck and call. For heaven's sake leave him in peace. You're on holiday. You always do exactly as the mood takes you . . . It's selfish, Amy."

I have just learned that her Christian name is Amy. At the moment, Amy is looking contrite.

"Yes, you're right. I did go too far."

She doesn't look crestfallen for long.

"But let's get back to Borodino," she says with an excessively affable smile – there's something rather carnivorous in this overdone amiability.

She continues quite sweetly:

"Do you remember the battle. Prince André is alone. It's sunset and he's looking at a birch grove. A feeling of foreboding is gnawing away at him. Perhaps he will be killed tomorrow. He sees his own death. The extraordinary thing is that he feels jealous of those birch trees. He's going to die and those trees will still go on living. He can vividly picture his absence from this life while the trees continue to exist. You know that Prince André admired Napoleon?"

"Yes, he admired him in the beginning, at the time of Austerlitz. But he changed his mind."

"I presume you've been to Austerlitz?"

"Yes. You won't believe me, but it was quite by chance. I was visiting Brno in Czechoslovakia. I learned that the battlefield was close by. I couldn't resist it."

"I don't believe you. I think you're in the grip of an obsession. You French are unbelievable! Yes indeed. You say that you don't like Napoleon, but you never stop talking about his battles. You love to see yourselves through the mirror of the Emperor. You were the strongest; you dominated Europe. Luckily we, the English, were there."

"You're right. No doubt we have a feeling of nostalgia for that period."

Her face lights up. She adores being right.

"I bet you've been to Eylau. You never stop talking to me about that battle. What is so extraordinary about it?"

She must have a sixth sense. I have indeed been to Eylau. It's no use telling her that once again I visited the battlefield by chance. She won't believe me.

"Do you know where Eylau is?"

"I've no idea. Probably in Germany."

"It's in Russia. But at that time it was part of Prussia. Do you know Königsberg?"

"Vaguely."

I tell her that the town annexed by the Soviets was renamed Kaliningrad in 1946. Today it's a Russian enclave in Lithuania. For a long time it was a forbidden military zone. The Russian authorities are now starting to grant visas. I admit that I've always wanted to see the capital of East Prussia.

"Why is that?"

"It's where Kant comes from."

"I don't understand. What interest is there in seeing the town where Kant was born? Wouldn't it be better to read his works?"

"One can do both. I must confess I have a liking for borders. Königsberg is the furthest outpost of Germany in the Slav countries. It's the town of the Teutonic knights. The kings of Prussia were crowned at Königsberg. But it always leads us back to Napoleon.

The Berlin court took refuge in this stronghold after the disaster at Iéna in 1806, so that they could prepare to retaliate."

It's obvious that I'm boring her. She listens dutifully. She tries to look as though she is concentrating, but I can see that her thoughts are elsewhere. I'm getting to know her. The only things about history that she likes are gossip and bedroom secrets. But she has some reason to be inattentive. Here we are in front of the monument to the Boers in the centre of the island of St Helena, and I'm talking about Königsberg and Prussia.

I interrupt my long-winded speech to see if she carries on from what she was saying earlier. Peace has descended on the cemetery once more and a warm breeze is blowing across the valley. The companion is straining her ears as though she were listening for a strange sound. Now the silence seems to be only a still surface, moved by a ripple or rather a kind of rumination.

I think of Eylau, of my astonishment when I arrived at the village now called Bagrationovsk in honour of Prince Bagration. He was the Russian General who distinguished himself at Austerlitz and Eylau, and was mortally wounded at the Battle of Moskowa.

My English lady may well be tiresome, but she's quite shrewd. Hasn't she found me out? Why indeed this relentless effort to resurrect the dead, this presumptuous wish to fill the unbearable silence of the past?

The love of what is irretrievably lost has led me to St Helena, as it did to Eylau. Am I too credulous, too trusting? This naïveté makes me inclined to think that places outlive memory; that the upheaval caused by a disaster or a tragedy leaves a mark, or at the very least a ripple in the air; that a site can reveal more than a book. Eylau – St Helena, a hidden thread connects these two names in Napoleon's tragedy.

6

After leaving Kaliningrad early in the morning, I had spent a good part of the day trying to trace the Eylau cemetery. Like the former Königsberg, Bagrationovsk is a rambling village. It's a common thing in the region. The soul of Prussia wanders amid the vestiges of the past. There is no longer a single German here, but can such ancient traces be erased? Hence, the little town of Eylau has two lives, two heartbeats. The Russians have replaced the Germans. They took over their houses, but have never had the means to maintain them. Roughcast is falling off the façades in sheets, laying bare the masonry underneath.

I questioned passers-by in Eylau, with the help of an interpreter-guide. I had a postcard of Baron Gros's painting in my hand. Most people showed no reaction. A foreigner . . . The first to visit the battlefield since 1945. And that photo . . . Perhaps they were expecting me to show them the face of a relative I was trying to trace, but a painting . . . I was indeed trying to trace something that had disappeared: a landscape.

When I arrived, I had nevertheless thought that luck was with me. A long funeral procession, with a brass band bringing up the rear, was moving in the direction of the cemetery. The deceased was lying with hands together, in the open casket according to Orthodox custom. One detail had struck me: the man at the head of the procession was carrying the coffin lid on his head. I thought that if I wanted to find the cemetery, all I had to do was follow these people. But that cemetery, below the village, could not be the right one. In Gros's picture and in many contemporary engravings, the cemetery is near the church with the pointed steeple. I had looked around the ruined nave of a church in the middle of the village. It was a red brick building open to the sky and full of birds. The walls and the transepts had been reinforced with cement. But the site didn't correspond at all to the church I was looking for.

I questioned the last people in the cortege. They passed the picture of Gros's painting around, nodding their heads. I was thinking, quite unfairly, that they looked rather stupid, when one face lit up. "There is a man, as you go out of the village, a former teacher . . ." In the remotest villages of the old Europe, one always manages to search out a non-professional scholar, generally a teacher, or, less commonly, a retired insurance agent.

He was an old man with prominent cheekbones, a limp and a rather excitable personality, but incredibly well versed in military history. He had read everything on Eylau and impressed me from the start by reciting a passage from *Colonel Chabert*. Readers of Balzac will know that Chabert was left for dead on the battlefield at Eylau after being struck down by a sabre during Murat's famous charge. When he regained consciousness, he was almost suffocating under a pile of corpses.

"Remember the account Chabert gives to the lawyer Derville, Frenchman?"

"To tell the truth, I can't recall it."

He then began to declaim sentences in Russian, which my interpreter tried to translate as best he could. It was about a "human dunghill" in which the poor Colonel is struggling to free himself.

"This is where it all happened, Sir."

He left long pauses between each sentence to give his words more weight.

"Everything happened here . . . In the snow . . . Corpses . . . Everywhere . . . Right here."

"But *Colonel Chabert* is a novel."

"Yes, it is a novel. But Eylau, Sir, is real."

He then took me outside the village to show me a grey building on the top of a small hill.

"That's where the church was. The cemetery was right here,

where we are standing. It all took place in front of the factory you can see over there."

I couldn't hide my feelings, that mysterious charge that shivers down your spine and leaves you deeply disturbed, like a shock. Why was I so moved? On the face of it, there was no real cause. The ground, furrowed by winter frosts, was poor, sad, and bare. A heavy smell of brown coal, soot and gunpowder, so typical of Eastern bloc countries, wafted over from time to time. The interminable sandy plain stretched out as far as the eye could see. The same landscape of moors and peat bogs, broken only occasionally by a hillock or a line of poplars or pines, goes on and on from the North Sea to the Ural. Geographers call this vestige of glacial expansion "a very ancient depression zone". It couldn't be better expressed.

Eylau, far from everything . . . I'd undertaken a very complicated journey to reach this mound where Napoleon stood on 8 February 1807. But what can one say about the Grand Army's seven-month march? They used to say: "It's our legs that win *Le Tondu*'s wars".[3] They had been victorious at Iéna and Auerstaedt, they had taken Berlin, then gone straight on into Poland. Chasing the Russians, who had given them the slip for several days, they reached Eylau in the heart of winter. The enemy was entrenched in the village and at last decided to join battle. Napoleon's soldiers of the old guard were hungry and weak from incessant encircling manœuvres. All they wanted was some rest. Napoleon could only muster 60,000 soldiers against the 85,000 Russians. Almost all the Empire Marshals first promoted in 1804 were there. Did they feel just as weary? Probably, but the wind of revolt was not yet blowing through their number. At the time of battle, most of them still burned with the zeal they felt at 20. At the beginning of the Revolution, Soult was only a corporal, Augereau a fencing master, Davout a sub-lieutenant, Murat a sergeant, Ney a book-keeper, Bernadotte a sergeant-major. Bessières intended to become a barber.

The engagement began on the previous evening, 7 February. After several bloody confrontations around the cemetery, the cavalry had finally dislodged the Russians. The enemy had unsuccessfully counter-attacked during the night. One doesn't need to know a lot about military strategy to appreciate the importance of this observation post, a panoramic viewpoint dominating the countryside all around as far as the eye can see. On the morning of 8 February 1807, the snow-covered plain looked like a white swell rolling towards the village of Eylau. A few little black islands emerged from this frozen sea, formed by marshes where the snow had not been able to cling to firm ground and had melted. Trampling feet, hooves and blood had not yet turned it into a quagmire.

A cavalry officer, Captain Parquin, writes: "A really difficult thing to cope with was the north wind lashing our faces with so much thick snow that we were blinded. The pine forests on the edge of the battlefield, so common in this country, made it seem even more dismal. Add to that a dull sky with clouds that didn't seem to rise any higher than the trees. They cast a gloomy hue over the whole scene, incidentally reminding us that we were 3,000 leagues from the beautiful skies of France."[4]

It's a desolate, hostile impression that I had also felt then at the end of winter. The wet, empty fields separated by straggly bushes, a stiff wind that seemed to have cut off the vegetation to ground level, gave me the feeling of being in a limitless, primitive landscape. No sign of human order, no hamlet or church tower to soften the bare land. The sharp smell of sulphur matches washed over us like a wave. This feeling of exile, which Parquin describes so well, was also felt by Napoleon, but in his own way. His progress towards the east distanced him from his bases and weakened him day by day. The barren site of Eylau was scarcely favourable to offensive tactics and unexpected movements aimed at disconcerting and trapping the enemy, as he had done at Austerlitz.

The presence of a foreigner had really galvanized my companion, but he was shivering just as much as I was. We were staring at the horizon, standing in front of the factory with faded walls, a roof surmounted by a red Soviet star and an entrance decorated with a bust of Karl Marx. He gazed out glumly over the battlefield just as we were doing. The corners of his lips were cracked, giving his face a disapproving look.

Why had the old teacher declaimed a few sentences about St Helena to me? That day he put an idea in my mind which, at the time, I found quite eccentric. "Eylau the turning point, Eylau the turning point," he repeated. The interpreter could not translate what the teacher meant. He cast about, using the words "change of direction" and "reversal", not really knowing what the other man wanted to convey. Perhaps he was indicating that the great war leader had reached his limit right here, in open countryside, at Eylau.

We gazed at the great rolling plain, where the grand strategist had floundered for the first time. Clouds of crows flew off with a terrible, nasal sound like a death rattle. The deafening echo of their cries made one think of a huge explosion. The weather was overcast, with some mist rising fitfully from the marshes. This uncertainty of shapes and sky, far from depressing the mind, actually encouraged the imagination.

It was then that the old teacher showed me the place on the left where Augereau's attack to relieve Davout began at 10.30 a.m. When the attack took place, Augereau was suffering so much from rheumatism that he could scarcely stay on his horse.

I stared at the piece of land that my companion was pointing out, trying to imagine the divisions formed in their columns all surging forward . . . And the catastrophe that suddenly faced the helpless Emperor. The still, leaden sky suddenly begins to move and snowflakes swirl in the air like thousands of insects. Whipped along by the east wind, they hit the soldiers full in the face. 6,000 of

131

Augereau's men are blinded. While they believe they are charging at the centre of the Russians, they are actually presenting their flank, and are torn to pieces at point-blank range by the 72 pieces of Russian artillery. It's a critical moment: a gaping hole opens in the French ranks. 4,000 Russian grenadiers then rush into the breach, coming so close to the cemetery that many of the combatants can glimpse the Emperor, his eyes, his face, his troubled gaze!

Thiers, who had first-hand information on this period, notes how the war leader behaved under these circumstances. When everything was going well, Napoleon was hotheaded, even irascible. "As soon as the danger became serious, he became calm, gentle, encouraging, not wanting to add difficulties from any outbursts of temper of his to those that arose from the situation they were in."

The old teacher worried me. I had the impression that he took himself for Napoleon and was conducting the battle in person. He limped as his small steps moved faster and his gestures became more and more grandiloquent. He had stopped answering the questions I put to him, absorbed as he was by problems of strategy. Basically, each of us was trying in his own way to bring the invisible presence of the battle to life. He had put himself in the Emperor's shoes, and for my part, I thought I could still see the waves of the 1807 earthquake moving in that landscape.

Indeed, if one studies it closely, it really was a seismic event that shook the Eylau plain on that afternoon of 8 February. Led by Murat, 10,000 cavalrymen, joined by the mounted grenadiers, would try to close the huge breach opened by Augereau. It was probably the most extraordinary, gigantic charge in all of Napoleon's history. It shows the danger the Emperor was in, forced to throw all of his forces into battle. Eylau, the place where the real obstacle begins ... Nothing happened as planned. For him, manœuvring had always been more important than fighting. This time it was the fight to the death that forced him to use a frontal attack.

"Murat! Murat!" shouted the teacher, holding his scarf like a whip.

He pronounced the name "Miourraht", rolling the *r* interminably as he leaned on one hip. His excitement was mounting all the time. His fervour frightened me . . . He looked like a prophet in a trance. The crows seemed to answer him: his curses loosed an enormous clamour, a harsh sound like the cries of the dying. The interpreter had long ago given up translating and kept making discreet signs to indicate that the old man was completely crazy! He wasn't altogether wrong, but today it seems to me that his madness and his rage had succeeded in forcing one of the portals in the labyrinth. He had let me glimpse a few images in the tangled web of time . . . The squadrons lined up in columns with sabres raised and trumpets blowing into the wind, the horses hooves stamping the icy ground, waiting for the signal, then the mighty surge of 10,000 men on horseback under the sky that had cleared at last.

The old madman had perhaps shown me that the skin that covers the past can sometimes tear, that the dead can sometimes be called back to life. Was it his fury that had summoned up the ghosts of 8 February 1807? In any case, thanks to him, for a few moments I seemed to go in a forbidden direction, to perceive a wave or a wind in the past. It was nothing really. Scarcely more than a vague presence. Could that be what is meant by the permeability of memories? With my back against the Eylau cemetery – which one can't see any better in Gros's painting than in the other engravings – I saw that what is finished is not shut up for ever in some reliquary. It's not past time that is fascinating, but the way it can stop for an instant, an isolated instant, when an interval is created in continuous time. I found myself in a *break*, in a space between two periods.

Nothing of what is past is inaccessible. I felt that its presence was less vague, that the wave was taking shape and coming towards to me. It had almost touched me. I had felt its icy breath. Places like

Eylau are divided between absence and excess, barrenness and retrospective illusion. The past is a grey light we all must colour in our own way, and the past had just dazzled me like lightning.

It's true that I was anxiously waiting for that presence one can never possess. Then I felt as though I too had been carried off course, dragged towards the forbidden passage, the hidden point opening on to the gates of chaos. One cannot with impunity displace what time has put in such order. Once the door had half-opened, I had taken fright and gone back on my tracks. One should not linger in the intermissions of time.

The fifty-eighth Bulletin of the Grand Army indicates that Murat's charge, carried along by its own momentum, overwhelmed the first Russian line, then the second. It failed to break through the third, which managed to fall back into a wood. Murat's cavalrymen turned round and, at the same pace, crossed back over the Russian defences that they had just overthrown. The Grand Army report calls this charge "brilliant and unheard of". It's certain that this legendary exploit, known as "the charge of the 80 squadrons", had a decisive influence on the course of the battle, but for all that, was not able to overcome the Russians. Napoleon had practically no reserves left; he was impatiently waiting for Ney's army so that he could win the battle. Instead of Ney, the Prussian general Lestocq suddenly appeared. Fortunately Davout managed to save the situation by containing the pressure until the arrival of Ney, who finally forced the Russians to fall back. "Lestocq arriving instead of Ney, is the foreshadowing of Waterloo, when instead of Grouchy, Blücher arrives on the scene."[5] The enemy had lost 25,000 men and a good proportion of the 15,000 wounded evacuated to Königsberg also died. The French had 20,000 casualties.

On the evening of 8 February, Napoleon did not know the outcome of the battle. He had retired for the night, fully dressed with his boots on, in a little farm near Eylau. He seemed downcast. Early in the morning of the ninth, Marshal Soult's aide-de-camp asked to see the Emperor. "Sire, the enemy is beating a retreat." It was only at that moment that he knew he had won . . . or more precisely, that he remained in control of the battlefield. Should he proclaim victory? He hadn't the heart to do it. The Eylau plain looked like a nauseating quagmire: trampled snow red with blood, the last cries of the dying, the whinnying of mutilated horses and above all, the mountains of bodies and the flocks of crows. "Everything I have seen and heard will stay in my memory forever," the surgeon Percy writes.

"Come!" The order had issued from the wild-eyed teacher.

As he walked he jerked his body to one side, then tipped it up again just when I thought he was going to fall.

The interpreter wanted to leave, but the other man didn't see it that way. He kept repeating the number 14 and the word "regiment". He made the gesture that Orientals use to signify death, that almost comic way of touching one's throat with the flat of the hand. From time to time a long whining sound like a circular saw could be heard over the moaning of the wind. I had thought that the factory built where the cemetery used to be was a sawmill. "A sawmill!" our guide had exclaimed, cut to the quick. "Why, it's our computer factory. It's very modern." Computers at Eylau! That weird telescoping of time seemed to me an example of life's great ironies, the comic element present in every tragedy.

"Come!" the teacher said again.

We had slowly covered 500 metres to the east of the cemetery, when he pointed out a hillock and said the number 14 once more. I realized that he was talking about the spot where the 14th Line Regiment was wiped out during Augereau's unfortunate attack. I was there facing the ultimate mark left by the battle. There were no others. I knew that all the rest came from the fact that

I liked conjuring with history – and from its madness.

On 9 February 1807 there were hundreds of bodies at the foot of this rise. Bessières, who was in command of the guard cavalry, accompanied Napoleon as he inspected the battlefield. Looking at that sight, he made this stupid comment:

"They're lying there like sheep."

"You should say 'like lions'," the Emperor said, correcting him.

Napoleon on St Helena says of him: "Bessières had cool courage. He stayed calm in the midst of fire." In Gros's painting, he is on the left of the Emperor, looking wary, chin tucked in, his face wearing a slightly silly expression. He was a brave, phlegmatic man. Why did he make that remark, which disparages the valour of those brave men? Perhaps he felt he had to say *something*. Napoleon only speaks when he has to – it's only on St Helena that he becomes verbose. What does he say the day after Eylau? "What a massacre! And with no real outcome!" Then he adds, rather sententiously: "A sight made to inspire rulers with a love of peace and a horror of war."

In the evening he invites the artillery officers to dinner. One of the guests relates that: "To go and dine with the Emperor, we had to pass between two mountains of corpses, shattered limbs, arms, heads, those of our friends, alas! No one was hungry. But what revolted us even more and nauseated us the most is that when each of us opened our table napkin, we found a bank note there."[6] A banknote to make them forget the horror! A puerile and extremely insensitive side of Napoleon's character. Money to buy silence! It's true that Friedland, then Tilsit, will soon destroy the disastrous impression made by Eylau.

A few electric light poles with two horizontal cross pieces on the top, which make them look like guillotines, flights of crows leaving the black line of the pines and the mound where the remains of 36 officers of the 14th Line Regiment lie buried: this part of the landscape seemed to have grown smaller, as if time had dried out and shrunk space.

Unlike Waterloo, the Eylau battlefield does not *represent* anything. That is its strength. Waterloo, on the other hand, evokes too much (too many columns, monuments, plaques, dioramas and above all, *too close* to Brussels). But in the last analysis, Waterloo doesn't suggest anything. Eylau is raw, primitive, impenetrable like the sphinx. That had struck me very forcibly as we left the wood. I saw then that the view was magnificent from there, much better than from the cemetery. The extraordinary thing is that the panorama of the battle laid out before me covered about the same space as Gros had tried to represent. In the distance on the right, I could see the computer factory. In front of me, there were only enclosed fields and small kitchen gardens (*ogorod*) that the Russians cultivate at the end of towns or villages to supplement their ordinary meals.

The old madman, who had been silent for a while, then proclaimed:

"All of Bagrationovsk is a cemetery. History is buried there: the dead, the past. But it's only buried, not disappeared."

I had forgotten that Eylau is now called Bagrationovsk. But what did he mean by "not disappeared"? I could see that the interpreter now needed a lot of persuading to translate our guide's wild imaginings. They exchanged a few lively propositions, then the interpreter's sullen face suddenly changed. Why had he begun to quote him? He stressed the bravery of the Russian army and its success at Eylau. I had suddenly realized the reason for their new understanding: the old teacher had persuaded the interpreter that this battle was a Russian victory.

"But," I pointed out, "doesn't victory belong to the one who remains in control of the terrain?"

"The Russians withdrew in good order. And you French were too exhausted to pursue us."

That was strictly true – I had noted what the interpreter was doing, his use of "you" and "we".

Napoleon was so unsure of his success that he stayed at Eylau until 16 February. He didn't usually do that, but Europe had to know that he remained in control of the battlefield. During the days that followed the carnage, he acted in an unusual way. He dictated to Bertrand the text of a tract entitled *Account of the Battle of Eylau by an Eye-witness, Translated from the German*. Bertrand – his companion in misfortune, the man who will accompany him to St Helena, one of the only messengers to come back alive. At Eylau, Napoleon had dispatched him to Augereau with the order to take the 7th Corps forward. It was a suicidal mission. Then came the turn of the 14th Line Regiment. A worrying coincidence, isn't it? To justify what he was doing, he said to the man who at that time was still his aide-de-camp: "This is how history will tell it." The person who knew the real history was faithful Bertrand. What did he think of Napoleon's trick and of the account of Eylau "*translated from the German*"?

Bertrand is the one who will oversee the construction of the rafts over the Niemen River at Tilsit a few weeks later. He's the essential intermediary. After all, he's the bridge specialist, and a bridge is a place for crossing and testing. He's the man who knows. And on St Helena, doesn't he take a sly pleasure in grilling his master about Eylau, the most delicate subject?

In less than a week, Napoleon writes five letters to Josephine. We know the first, written the day after the slaughter ("Victory is mine, but I have lost a lot of people"). There is another, which expresses feelings he very rarely writes about: "The countryside here is covered with the dead and wounded. It is not the best part of the war; everyone is suffering and the air is *oppressive* with so many victims." "Oppressive" is a word he won't even use on St Helena. He is overcome by the horrible details relayed to him by the surgeon, Percy.

The Tzar himself congratulates Bennigsen, the general in chief, "for having conquered the man who had never been beaten until that day".

"So, Eylau is a Russian victory," I had suggested to my two companions.

They had protested rather affectedly:

"No, no. You're exaggerating. There was neither winner nor loser. Look, today Eylau is a potato field."

The teacher obviously didn't believe what he had just said. Was he really so demented? The countryside around here still had that false stability of land that is not completely at peace. An obscure upheaval marked the ground as if the storm of battle still shook it and would shake it forever. Only the crows, those indestructible birds of ill-omen, brought to mind the rotting bodies that had lain there.

The visit to Eylau would lead me to St Helena; I couldn't resist its urgent call.

Eylau is an unwieldy name, almost banished from the national memory. The Avenue Victor-Hugo in Paris was called the Avenue d'Eylau from 1864 to 1881. Then the name disappeared for a few years before surfacing again, attached unexpectedly to a new thoroughfare near the Trocadéro. It's a shortened, you might say amputated, road since initially it was supposed to go as far as the Porte Dauphine. It's an altered, distorted, mutilated road in the eyes of the church that bears its name: Saint Honoré d'Eylau has nothing to do with the eponymous avenue.

I had landed up in East Prussia, where history had pulled back rather like the Russian retreat from Eylau: in distress but in good order.

The same hybrid world, the same kind of silence, the dreamy sadness, the permanent presence of the past – I found them all intact at St Helena. There are two sides to these places: they convey absence yet they still brood with a deviant, silent life. Eylau and Longwood have the same vibrations, the same magnetic field attracted towards an unknown pole, which is none other than the hope of a resurrection. When we can't see anything, we always think we can see ghosts. But the old madman wasn't a ghost; he was the *envoy*, a kind of courier from another time, sent into the present to enthral impressionable souls like myself, a plenipotentiary of the irrational, a lost messenger who is not sure to whom he should entrust the tragic message.

I took my leave of the strange emissary in the centre of Eylau in front of the bust of Prince Bagration, the moving spirit of the Russian retreat. I appreciated the fact that Prince Bagration, who plays such a large part in *War and Peace*, should witness our parting. Tolstoy states that he had a rugged face with olive skin, and a very pronounced Georgian accent. He appears at the Battle of Schoengraben – a confrontation that took place before Austerlitz – where Prince André distinguished himself. I had noticed that the gold paint that covered the bust gave Bagration's severe expression the same comic air that he had at the triumphal welcome organized at the English Club of Moscow by Natasha's father. The inscription below the bust reads: *He spent thirty years of his life making war.*

"Always remember Eylau, Frenchman. The first blow of fate was dealt right here . . ."

After taking his leave, the old man had waved his scarf in the air and made it crack like a whip.

7

He's sitting in the darkest corner of the sitting room, looking somewhat aloof, obviously torn between wanting to talk and not wanting to.

A wall of rain surrounds the property. The intermittent drizzle falling in fine droplets, forms a kind of insulation around the house that muffles all sound.

On the wall are two portraits of Napoleon: one is a naïve oil painting showing him on horseback while in the other he has sat for the portrait at the Tuileries. These two canvasses are fascinating, as once again it is obviously not the same man who has been depicted. Naturally everything has been done to show us that it is indeed the Emperor. The uniform and the Titus hairstyle are details that explicitly indicate who he is. But it would seem that there is always an essential, elusive feature in that face, an expression which painters cannot render. Yet the real paradox lies in the fact that Napoleon is still always recognizable. Also on the walls hang a series of roses signed Pierre-Joseph Redouté, the artist who painted the garden at Malmaison.

"They're original plates," Michel Martineau comments. "I should tell you that my father is a born collector. If there's a document, an edition, he must have it. While I'm more of a curator, conserving and rescuing – you know the sort of thing . . . To tell the truth, I'm not very interested in the sentimental side of an object." Martineau senior mutters in his corner. He has a square face with his hair parted on the side. With his pale grey waistcoat he looks like an Englishman – at least that's the style he affects. Prominent eyebrow ridges and searching eyes denote keen observation. The Martineau's sitting room, where we are having drinks before dinner, is in the part of the house formerly occupied by the Montholons.

It often rained in their quarters, as the roof had only been made of tarred canvas. Nothing like the Martineau's residence now. Everything in this room, where I'm sitting on a Louis XV armchair upholstered in cock-of-the-rock red velvet, exudes solidity, a very British sense of comfort. Countess Diane is snoring gently at Gilbert Martineau's feet. She suddenly wakes up and rubs her piercing eyes. Countess Diane may well be of indefinite breeding, but she holds herself with dignity. She's very affectionate and sure of her master's attachment to her. At Longwood this dog is looked upon as a real person.

Michel Martineau was telling me a while ago that his father was working on Hudson Lowe's papers, some of which are in the British Museum. These enormous bundles, which contain notations of the slightest fact, the slightest rumour, have not yet been completely examined and could contain a few surprises.

"Have you discovered anything interesting?" I ask politely.

"Interesting! What do you mean by that?" the father replies in a rather haughty tone.

"Well, I don't know. Some revelations perhaps . . ."

"Revelations about what?"

"About Napoleon's companions or the servants. Cipriani, for example. What role did he play? Could he have given any information to Hudson Lowe?"

"Ah! Cipriani . . . A strange business."

His tone became a little more cordial. He hesitates . . . Is he going to say anything? I know that he's fascinated by the butler's story. His brown eyes look at me coldly.

I try to press my advantage.

"You say in one of your books that Hudson Lowe placed a certain amount of trust in him . . ."

"Hm, that's right . . ."

He clears his throat.

"There are some letters . . . yes, letters from London, encouraging Hudson Lowe to use Cipriani. But you know how Cipriani ended up . . . He died suddenly in February 1818. Was he poisoned? I admit I have no idea. Other people at Longwood, notably one of the Montholon's chambermaids, had come down with the same illness. He was buried in the Plantation House cemetery. His death has always intrigued me. I wanted to be clear in my own mind about it. I actually wanted to find out where his grave was. I did some excavations. Well! You won't believe this, but Cipriani's body had disappeared. It's strange . . ."

He's said too much and he's not happy about it.

"Right. That's enough. We'll have dinner." He cuts off the conversation and sounds definitely frosty.

The dining room is in the O'Meara section. Napoleon's Irish doctor stayed at Longwood until July 1818, when he was sent back to England by Hudson Lowe. At the beginning of Napoleon's captivity, O'Meara had had a foot in both camps, but he finally sided with the prisoner. His book, *Napoleon in Exile*, published in 1822, played an important part in the St Helena legend. He was the first to inform Europe of the jailer's pettiness and persecutions.

The walls of the dining room are hung with engravings of members of the Bonaparte family. I notice a bottle of Château Batailley, 1986 vintage, standing on the sideboard. Pictures of the old parasol pine that covers almost the whole facade of the château and the peaceful library of the proprietor Émile Casteja flash into my mind. I've always been fascinated by the Louis XIV clock sitting in the middle of the mantelpiece. Why does the effigy of an old man holding a scythe come to mind? Perhaps because of the inscription *The last minute kills*, an image of Time and its pitiless law. Wine may be the only living matter that avoids the irreparable damage wrought by time – it only becomes more delectable as it ages.

The beginning of the meal is not very lively. Gilbert Martineau says nothing. His son tries to get his father to talk about the Hudson Lowe papers, but the only time he speaks is to see to my glass or my plate. He is very attentive and insists on me taking a second helping. I'm not taken in by this solicitude, as I know it's meant to cut short any conversation about Napoleon. He does, however, ask me a few questions, or rather he uses the question form to dwell on points of detail about the Emperor's companions. For example: "Montholon, now what a shifty character he was, don't you think?" I'm meant to add something here . . . These soundings are obviously intended to test me. He wants to know if I've done my homework. It's true that there's no great merit in my displaying knowledge that I've only just acquired. I certainly swotted up a lot on the boat. He seems to be satisfied with the books I've read.

"Yes . . . One definitely must read the first-hand accounts," he mutters. "The rest is only paraphrase! Well now, this 1986 Batailley, what do you think of it?"

"Excellent. It hasn't completely opened out yet, but it has a nice texture nonetheless."

My comment amuses him.

"A nice texture! I didn't know that wine had anything to do with weaving," he says ironically.

"It's truer than you think. People also talk of the fabric of a wine . . . Above all for a bordeaux."

"You know that at Longwood the English gave Napoleon nothing but bordeaux."

"That's quite usual. The English generally prefer a bordeaux to a burgundy."

"Yes, but Napoleon much preferred burgundy. In France he only drank Gevrey-Chambertin – with water, it's true. In any case, he didn't particularly appreciate the pleasures of the table."

This subject has suddenly made him quite talkative. He goes into his study to look for a document. It's a letter from Lord Bathurst to the Governor. He reads out what the English minister writes to Lowe: "I know that Napoleon has a preference for burgundy, but I have good reason to believe that this wine does not travel well: and if some burgundy has turned sour when it arrives at St Helena, he will swear that I am trying to poison him!"

"But where does this myth about bordeaux travelling better than burgundy come from?" asks Martineau senior.

"It's the tannins . . . Bordeaux wines are very high in tannins. That's why they're so harsh when they're young. That's why they sent them by ship so that they'd soften. This Bathurst was a connoisseur . . ."

"Perhaps. But he was also a swine."

We discuss the large numbers of bottles drunk at Longwood. He quotes Gourgaud who often mentions in his *Journal* the amount of waste that went on in the house. "I confirm the fact that the servants waste a lot and that 17 bottles of wine, 88 pounds of meat and nine chickens cannot be consumed per day: that gives them something to hold against us. In our position, it is best to take as little as possible." A note to Hudson Lowe instances a daily consumption of nine bottles of bordeaux, 24 of Cape wine, six of Tenerife, Graves, Constance, one of madeira, plus 14 bottles of champagne and six of port per month.

"Out of interest I did a calculation just for the last trimester of 1816," said Gilbert Martineau. "It's an impressive total: 3,724 bottles. One then gets an average of 3,300 bottles."

"So, they were heavy drinkers at Longwood!"

"Yes, but Napoleon and his companions were sober. The servants were the ones who drank like fish. Life was far from boring in the staff dining quarters, let me tell you. Hudson Lowe was irate when he came to Longwood. He had insisted on the empty bottles being given back to him, but Napoleon's servants took pleasure in smashing them to annoy him. Broken glass littered the ground all around Longwood.

Gilbert Martineau is becoming more and more talkative. He thinks that history has been too hard on Hudson Lowe. According to him, Lord Bathurst, the Colonial Secretary and therefore the person in charge of Napoleon's detention, was a far worse individual than the jailer. He had an almost pathological resentment of the former sovereign, and in London he would lay down rules and regulations with an obsessive attention to detail. These edicts had no other purpose but to humiliate the prisoner and make his life miserable.

Lowe, who was unintelligent, suspicious and mean by nature, slavishly applied the Minister's injunctions. "The Henchman", as the prisoner liked to call him, had the profile of the perfect scapegoat. His stupidity and evil-mindedness tend to make one forget the overwhelming responsibility of "the English oligarchy" – an expression Napoleon often used. The cruelty, the baseness and the humiliation come first from the cabinet in London, which was responsible for the two major decisions: the choice of St Helena and of the jailer.

We discuss the sixth and last meeting between Napoleon and Hudson Lowe on Sunday, 18 August 1816. The weather had been frightful. Taking advantage of a brighter interval, the Emperor decided to take a walk in the gardens. He is there when the Governor appears on the scene. Napoleon is very annoyed. Lowe announces that he has received instruction to reduce expenses at Longwood. The conversation very quickly turns sour.

"You are the instrument of Lord Bathurst's blind hatred!" exclaims the captive.

"Sir, Lord Bathurst does not know the meaning of the words 'blind hatred'," Lowe retorts.

"In 500 years the name of Napoleon will shine brightly and those of Bathurst, Castlereagh and yours will only be known for the shame and injustice of their conduct towards me."

Napoleon then adds:

"If you do not wish to provide us with food, I shall take my meals with the officers of the 53rd or with the soldiers."[7]

"Fortunately, all of that makes little impression on me," replies the Governor, getting quite annoyed.

"No doubt. The executioner laughs at his victims' cries."

This altercation will be the last. Lowe, very red in the face, turns on his heel and leaves without another word. The next time he sees his prisoner again is five years later when Napoleon has died, on the morning of 6 May 1821. This last quarrel bothers the prisoner, who regrets having lost his temper:

"That is the second time I have caused my dealings with the English to deteriorate. Their composure lets me go too far and I say more than I should. It would have been better not to answer him . . ."

He admits to Las Cases that he had criticized Lowe "very harshly" and admits that the Governor "had never actually wronged him".[8]

"Hudson Lowe is a useful character for everyone," continues Gilbert Martineau. "He's criticized on all sides. But he had real qualities as an administrator. Did you know that he was the one who abolished slavery on St Helena? Far be it from me to defend him, but between ourselves, where would the legend be without persecution? Where would the Passion and Redemption be without the executioner?"

"The jailer often explains a lot about the prisoner," I said.

"Exactly. And also, his assiduous side, his obsession with detail, is of benefit to people like me who are working on Napoleon's captivity. Just think of it: 104 volumes in the British Museum! 98 are devoted to the administration of St Helena . . . A real mine of information."

The expression on his face suddenly changes. He knits his brows and purses his lips. His whole face retracts.

"Why did I tell you all that?"

The tone of his voice shows that he's not at all pleased. He has his surly look again. I'm beginning to know his sudden changes of mood. This type of solitary individual likes to let himself go when he has been self-contained for too long, but then he regrets having said so much.

A long silence settles over the dining room. The weather is

overcast. A miserable rain falls relentlessly over the gardens. This wind hits the woodwork of the doors, making a constant thudding noise against the background of the eternal moaning of the trade wind. During the end of the meal, Longwood melancholy gently seeps drop by drop, like the dull drumming of the rain falling from the roof on to the ground. I'm beginning to get used to this endless flow of water; it's Longwood's only song. It steals into people like a mild vexation or an almost salutary suffering.

I sometimes feel affected by the same sickly languor, the same disillusionment, the same inclination that comes upon me suddenly but doesn't last. But don't imagine that Longwood melancholy is the pleasure of being sad. It's rather the lassitude that comes from an inevitable relapse, the despondency of knowing the vicious circle will never end. The same wittering of the wind, the same old song of the rain, the same old words that tell the same stories about Napoleon's captivity over and over again. Yesterday, tomorrow, forever. Napoleon himself suffered the martyrdom of repetition. He in turn imposed it on his entourage, not without a certain sadistic pleasure. The dictation of his memoirs is repetition: they harp on the same depressing theme. Fortunately there are numerous false notes, and those discordant passages are the best part of the imperial *miserere*. Unlike Eylau, which he doesn't want to recall, the vanquished general constantly ruminates over his defeat at Waterloo. This is one of several examples from Montholon: "The Emperor is taking up his work on Waterloo with Gourgaud for the tenth time. In the evening he tells us: 'I still cannot conceive how the battle was lost'." (20 May 1817). Is it this constant repetition of the same theme that causes old Martineau's misanthropy?

He no longer wants to trot out the same story. He's not aware of what I know about him. I know that he turned his back on the world for good in 1957, voluntarily accepting exile. Why did he choose to live his life in isolation? Martineau was a fairly familiar figure in

Parisian salons after the war. These were the last brilliant days of literary society. Every Thursday he went to the Rostands and he frequented Jean Cocteau. "He was a taciturn figure, enigmatic, rather austere and critical of the frivolous side of our group."[9]

He worked for Nagel for a long time, publishing numerous travel guide books, rubbing shoulders with Jean-Paul Sartre – many of the philosopher's works were published there.

What I find intriguing are the two years spent in Corsica at the Aspretto naval airbase. Aspretto was the training camp for naval frogmen and the nerve centre for clandestine activities. What exactly was his role there? Officially he was "Chief of General Services and Operations".

Then one day he had enough . . . What was the cause of his departure to St Helena? At one time during the meal he condemned "the rush to be rich, indifference, selfishness".

He lights his cigar, sighs, then declares gruffly:

"We'll have coffee in the sitting room."

Among the brandies, I notice a liqueur Napoleon brandy with the famous hat on the label. Did he notice I was looking at it? He smiles and takes the bottle.

"You'll try this," he ordered. "I'm sure you'll agree that this brandy is part of the process of immersing yourself in the atmosphere. That's what you're trying to achieve, isn't it?"

I don't object to the touch of mockery he always puts into whatever he says. The purpose is no doubt to create a distance from others and from himself. "I am extravagant by nature," he says, quoting Byron. His son, Michel, had told me that he has written the memoirs of a dog called Marmaduke. Men and their foibles are seen through the eyes of a cocker spaniel. Marmaduke's master is a diplomat with a posting on an island. It seems that in the preface Martineau states that his book belongs to "a hybrid genre of humorous writing", and that it will therefore never be published.

An English humorist once said that "the most human thing about man is his dog". Gilbert Martineau seems to have made that assertion his own. I remember another remark of his son's: "My father has seen it all before. On St Helena he has created out of his disillusionment an art of living." His book on Byron describes the disappointments of a life that had been lived "too much in his imagination" during adolescence. *La Malédiction du génie* is essentially the story of a young man who was "naïve but demanding, gifted but temperamental, affectionate but sly, impetuous but frail, merry but sarcastic."[10] That's just how I imagine him in the 1930s – he was born in 1918.

The video room was formerly occupied by Gourgaud. Michel Martineau shows me some pieces of wood: they are the last vestiges of the original floor. I feel these worm-eaten bits of oak and weigh them in my hand. There it is again – my neurotic attachment to relics and the illusion that they possess *mana*. But for all that, I'm well aware that they don't hold any supernatural power, and I'm not naïve enough to believe that by squeezing these bits of wood in my hands I'll make the original floor appear. And yet, I sometimes feel I'm searching for this lost ingenuousness . . . Dear objects from the past, time hasn't destroyed you because you harbour the regret for lost innocence in every human heart, that touch of eternity which is nothing but the memory of childhood.

The impossible task of recreating the past, of capturing its vividness – I love that battle, even though it's lost before it begins.

Contrary to our museums crammed with an indiscriminate host of objects, Longwood is irreplaceable because the few pieces of debris saved from the wreck are never insignificant. They have a meaning. Hence, this worm-eaten wood that I have in my hand tells the story of a rescue. Longwood nearly disappeared, victim of a plague that descended on the island at the beginning of the century: termites.

Michel Martineau tells me about the adventure of an engineer from Bordeaux called Maurice Décamps, who was sent to St Helena in 1935 to save Longwood from the termites. The operation had been decided upon by the Minister for Foreign Affairs at the instigation of the Friends of St Helena. The process involved was theoretically quite revolutionary. The anti-termite specialist stayed at Longwood for about ten days, then went back to France. Several letters sent to him from the curator at that time, Georges Colin, confirmed that the treatment had been successful. In reality, the termites were secretly continuing their work of destruction, to such an extent that in 1945 it was impossible to ignore the obvious: Longwood was about to collapse.

In 1947 Georges Colin's successor, Georges Peugeot, had to concede that "the Emperor's house is in a disastrous state". When King George VI and his family called at St Helena, they noted the enormous damage caused by termites. Longwood then had to close its doors to visitors. The restoration work did not begin until 1950, and would last for five years. A mistaken measurement in the rebuilding of the billiard room meant that the work had to be started all over again.

I carefully place the pieces of wood on the table. Michel Martineau is well aware of my little obsession. It amuses him and he enters into the spirit of the thing in a very urbane way. His perfect courtesy is his way of keeping himself at a distance. He's an imperturbable giant with a piercing gaze, who observes, usually in silence, and frowns when his attention is engaged by something. He's amused by the surly side of his father's nature, in rather the same way as one watches a well-rehearsed act. He must know all the techniques and all the little tricks his father uses, but he's careful not to intervene. One doesn't interrupt an artist while he's performing. Gilbert Martineau is certainly an old bear, but is he bearish in the sense of unmannerly? Out here on his rock, the old misanthrope loves to intrigue people, to arouse their interest. He's chosen to bury himself here, but not as someone insignificant and unknown. He represents France. At the same time, he dislikes performing. I know that he hates the role of the old scholar in which I've typecast him.

He joins us in the video room smoking a cigar, looking as impenetrable and cross as ever, mumbling something about the weather which seems to be clearing. Among the hundreds of cassettes I notice recordings of concerts (*La Bohème*, *La Traviata* by Ileana Cotrubas, lots of Beethoven) as well as numerous tapes of *Grosses Têtes* [*Big Heads*]. I'm not at all surprised that he likes to look at that kind of TV programme with its mixture of erudition and broad humour. I'd already noticed that his language has a certain roughness reminiscent of the ex-naval officer. He spoke to me a while ago about his time at the Naval College. I learned that he had joined the Free French in 1940. He began as a leading seaman on a submarine in England, became an interpreter, then was sent to Port-Étienne in 1943.[11] At the Liberation, he had reached the rank of lieutenant. This native of the Charente region loves islands. He owned a house on the Île de Ré for many years.

"What are you up to?" he asks us.

"We were talking about termites, Dad," says Michel Martineau with an amused smile.

"Ah! The termites," he says, looking thoughtful. "Do you know that after the war, given the enormous extent of the damage, they had even considered completely demolishing Longwood and building a commemorative monument in its place? Right. Let's take a walk in the gardens. The weather is clearing."

We've stopped in front of a bed of agapanthus, at the very same spot where the last meeting between the prisoner and his jailer took place on 18 August 1816.

Why do I feel the same quiver each time I look at the blood-red walls of the house? Why do I get that uneasy feeling? There's something about the sight of that house and the clouds that zoom down on Longwood and then fly off as though the devil were chasing them that gives an impression of both destruction and energy. The aerial assault on the plateau – an invasion of incredible proportions – is just like a cavalry charge. Bands of mist like long scarves engulf the sky, flow over the rooftops and then race off towards Diana's Peak.

Nothing lasts, yet everything survives ... I'm thinking of this house: it continued to exist even when no one was left there to see it. Out of sight and out of mind, it held its own against the excesses of time, the powers of darkness and the fearsome blast of the storm. The dark room was used as a stable, the sitting room as a barley mill. The fragile but resistant "cardboard house" is a marvellous symbol of triumphant reality. It didn't need to be admired to survive; it did without love and the worshipping gaze of pilgrims to the shrine. The realm of sadness and death miraculously held out against disintegration, collapse and nothingness.

One of the paths in the garden bears the name of Paul and Édith Ganière. The author of *Napoléon à Sainte-Hélène* first came to Longwood in 1954. The gardens were bare and the house in ruins. He was a doctor who had wanted to go to the actual location to study "the sick man". The general survey he wrote on Napoleon's exile is the work of an historian who has breathed, touched and examined the Emperor's troubled time on the island. A little stone pyramid marks the grave of a French naval lieutenant who died on St Helena in 1850. A few stone benches ... The peaceful, rather arcadian view of a mausoleum. A piece of unpretentious theatre scenery.

One thing I like, especially in the gardens, is this idea of *reappearance*.

The beds, the paths and the pond had disappeared. The old plans were retrieved and, with a lot of patience, everything has slowly taken shape again.

"You could say that from 1990 the gardens have come back to what they were," says Michel Martineau. "We've favoured tropical plants that don't need much water. You won't believe me, but it rarely rains at Longwood. We're constantly shrouded in mist and damp. We're the ones who get the first clouds, but they generally burst over Hutt's Gate. I should also tell you that the gardens you see here are made to the plans drawn up in 1821. At the beginning of the exile, the land around Longwood was barren. The only trees were gum trees. All that existed was a sparse little garden under the windows of the Emperor's bedroom and study."

"We haven't taken our concern for authenticity as far as rebuilding the three-metre ditches dug by Hudson Lowe," the father adds, quite pleasantly. "You know that he had built what amounts to fortifications around Longwood."

He's in an affable mood once more. It's not that he's rude; he even has all the appearance of a refined gentleman. The fact is that he wears a mask and doesn't know whether he should take it off or keep it on. And yet he came here to be rid of it. A while ago I heard him speak of "the studied savagery of the world at large". No doubt he imagines that I belong to this cruel, conformist world. He doesn't know what position to take.

"All the same, these araucarias, Norfolk pines and cedars weren't there in Napoleon's time," I reply. "Can you explain something to me? Longwood gives the impression of being a refuge hidden in a wooded bower, whereas Napoleon complained bitterly of the lack of shade."

"There were a few trees," Michel Martineau informs me. "There you are. I can show you two of them."

He points out two pines bent by the wind. These two veterans are not as strong as they were, but their reflexes are still good. They struggle on, but they obviously haven't reached the point of giving up the ghost. I run my hand over the deeply etched bark covered with lichen. The light, rough skin is furrowed with grooves that look like fluting on a column. I like to think that one of these pines is there in Marchand's watercolour painting. Couldn't it be the tree on the right of the gardener – the one digging the earth?

"I couldn't swear to it," Michel Martineau replied. "But if it pleases you to think so, why should you deny yourself something that may only be an illusion? . . . Also have a look at that green oak. I think that it's the last survivor from that period, together with the two pines. Please don't think I'm being ironical. I've told you that I like to preserve things, to rescue them. At least I try to . . . Survival . . . Perhaps it's my way of believing in immortality. Nonetheless, I don't like relic hunters."

"Do you see a lot at Longwood?"

"Napoleon seems to arouse a very strange kind of fetishism in people. They couldn't care less about Louis XIV's shirt or the bed he slept in. Napoleon is the only French historical figure who inspires such a craze. One day I came upon someone stretched out on the sitting room floor in the position where Napoleon died. Lots of people want to take away with them some earth from Longwood or a plant. We have to keep a close watch in the house. There are people who wouldn't hesitate to break off a piece of the billiard table. I regularly get letters addressed to Napoleon! It's exhausting! They ask the Emperor's advice on the Gulf War; they suggest an amorous adventure. I don't know why the postman sends the letters to me. But look at this green oak . . . another survivor."

This usually leafy oak is also quite leafless with age and in a worse state than the two pines, as it is supported by a crutch.

"It's crippled. Like a soldier of the Napoleon's old guard after the great battles were over. But the old man doesn't want to die," I say to him.

"It's funny you should say that. What a coincidence! Do you know, it's the name of a plant that's endemic on St Helena. Here it's called 'Old Father Live Forever'. I'll show you a specimen. I'm trying to acclimatize it here, but it's not easy as this plant likes dry areas."

We stop in front of a pot plant. It looks like a geranium with creeping roots.

"There are about 20 endemic plants like that on St Helena. Just a moment. I'll show you the 'Baby's Toes'."

"I can hear the painter waxing lyrical over his models," I remark rather subtly.

"The painter? I'm not so sure. I'm essentially a botanist who has strayed into painting. I haven't even painted the 'Babies' Toes' yet. Look, it's very unusual."

He points out a plant with numerous stems that look like toes. They are round and full and the light green surface is smooth, in fact very much like the toes of a plump baby.

At the moment a heady, slightly gamy odour typical of tropical rot is being drawn out of the ground by the warmth of a bright shining sun. The beds of brilliant irises, the amaryllis and the plumbago growing in profusion cannot make one forget that subtle smell of decomposition – the secret sign that things progress much faster towards their end here than elsewhere.

Behind the Chinese pavilion where Napoleon used to watch the ships coming and going, in a gap in the silvery beeches that act as a wind-break, one can see the sea in the distance like a lapiz lazuli fountain. The jet seems to have suddenly frozen in mid-air, above the shimmering silver metal of the trees.

The ocean, the whispering shadows, the dazzling, despairing light. From this plateau, any dream of freedom must inevitably come up against the dispiriting permanence of that blue.

1. The footnotes of history. [Tr.]

2. Fonds Jourquin [Jourquin collection], unpublished.

3. General Bonaparte was often called "Le Petit Tondu", the little man with the close-cropped hair [Tr.]

4. The lively, vivid *Souvenirs* [*Memories*] have been published in a critical edition by Jacques Jourquin (Tallandier). They are a fascinating account of Napoleon's campaigns.

5. Louis Madelin, *Vers l'Empire d'Occident* [*Towards the Western Empire*].

6. Michelet, *Histoire du dix-neuvième siècle* [*History of the Nineteenth Century*].

7. The 53rd Infantry posted at Longwood to keep the prisoner under surveillance.

8. Octave Aubry finds that "He was not without a certain natural benevolence", and this author is not usually indulgent as far as the jailer is concerned.

9. Told to the author by Éric Ollivier.

10. *La Malédiction du génie* [*The Curse of Genius*].

11. Port-Étienne, now called Nouadhibou, is in Mauritania. [Tr.]

The Sixth Day

I

I HAVE DINNER EVERY DAY IN JAMESTOWN'S ONLY RESTAURANT, Anne's Place, situated in the middle of the town park. The bars of the iron grille fence are lance-shaped. They come from the fence at New Longwood, the house that Hudson Lowe had had built to receive Napoleon. The prisoner always refused to live there.

The specialties at Anne's Place are fishcakes and chicken curry. Fishing is the island's only wealth. Everything produced is exported to the United Kingdom.

With my meal, I always have the same heavy, South African wine. Anne, the proprietor, is a matronly woman with gentle ways, who has taken "the Frenchman" under her protection. Anne takes it upon herself to contribute to my well-being and to the convenience of my stay on the island.

"See that woman over there," she whispers. "She's with her husband, the Attorney-General. You should have a word with her. I think she's half French."

She's referring to a red-haired woman with a pleasant, lively face, who is sitting near the cash register. Anne must have mentioned me to her as she gives a small wave of her hand. The attorney nods his head. As I cross the room after paying my bill, the couple call me over and ask me to sit down.

Once the introductions have been made, we are soon conversing like old friends, sitting under the lights that Anne has hung on the branches of the trees.

"My name is Marian."

She speaks French extremely well. Her mobile features and fresh complexion make her little face very expressive. One can imagine she has a subtle and keen sensitivity.

"I've noticed that the Saints are naturally open and friendly," I say to start the conversation.

"That also means that they're very curious and love to gossip," Marian replies. "But you know, both of us are expatriates."

The attorney explains that his responsibilities are like those of a Minister of the Interior.

"It's a very peaceful island. Delinquency and crime scarcely exist here."

He almost apologizes for it and seems to be sorry that this peace and quiet might lessen the value of his office.

"But in spite of that, it's not easy coming here from Britain," she warns me. The Saints are suspicious of all high functionaries. That's to be expected. They have always been told what to do. Before the English Government, there was the East India Company.[1]

Like Nick Thorpe, whom I had met at the beginning of my stay, she calls St Helena "a museum".

"No industries, no pollution, no television! It's a real paradise . . ."

Then she adds, *mezza voce*:

"But one sometimes regrets having entered this paradise . . ."

What does she mean? That one gets bored here? I don't dare ask her to explain. Her husband has started a conversation at a table nearby, but I have the impression that he's listening with one ear.

"All the same, it's reassuring," she says, correcting herself. "Here the violence of the world is something abstract. As they don't have television, the Saints imagine war is like a film on video. For example, they had no really concrete idea of what the Gulf War was like. I think they imagined it as a sort of kung-fu – a type of film they adore. The world moves quickly, violently. St Helena is snug in its peaceful little universe."

"That's a privilege, don't you think?"

"Oh! Certainly. You've seen Jamestown . . . the cars, the shops. One would think that life stopped in the 'fifties, 'sixties. I don't deny that living conditions are pleasant and easy for expatriates. Domestic work isn't expensive, there are receptions every week, alcohol is cheap. And also they can allow themselves to act in ways that often wouldn't be accepted in England. Wives of government officials haven't a great deal to do here, apart from organizing local charities or doing a bit of free teaching in the schools."

"Patronesses, as we say in France."

"Well! I didn't want to be one of these patronesses."

"Ah! What do you do then?"

"I was lucky enough to be able to work in the St Helena information bureau as chief editor of the local paper. Between you and me, I was the only applicant for the job. You can't imagine what problems I've had. For example, I've never been able to get confirmation of a burglary at the presbytery, as the police are very reticent about giving the slightest information. In any case, people here think that the wife of a civil servant shouldn't work. Still, it's allowed me to get an idea of the frustrations the islanders have felt towards the British bureaucrats, who tend to act like Big Brother."

"Does this criticism worry your husband?"

She smiles but says nothing further. Her husband hasn't heard and is still in discussion with our neighbours. He gives us a smile from time to time.

"Let's just say that official decisions are often taken here in a rather clumsy way," she proffers. "There's a problem of communication, as they say today. The result: people latch on to what they hear in the street. Rumours and tittle-tattle circulate quickly here.

Personally, I often have the feeling of living in a goldfish bowl, given the huge interest in my private life."

"Right. We're going home," mutters the husband, out of the blue.

Even though he hasn't taken part in our conversation, the looks he keeps giving his wife seem to signify that he doesn't much like her plain speaking. But perhaps it's only my impression. The attorney looks tired. Seeing the disappointment on my face, Marian exclaims:

"St Helena is so small! . . . We'll finish our conversation one day or another."

"The only thing is that I don't have many days left. The boat leaves the day after tomorrow."

"But two days is a lot . . . You'll see . . ."

2

It's the 25 November 1816, and the Emperor is walking about the garden. "The wind had grown cold," notes Las Cases, who accompanies him. The two men hurry back to the billiard room. As usual, the prisoner is reeling off his memories, walking up and down the room. The subject on that day is his marriage to Marie-Louise. Through the casement, he suddenly notices that a large detachment of English officers has appeared in the middle of the garden. A servant rushes up to announce that Colonel Reade wants to see Las Cases very urgently. Napoleon's confidant indicates that he is in conversation with the Emperor, but the latter says to him:

"My dear man, go and see what the fellow wants . . . and make sure you come straight back."

These were the last words Las Cases heard from Napoleon's lips. The author of the *Memoirs* writes:

"Alas! I never saw him again! I can still hear his accent and the sound of his voice."

On Hudson Lowe's orders Las Cases has just been arrested. He is immediately put in solitary confinement with his son, then questioned by "The Henchman" in person. What "crime" had the Emperor's favourite committed? It's a mysterious affair that has never really been explained. Las Cases had a mulatto servant called James Scott, a smart, unscrupulous lad. Hudson Lowe was suspicious of him and managed to get him dismissed. In spite of the Governor's orders, Scott reappears at Longwood on 20 November. He informs his former master that he has decided to leave for England and offers to take back some messages, unbeknown to Hudson Lowe. Las Cases mentions it to Napoleon, who is not very enthusiastic about the idea. The former chamberlain, however, takes the initiative on his own behalf to send two letters: one to Lucien, the Emperor's brother, and the other to his old friend Lady Cleveland. These were written on two pieces of white silk and then sewn into the lining of Scott's jacket. Once home, the young man confides in his father, who denounces him. Lowe discovers the secret and has Las Cases arrested.

All the historians have been struck by Las Cases's rashness. Napoleon himself will be appalled by it. The worst thing is that Lowe seized Las Cases' voluminous journal. The prisoner is worried . . . He calls Ali, who is familiar with Las Cases's papers, since he spends a good part of his time making a fair copy of them. He asks the scribe if Las Cases has written down the things he said about his jailer:

"Does he repeat that I said he is a vile man and that his face is the most vulgar I have ever seen?"

Ali confirms the fact.

"Does he say that I called him 'a Sicilian henchman'?"

"Yes, Sire."

"That is his name," says the Emperor.

Was Las Cases acting rashly? It's difficult to believe that this intelligent man would be so imprudent. So, one has to admit that he probably engineered his departure. Several reasons have been put forward: the ill health of his son Emmanuel, who had come with him, the growing hostility of Napoleon's entourage towards him, and above all, the completion of his work as historiographer. Las Cases had collected a considerable amount of material and considered his task as the writer of memoirs was over. The publication of his journal would contribute much more effectively to Napoleon's cause than would prolonging his stay, which he had found less and less bearable. He thought that he could once again be useful to the prisoner's cause by leaving St Helena and becoming a sort of roving ambassador in Europe. It's also possible that Lowe sent Scott to trap Las Cases. The Governor knew of the ex-chamberlain's notes and was very eager to know their contents. "The truth, if one can ever establish it, seems to lie somewhere between the two. Las Cases and Lowe used Scott for opposite purposes: one to get himself sent home under the guise of breaking the rules, and the other to seize private papers among which he hoped to discover references to a plan of escape by Napoleon."[2]

Las Cases's departure had a great effect on the prisoner, who appreciated the man's culture, his subtlety and his deference. "The Jesuit", as Gourgaud called him, was intellectually far superior to the other three companions of the Emperor who sought his company, and evidently aroused the group's jealousy. "His favour with Napoleon, though perfectly explicable to us from his experience and his contrast with the too domestic Bertrand, the less cultivated Montholon, and the impracticable Gourgaud, was a constant irritation to them," Lord Rosebery writes.

This month of November 1816 marks a change in Napoleon's captivity. On 31 December, Gourgaud describes the prisoner as "very downcast". Napoleon confides to Bertrand: "I am in a tomb." During the little party on the following day, he declares:

"I am only waiting for death to put an end to my torment."

From then on, that lament will never cease. It will resound throughout Longwood until his death. Now, he has a clear awareness of his end. The birth of Arthur Bertrand – "The first Frenchman," as his mother says, "to arrive on St Helena without the permission of Lord Bathurst" – will bring a smile to the captive's lips, but he seems more and more a prey to sadness. Gourgaud recounts a pathetic scene on 15 January. The Emperor is leafing through the Imperial Almanac to verify a figure. His eyes linger over names that were well-known to him: "It was a fine Empire! I had eighty-three million human beings to rule, more than half the population of the whole of Europe!" And then, to hide his emotion, he begins to sing. Gourgaud is overcome: "What a man, what courage, what a fall! Went to bed at midnight."

When things are going badly at St Helena, you can bet that Waterloo is not far away. On 25 February 1817, he is going through the battle once again. "I should have put Soult on the left . . . I should not have used Vandamme." All his sentences begin with the past conditional. On 8 March, he only says one thing: "Let us work on Waterloo." Gourgaud is not in form.

An incident then takes places that is very revealing about the relationship between Napoleon and his aide-de-camp. The feat of arms in which Gourgaud takes great pride after the French campaign is, as we know, to have killed a hussar who was rushing at Napoleon. The whole of the entourage knows about this exploit and the party concerned boasts about it incessantly. He is careful not to mention the episode in front of the Emperor, thinking that Napoleon knows that he saved his life. However, one day after a quarrel, he lets drop an allusion to this feat. The Emperor is surprised and replies: "I don't remember."

"I'm stunned!" Gourgaud exclaims. "How could Your Majesty not remember? The staff officers witnessed it, and that same evening Monsieur Fain came and asked me if it was with the little pistols that I always had in my pocket or with horse pistols. It was the talk of Paris."[3]

"You should have told me about it."

"Sire, I was sure that Your Majesty had seen it and I thought that if I boasted of having done Your Majesty a service, he would hold it against me."

"I know that you are a fine young man, but it is surprising that with your intelligence you should be so childish."

Gourgaud, who is relating this scene, does not take kindly to being called "a child" in that way: "His Majesty is angry and I shall remain silent." This is a comment that is found on almost every page of his *Journal* for that year, 1817.

"Come now Gourgaud. Play! It will put you in a good mood."

"No, Sire."

The next day, Napoleon insists:

"You are a child. You should still finish Waterloo, while I am inspired to work."

Gourgaud is nearly always the one who provokes an argument.

"You want to get everything by force. You want to be like me," Napoleon retorts.

They tried to pick arguments over money matters. The Emperor tactlessly dangles the prospect of a tidy sum of money before the young man, who is poor. "If you leave, rest assured that I will give you 300,000 francs, at least."

Of all the accounts, Gourgaud's is the most spontaneous and lively. The author's impulsive nature gives his *Journal* a ring of inimitable sincerity. This spontaneity contrasts with Las Cases's grandiloquence and the dull reports of Grand Marshal Bertrand. This absence of affectation is not without a certain puerility. Napoleon also succumbs to this childishness. Gourgaud often gives him the cold shoulder. Napoleon advises him to be more accommodating with the Montholons. "I prefer to stay in my room with the rain coming in," Gourgaud replies crossly. Voices are raised. "I prefer Montholon to you!" Napoleon says, flaring up. The two men almost break off relations with each other, then their quarrels die down. Gourgaud returns to the Longwood fold. "Bertrand dines with us. The beans are good" (23 March). Gourgaud may well be under his hero's spell, but he doesn't treat him with any great respect. Sometimes he even makes fun of the prisoner, who is very concerned with what others think of him. The Grand Marshal notes that during the course of the Egyptian campaign Napoleon had the water of the Nile measured "by the chain". The Emperor interrupts him: "Don't say that. That is all that is needed for someone writing a lampoon to say that I have forgotten my mathematics."

On another occasion, an English officer cadet is introduced to Napoleon. The young soldier was on the frigate taking the defeated general to Elba. "The Emperor tells the cadet that he recognizes him, but that he has grown." He later confesses to Gourgaud that he doesn't really remember, but that he said that to please him. The great charmer, the infallible reader of the human mind, is not dead. Gourgaud is astounded. "That is how to be a leader of men," he sighs.

One of the few notable events of the year 1817 is when the Emperor receives the bust of his son, the King of Rome. He has it put on the mantelpiece in the sitting room, commenting that he looks a little too much like Marie-Louise, but that fortunately the upper part of the face is his.

Reconciliations follow quarrels between the captive and Gourgaud. "Boredom is wearing you down. You need a pretty little woman," says Napoleon. Whereupon Gourgaud makes an aside: "That is what I think to myself."

Wandering memories, experienced by all captives confined in their prison, slowly make Napoleon become sluggish. He isolates himself more and more. This confinement takes the form of long periods spent in his bath. He sometimes has his lunch there. On 12 June 1817, he stays there for four-and-a-half hours. He *submerges himself*, sunk in amniotic warmth, far from Longwood. The exile is 48 years old.

He is so racked by guilt that sometimes he gives up. One day he has his accounts of the Russian campaign brought to him so that he can "go to work". He soon stops: "It is too painful. It recalls too many mistakes. Let's go for a walk" (10 May). When Gourgaud complains, he exclaims: "You may have your troubles. What about me? What troubles I have had! How much to reproach myself with!"

On 21 September 1817, Napoleon is woken up by a very loud rumbling sound. His bed moves. He goes back to sleep. It's 9.48 in the evening . . . "All we needed was an earthquake to make our stay on St Helena a pleasant one," remarks the Emperor, who immediately has the story of the Lisbon earthquake read to him. The captive regrets not dying in the quake. "It's a pleasure to die in company," he says, deadpan, to Gourgaud and the Montholons.

He rarely leaves the dark room. So much reserve arouses curiosity. On 4 December 1817, Lowe's chambermaid is allowed by the servants to look at the prisoner through the keyhole.

The first of January begins badly. There is another altercation between Napoleon and Gourgaud. "You insult me!" the Emperor cries out, extremely angry.

For months Gourgaud has suspected Mme de Motholon of being Napoleon's mistress. It has become a real obsession. He watches her, notes her comings and goings with the Emperor. More and more jealous, he decides to challenge Montholon to a duel. Napoleon and Bertrand try to reason with him.

"And if I should sleep with her, what is wrong with that?" Napoleon says finally.

"None, Sire. I do not imagine Your Majesty to have such depraved taste."

It is 2 February. A break-up is inevitable. Gourgaud seems to have taken leave of his senses. Bertrand finally finds the solution by suggesting to Gourgaud that he leave because of ill-health. On Wednesday 11 February 1818, Gourgaud sees Napoleon for the last time. "His Majesty has mellowed and gave me a little tap on the face: 'We shall see each other in another world. So farewell . . . embrace me'."

Napoleon later makes this crude remark about Gourgaud: "Every day he wanted to b——r me against my will."

Twelve days later, another event sends the little community into confusion. Cipriani is suddenly taken ill. He dies on 27 February. Much affected by this loss, Napoleon the funerary accountant can no longer spend all of his time assessing the past. Now that Longwood is emptying of its inhabitants, he must list those who leave: Las Cases, Gourgaud . . . soon O'Meara, then Albine de Montholon, not to mention the servants: Santini, one of the Archambault brothers, the cook . . .

In the year 1818, the Longwood biotope will be significantly transformed.[4] The half-way mark of Napoleon's captivity on St Helena has just passed. Competition for the prisoner's favour becomes less noticeable within the community. There's no longer any lack of it for those who remain. The Longwood ecosystem, that association of beings living in a damp environment, is now functioning better.

In April, Napoleon decides to embark on "a recapitulation of his mistakes". He lists seven, which all arise out of the Russian campaign. The previous month, he had confided: "The marriage to Marie-Louise is the biggest mistake. I should have married a Russian."

After this *mea culpa*, he comes back to Waterloo and enumerates the many blunders. But they are those made by the victor,

Wellington. Bertrand has now replaced Gourgaud. He is a scrupulous clerk, who notes down the slightest phrase, the least murmur.

"Bertrand, what time is it? Another day less. Let's go to bed."

3

The wind bends the yew trees in the cemetery, blows the needles up like bristles. A battleground sky lowers over Plantation – one of those tussles in which the wind and clouds seem ready to mount a frontal attack on the trees.

In the mêlée the vases have fallen over, rolling over the graves, spilling water and flowers. Michel Martineau has described the French section of the cemetery, where Cipriani's grave is located. I examine the sunken moss-covered gravestones one by one, but none corresponds to that of the Corsican butler. Many crosses have fallen over and the vegetation is slowly but surely burying the gravestones. In a few years everything will be swallowed up and covered with a jungle of vines.

I have to take shelter from the storm. I finally take refuge against a wall of the chapel.

"Foul weather, isn't it? Can I be of any assistance?"

A man dressed in a red soutane is standing in the doorway. He's wearing a weighty pectoral cross that swings about at the slightest movement. He has a heavy jaw, an energetic expression and a furrowed face, which gives him a warm, habitually eager look. Around his waist is a very rough leather belt, almost a strap.

"I'm Bishop John Ruston," the man says in a clear voice. "Are you looking for something?"

"No . . . well, yes. But it's complicated."

I tell him the story of Cipriani.

"I fear I can be of very little help to you. I didn't know about this man. To tell the truth, I've only been here for two years . . . It would be interesting to draw up a list of all these relics of the Napoleonic period, a kind of itinerary . . ."

"It's true . . . One can hardly claim that the St Helenians have over-exploited the Emperor's memory."

"Oh! That's not the island mentality. The Saints abhor self-promotion. They don't like putting themselves forward and they don't know how. Anyway, they know absolutely nothing about this part of their history."

"I've visited the little museum in Jamestown. It's significant all the same that there's not a single object or document on Napoleon's captivity."

"Are you sure? Hm . . . Napoleon lived very much apart. I would say that the Saints didn't really see him until 1840, when his ashes came back. His mortal remains were taken back to Jamestown. You know that he had never returned since that first night in 1815. It should be said: his death was a relief here. St Helena had become a veritable fortified camp."

I have the impression that in spite of his affability, the Anglican bishop has a slight antipathy towards Napoleon. When I mention the French domains on St Helena, he interrupts me.

"It's not correct to call them 'French domains'. When a person buys land or property, it doesn't automatically take on the national-ity of the purchaser. Longwood is the *property* of the French State. It's an important shade of meaning."

"And yet there's a French consul."

"An honorary consul . . . Because of Napoleon . . ."

I'm careful not to engage in controversy. After the war, the Anglican canon of Jamestown still recalled the anniversary of the English victories over Bony's troops in the parish magazine, which very much upset our agent, Monsieur Peugeot. "For many Helenians, the French representative is seen as a defeated adversary or an undesirable," he wrote back sadly to his department in 1947.

Beyond their much vaunted lack of interest, in the end the people here are rather sensitive about Napoleon's captivity. It's a vague feeling that includes feigned indifference, a certain annoyance at having been excluded from a decision imposed at the time by the European powers, St Helena's image as a jail. All these ill-defined complex impressions still weigh on the memory of the inhabitants. Perhaps Napoleon's captivity gives them the consciousness of always being offside. The bishop speaks of the Saints' "non-independence syndrome".

"What do you mean by that?"

"It's very strange. Everyone comes under the same authority – London – so there's total equality of the Saints as far as this dependence is concerned. They're ultimately very united. A colony implies the existence of colonials. Well! That's not the case for St Helena. They all have the same origin: they come from somewhere else. There are old families, but this age doesn't give them any patrician superiority."

"Are they church-goers?"

"Hm . . . That's another problem. 85 per cent of the population are Anglican, but there only 5 per cent of them are practising."

"All the same, they seem to show religious zeal, judging by the numerous places of worship I've seen in Jamestown . . . Baptists, Adventists, Jehovah's Witnesses, not to mention other religions."

"The large number of religions doesn't mean that people are more religious. In recent years there has been an increase in the number of sects. St Helena hasn't escaped this phenomenon. The island is entering the modern world in its own way . . . But it's a population whose lives are uneventful: isolation obliges them to be virtuous. Well, I think you can go out now. Look, the sun's out."

I glance outside. Wind and the cloud have beaten a retreat. The yew trees are still. They look rather prim and proper, as if the calmness they affected was trying to hide the storm just past.

The vases and pots of flowers are no longer scattered everywhere. Someone's hand has picked them up, put them where they should be, and cleaned them . . . But a few petals still lie on the graves.

4

The soft drizzle of gleaming, almost pearly, rain gives a gloss to the foliage of the araucarias in the large garden. Two giant tortoises are walking on the lawn. The moisture makes their shells shine; they look as though they've been waxed and have blue spots on their breastplate. The turf has been closely mown and is so smooth and even that it looks like a piece of felt placed on the ground. The house itself, like a Portuguese *quinta*, sparkles in the short burst of sunlight. The black lava stone window and doorframes stand out against the whitewashed facade.

The Union Jack flying over the pediment of Plantation House signifies that we are on British territory. I cross the Georgian-style portico. Alan Hoole, the successor to Hudson Lowe and sixtieth Governor of St Helena, will receive me in a few moments. Portraits of the royal family dating from the beginning of the reign hang on the walls in the hall. The thick carpets are delicately woven, full, springy, almost spongy underfoot. The dark, polished floorboards are evidence of two centuries of good housekeeping. The furniture is Regency: rosewood occasional tables with brass inlay, Coromandel console tables decorated with mouldings.

"The Henchman" lived here in this house, built in 1791. On his arrival in 1816, he extends Plantation House so that he can house the army of scribes and functionaries who have come with him to coordinate the enormous administrative and military machine of the island that had been turned into a bunker. The offices, reception rooms and private apartments spread over 27 rooms were all housed under the same roof.

"Welcome to the torturer's house!"

This introduction, albeit good-natured, certainly surprised me. The Governor is wearing one of those loose, dark suits with cream stripes which only the British can wear with distinction – while on others they look *mafiosi*. He has a pointed nose, thin lips and a heavy signet ring on his left hand. But humour does not exclude caution. His piercing eyes seem to be saying, "Who am I dealing with here? Can I trust him?" he wonders with a frown. "Care is recommended where Napoleon's captivity is concerned. The French are so unpredictable on that subject."

The Governor tries first of all to sidestep the question by talking to me about the official status of St Helena. He insists on explaining to me that the Legislative Council has fifteen members, of whom three are appointed by the Crown. The Executive Council is led by the Governor and comprises eight members. Five come from the Legislative Council and the other three are high officials.

"Could you explain something to me?" I ask him. "The Saints are British subjects, aren't they? Why do they need a visitor's visa to enter Great Britain?"

"Oh! That's quite simple. The Government in London wants to control immigration."

The Governor's explanation isn't clear.

"But the Saints aren't immigrants. They're British. Or else, they're second-class citizens . . ."

"Second class!" he replies with a horrified expression. "That's not right. London has done a lot for this island you know. Nine million pounds a year! That's not what I call nothing. It's the biggest budget per person" – he stresses this last word – "in the United Kingdom. St Helena has no mines, no industries. Its only wealth is fishing, and to a lesser extent, wood."

A woman enters the sitting room. Her bronzed face has a delicate, serene beauty that bespeaks harmony.

"My wife Delia."

I learn that she comes from St Helena. "From Longwood village," the Governor explains to me with a hint of mockery in his voice. At the beginning of the 1980s, Alan Hoole was Attorney General of St Helena, like Marian's husband.

The "First Lady" of St Helena gives a timid smile. Her husband looks at her lovingly, then continues.

"I'll show you something. In the library."

He asks me to sit down in a well-upholstered armchair.

"The room we are in was added by Hudson Lowe. It was built on the central courtyard."

I think I can see the curiosity that the Governor wants to show me. It's a picture on the wall near the bookcase – a surprising, disturbing portrait of Napoleon. I'm taken aback by the sorrowful, distracted expression on the face. I confess that I didn't know this picture of the captive.

"What do you think of it?"

"Of the picture or its presence in Hudson Lowe's house?"

He's delighted that I seem so disconcerted.

"Yes it's true. What a revenge, isn't it?"

"Where does this work come from?"

"Oh! It's a charcoal drawing. It was a study for an oil painting on canvas in the Glasgow Art Gallery. The picture is called *Napoleon: the Last Phase*. It's the work of James Sant, a Scottish painter best known for his portraits of the English aristocracy and the royal family."

"*The Last Phase*? But that's the title of Lord Rosebery's book on Napoleon's captivity!"

"Precisely. It was painted to illustrate Lord Rosebery's book. I think the portrait was shown at the Royal Academy in 1901. The

painting belonged to Lord Rosebery, who made a gift of it to the Glasgow Art Gallery.

"So, it's a completely imaginary portrait."

"Imaginary! I don't think so. You yourself identified it immediately as a portrait of Napoleon. Sant imagined it no doubt, but with the help of contemporary painters."

I can't make the objection that no depiction of the Emperor is really exact. And it's hardly the place to debate the point. I remain silent, hypnotized by the captive's appearance. The Governor standing next to me is also silent. We look intently at the suffering face. It really is Saturn stripped of his kingdom forever, eaten away by time after he himself has eaten his children. There's no more frightening depiction of hopelessness. Everything is there: the withering of the soul, the melancholy of memories, the fading of the dream. The exhilaration of the past has disappeared for ever. It is indeed *the last phase* before the spectral state. Moreover, Lord Rosebery understood it well. Doesn't he say that he wrote his book to exorcise a ghost!

One room in Plantation House is haunted: the west bedroom. Joshua Slocum, the first man to sail solo around the world, spent several nights there watching for the ghost to appear, but all he saw was "a horse-shoe nailed to the door".

Those who write on Napoleon have at least one thing in common: at some time or other, they are all paralyzed by their subject – dumbfounded, terrified. They have seen something. But what? "When did his faculties become unbalanced?" Lord Rosebery wonders. He doesn't go so far as suspecting him of madness.

At the end of his book, the author does a strange thing. One would expect that a book written by a former English Prime Minister would contain documents on serious subjects like foreign policy or unpublished accounts of the Emperor's captivity. In actual fact, the author's only real enthusiasm is Napoleon's physical appearance. He makes a note of many clues to the contradictory and finally elusive nature of his physical being. The secret that James Sant has unravelled so well has its origin in these final pages. I'm convinced that the painter read them carefully, so that he didn't have to think about them when he was painting.

Descriptions agree on only one aspect: Napoleon's portliness and the disproportion of the head in comparison with the body. On this subject Lord Rosebery cites the account of Dr Henry, surgeon in the 66th Infantry Regiment, who saw him for the first time on 1 September 1817. "His general look was more that of an obese Spanish or Portuguese friar than the hero of modern times."

Now, James Sant's Napoleon is not bloated. On the contrary, the artist has painted a much thinner face. You can see that the flesh is beginning to sag. An unpleasant line cuts across the left corner of his mouth and the bottom of his chin has become emaciated. The fleshly frame seems to float. It's the beginning of *disembodiment*. The prisoner, who can observe himself better than anyone else, will one day announce: "Every day I cast off a little more of my tyrant's skin."

Yet the thing that intrigues you most is the desolate, shining eyes, frozen in a penitential attitude as though they had just been weeping. Those eyes have no more desires. They are waiting for death. In the painting at Eylau, the Emperor turned his head away, not wanting to look. Napoleon at St Helena, on the other hand, gazes searchingly at a force we cannot see. The king of suffering knows that he has arrived at the end of his ordeals. He looks at the monster of night, not with terror but rather with stoical attention. There's already a sense of lofty elevation. He's preparing himself to rise above death and he senses that he will soon be released. Soon he will transmigrate, leave his mortal body and be transformed into an immaterial being, a figure in history.

"What is he staring at? That's a question that I always ask myself," the Governor murmurs. "Whenever I come into this library, I always see that look. It becomes obsessive."

"No doubt the obsession with past misdeeds," I say with a laugh.

"Misdeeds? I don't understand." The Governor contains himself, but gives me a rather prim look.

I shouldn't joke about things like that, but the desire to provoke is stronger than anything else.

"I only meant that the presence of this portrait in Plantation House seems to indicate a desire to make amends."

"Make amends for what? English persecution?" (Then his face resumes its more diplomatic expression.) "It's all ancient history . . . Besides, it's not me, but one of my predecessors, who was responsible for that," he says, pointing to the painting.

"Well then, let's say that it's an expression of English humour."

This bright idea lights up his face.

"Ah! Humour. Yes, indeed," he mutters. "But what do you mean by that?"

"Nothing . . . Humour makes you feel better, doesn't it? You exorcise something, and at the same time you perpetuate it. I can't remember who said 'Humour is a way of getting out of a difficult moment, without getting out of the difficulty'. That's the case here, don't you think?"

He gives me an uncertain look.

"If you like . . . So, we'll never be rid of our difficulties with Napoleon?"

After all's said and done, this governor is a kind man. He's agreed to see me and give me his time. He's introduced me to this surprising work by Sant. And I pick a quarrel with him.

The Governor breaks the silence to tell me:

"Did you know that one of my predecessors was French?"

"A governor, like you?"

"Yes. When the island was administered by the East India Company. His name was Etienne Poirier, a Protestant. He'd left France after the Revocation of the Edict of Nantes. He was a wine grower."

"A *bon vivant* then . . ."

"I wouldn't say that. He was very puritanical. He brought in some very strict laws here, as he found the local ways too lax. I believe he was finally relieved of his duties."

I'm dying to talk to him about one of his predecessors, John Massingham, who was Governor from 1981–84. He loathed Napoleon, whom he saw as a "dangerous war criminal."[5] But do I really need to provoke the man I'm speaking to? He's so courteous. He talks to me about the French Consul, whom he sometimes invites to Plantation House.

"We'd obviously get on well. We're both here in the middle of nowhere . . ."

"Do you mean that the island you administer doesn't exist?"

"That's not what I said . . . How many people know exactly where St Helena is?"

"You're right. It's an island marked by its deceitful origins."

"Deceitful!"

"Yes indeed. You know that the Portuguese had given false geographical coordinates to hide their discovery. I'm convinced this original act has had its consequences."

The drizzle has stopped falling. We go out and walk in the grounds. Plantation House is the antithesis of Longwood. Everything is delightful here: the charming location, the harmonious view to the sea, the soft green of the lawn stand in opposition to the disturbing harshness of the plateau. Longwood is a building besieged by wind, rain and ghosts. The tranquil ease of Plantation House, where everything is designed to favour the pleasure and peace of mind of its inhabitants, is in contrast to the discomfort of Longwood, a cage in the air, badly secured to the ground, rickety and open to the elements. There was a moment at the beginning of his captivity when some thought was given to allowing Napoleon and his entourage to live in Plantation House. What would the legend have been if the prisoner had lived in the Governor's house?

Alan Hoole is proud of his two giant tortoises. They give his residence a pleasing tropical look, a sort of Eden where animals, rare species and humans can live together in a state of innocence.

"These tortoises are very old," the Governor assures me. "In fact, it's said that they were brought to St Helena in Napoleon's time."

One of them opens its beak-like mouth and sticks out a tongue tapered like a snake's. The little black protruding eyes blink, revealing a bubo instead of an eyelid – a diabolical sight that suddenly disturbs the dream.

The two monsters stare at me coldly. The pattern on their shells formed by yellow lines and orange patches looks like a mosaic. They say that tortoises come from hell: after all, their name derives from Tartarus.

1. St Helena belonged to the East India Company, which transferred the administration of the island to the British government during Napoleon's captivity. It took up the enjoyment of its rights again after the Emperor's death. It once more became the property of the Crown in 1836.

2. Guy Godlewski, *Sainte-Hélène, terre d'exil* [*St Helena, Land of Exile*].

3. Napoleon's secretary (see p. 19).

4. A biotope is an ecological term for an area, usually small and of uniform environmental conditions, characterized by relatively stable biotypes. [Tr.]

5. Quoted by Gavin Young in *Slow Boats Home* (Hutchinson).

The Seventh Day

I

A PRETTY PROMENADE BORDERED WITH LINDEN TREES; THE same spear-shaped iron railings as at Anne's Place. A peaceful provincial square with seats and worn granite bollards stopping motorists from parking on the open space. There's something about the avenue that reminds you of a ship; you have the feeling that the stem is going to touch the Cordeliers' monastery close by.

A soldier stands in the bows presenting his sword, which is wrapped in a flag. From a distance, it looks as though he's brandishing an umbrella – an insulting detail to say the least – for this soldier has a baton in his cartridge pouch . . . a Grand Marshal's baton.

Henri-Gatien Bertrand, a count of the Empire and Grand Officer of the Legion of Honour, played an essential role at Wagram and Lützen. For nearly 150 years he has been watching over St Helena Square, a paradise for *pétanque* players and obligatory stop for dogs accompanied by their owners.

It's always easy to make fun of the grandiloquence of these statues, spattered by pigeon droppings and forever frozen in mid-action. Although it still shows evidence of the academic tradition, this work by François Rude, sculptor of *La Marseillaise* on the Arc de Triomphe, expresses a feeling that is essentially romantic. Behind Bertrand, the sculptor has discreetly placed a symbolic object that links the "Vauban of the Empire" to the legend. It's a stylized boat sinking in waves; on it are inscribed the words: *St Helena 1821*.

Bertrand's head is almost bald. Rude wanted to show the man's modesty, fidelity, honesty and gentleness, but also his moroseness. Napoleon sometimes liked to chide him for being over-cautious, as at Bautzen, when his lack of drive contributed to the loss of a decisive victory.

For all that, Bertrand is the most sublime figure of those involved in the tragedy of St Helena. He was in no way obliged to follow the vanquished Emperor into exile. He was faithful to him to the end, always benevolent, a bit boring, stubborn, depressed, wise, calming the tensions of the quarrelsome group of which he was a part. He was a good father and a good husband, saying no to his god when the latter ordered him to live at Longwood. A rather dull, irresolute man, he was passionately in love with his wife, the beautiful Fanny Dillon, a Creole of English descent and cousin of the Empress Josephine. Bertrand and Fanny's correspondence, written when the General was travelling all over Europe, is one of the finest examples of conjugal love. Almost every letter from the General, bearing the inscription "by courier", was written in the bivouac the day after a battle. These missives end with "Good day, dear Fanny", words that echo the adoration the chief of the 4th Corps of the Grand Army felt for his wife. She was a woman with an intriguing, independent and daring personality. "What love! . . . I've never seen anything like it," Napoleon will exclaim, a little envious.[1]

Her refinement and elegance won the hearts of the small English colony on St Helena. She was on friendly terms with Hudson Lowe's wife and with the Russian Commissioner Balmain. Her intimate knowledge of English society was invaluable to Napoleon, but he never knew how to take her. As she was capricious by nature and valued her freedom very highly, she continually declined invitations to Longwood, which the Emperor took as an affront.

It's relatively easy to overlook St Helena Square in the middle of the town of Châteauroux. On the other hand, the traveller can't help being intrigued by the presence of a Marcel Duchamp College. The dark, old-style door in the main entrance makes an incongruous contrast with the radical modernity of the man who invented the ready-made in art. However, if you look closely, the cast-iron frames of the seats around St Helena Square are manufactured objects that could well attain the dignity of works of art. You scarcely see them, but they are actually a nice piece of work. Their motifs are in praise of the faithful Bertrand: the count's coronet, the "B" monogram of the Grand Marshal, the imperial eagle and the officer general's laurels.

Châteauroux, the principal town in the Department of l'Indre, has dedicated a part of its memory to the most worthy of the Emperor's companions. On the death of his hero in 1821, Bertrand left St Helena with his family and retired to the city of his birth. After the July Revolution, when elected deputy for l'Indre, he sat on the left. Just when he was quite sure that he would never see St Helena again, he joined Prince Joinville's expedition to return the ashes of the Emperor to France.

The Bertrand Museum, a fine aristocratic mansion where the Grand Marshal lived and died, houses the numerous souvenirs of St Helena, for the most part brought back on the 1840 voyage. The most original is a stuffed dog, Sambo, who played with the Bertrand children.

Sambo probably sniffed and licked Napoleon. He barked when the Emperor approached. It's easy to see that Sambo is no ordinary dog. His smooth spotted coat is like a sea-lion's, his eyes, like two black glass balls, are quite fearsome, but the strangest thing of all is his neck. Sambo has no ears. They were probably cut off in the Chinese tradition. A group of sinologists have studied this dog. Their conclusion is that he can't be classified in any category:

he belongs to an Asian breed that has been crossed with other dogs on St Helena.

Sambo is lying with his head up. The iris and pupil seem to have merged, giving his basilisk's eyes a look that is at once savage, piercing, and almost intelligent. He stares with fixed attention. Sambo, too, *has seen it all*.

2

Countess Diana growls as I approach. Michel Martineau holds her back. She lets me pat her, growling all the while. This morning the wind has chased the clouds away, clearing the air of the fine mist that usually hangs over Longwood. The blue of the agapanthuses and irises is hard and bright, the drops of moisture on the petals look as though they have frozen, like beads of frost.

"I'll show you my studio later. In the meantime, I'll let you look around Longwood. If you want to become thoroughly steeped in the atmosphere, you need to be alone. It's an exercise that requires solitude. I believe you like that . . . What room are you going to explore today?"

"I can see you're starting to know my habits. I've seen almost everything. Today I'd like to spend some time in Napoleon's study."

"I'll let you get settled in there. At all events, you can go wherever you like. I've had all the doors unlocked."

The study, which is scarcely bigger than the adjoining dark bedroom, is lit by a window and a door with a glass panel, both facing north. A desk stands against the wall.

"Well now, you'll be like Napoleon. You can take notes at the desk."

Just as I'm pulling the chair towards me, imagine my amazement when I see James Sant's *Napoleon: The Last Phase* on the wall. It's all very well to be fond of apparitions – and Longwood hasn't lacked them since I arrived – but I can't help wondering whether the numerous souls in torment who roam this house aren't playing a trick on me.

"What's the matter?" the Consul asks.

"On the wall . . . I know I'm not dreaming."

"It's *The Last Phase* . . ."

"Yes, but it wasn't there on my other visits."

"I can't understand your surprise. It's been there on the wall for a long time. It was my father's idea to hang it there. You just never noticed it."

"All the same . . . It's an eye-catching portrait. My surprise comes from the fact that I saw it in the Governor's house. The painting gives you such a shock!"

"I can assure you that it's always been there. This room is nearly always dark and gloomy. On your other visits, you didn't open the shutters. You didn't see it there."

I hadn't seen it because that face *belongs* in this place. *Il desdichado* is at home here.[2] Yet you can tell that his stay on earth, now so painful to him, is nearing its end. As they say, he has an other-worldly look. The god-like gaze that used to sweep the battle-field in an instant, to plan and act, has been extinguished for ever. "Here more than anywhere else, one can understand how he, the conqueror of Europe, must have suffered from being shut up in this hovel."[3] Shut up is the right expression. This part of Longwood is an *in pace*. *Vade in pace* (Go in peace) is a ritual expression, said when closing the cell door behind a prisoner serving a life sentence. Michel Martineau, who knows the dimensions of every room by heart, informs me that the area of the study is no more than 17 square metres.

"It was as damp as the tomb here in the rainy season. Napoleon said that he felt as though he were going into a cellar. It must be noted that the room had no chimney. I have the impression you like chimneys . . . Do you know that there were 23 fires to be kept going at Longwood, including Bertrand's house? They sometimes had to break up barrels to keep them lit. One day, they even had to saw up slats from a bed. I'll go now and let you reflect in peace."

I put my notebook on the bureau. I begin to record the furniture and objects within the room, but my heart's not in it. I'm haunted by the presence of the head above me. I sometimes have the impression that the weary eyes are looking at the camp bed. It's identical to the one in the dark room in every respect: standard issue to senior officers under the Empire, with folding frame, webbing, and a canopy like a tent over the top. As the Consul isn't here, I can't resist the desire to sit on it again; the same feeling of instability. At one moment I fear it might collapse and fold in two on me.

When he was in the dark bedroom and couldn't sleep, the prisoner went into the study where a bed had been prepared. "The soul of the world" (as Hegel saw him at Iéna) would have more and more difficulty getting out of bed. He does not even try to hide the fact from himself. "I find that bed has become a delightful place. I wouldn't exchange it for all the treasure in the world. What a transformation! How I've fallen!"

I can't help thinking of Tilsit, of what he said about happiness. "I had had worries at Eylau a short time ago . . . Now I was victorious, dictating laws, having emperors, kings come to pay me court."

At Tilsit I spent hours watching the flow of the Niemen, the river that marks the border between Lithuania and the Russian enclave of Kaliningrad. How could Tsar Alexander and Napoleon have managed to stay on a raft with such a current? Luckily Bertrand was there, Bertrand, *who always accompanied him*, the cardinal witness, present at his peak, his decline and his end. This bridge expert notes the high water marks of the reign, the spring-tide as well as the ebb-tide.

Bertrand will build a footbridge using small boats placed side by side and secured to the river bank. "A very prettily furnished little house" had been built. It comprised two tents: one for the two monarchs and the other for the staff officers. "Sire," Alexander is reported to have said when they embraced, "I hate the English as much as you do."

"In that case, our peace is made," Napoleon replied.

Today there is no monument to indicate the raft at Tilsit. The Russians who live in this town, so long out of bounds to visitors, are for the most part soldiers preoccupied above all with the present. Tilsit had a strong contingent of SS4 nuclear missiles. If an atomic war had broken out and Paris had been destroyed, "the city of the raft" would have fired the fatal salvo.

"The only certain things in this world are coincidences," the Italian author Leonardo Sciascia once wrote. Tilsit, the symbol of Napoleon's happiness and of Franco-Russian reunion; the allusion to the English, a sign of catastrophe. I like to think that these encounters are never fortuitous, and that fate likes to play at situation comedy.

On the banks of the Niemen, there is a construction honouring river transport in the shape of an anchor sitting on a base. The raft was situated where the monument is now. It's true that the Germans had nothing to celebrate in the Tilsit meeting, which was to the detriment of Prussia and mortifying to Queen Louise. Her memory remains present in the town, now part of Russia. The bridge built over the Niemen still bears her name. The beautiful Queen tearfully tried to charm Napoleon, who showed little appreciation of her charms. "I am like an oilskin: everything slides off. It would be too much of an effort to play the ladies' man," he rather churlishly writes to Josephine.

Very few traces of the meeting remain today. The French were housed in one half-timbered house. The building Napoleon occupied has been demolished. I wanted to know where it had been. I was directed to a vacant lot closed off by wire fencing. I came back later. I had noticed a loose piece of wire netting, which I lifted. As was the case at Eylau, there was nothing to see. On the spot where Napoleon's house once stood was a dilapidated greenhouse. The broken windows reflected flashes of orange from the setting sun. It was on this little estate, now in ruins, that Napoleon knew real happiness. The monarch was at the high point of his power. Vigorous plants with hairy leaves, like those seen growing rampant over rubble, had taken over the house of happiness.

Tilsit makes up for Eylau, but after Tilsit, the autocrat will never be the same. Marmont describes this reversal very well in his *Memoirs*. This man who negotiated the capitulation of Paris in 1814 and withdrew to Normandy instead of protecting the Emperor, paints two portraits of him: *before* and *after* Tilsit.

"The first is thin, abstemious, immensely active, heedless of privation, dismissive of well-being and material pleasures, concerned only with the success of his enterprises, far-sighted, prudent, except when carried away by strong feeling, able to take a chance while avoiding anything that prudence can foresee.

"The second is fat and heavy, sensual and concerned with his comfort to the point of making it a major preoccupation, nonchalant and easily tired, blasé about everything, indifferent to everything, believing the truth only when it happened to coincide with his passions, his interests and his whims, proud as Satan and disdainful of men, dismissive of the interests of humanity. His sensitivity had dulled without making him unpleasant, but his goodness was no longer active: it had become quite passive. His mind was just as it had always been – the vastest, deepest and most productive that ever was. Yet there was no more will power, no more resolution, and an instability that resembled weakness.

"The Napoleon I have painted first was outstanding until Tilsit: it is the zenith of his greatness and the time of his greatest brilliance. The other succeeded him, and the complement to the aberrations caused by his pride was his marriage to Marie-Louise."

"How I've fallen." I glance at the adjoining room. A beam of light has cut across the floor of the *camera obscura*. The shutters of the combustion chamber are closed. Shaken by the wind, the aperture blades sometimes close off the light. The bursts of brilliance flood the room with a bright whiteness, like a magnesium flash. The brief illumination only serves to highlight the sombre, funereal atmosphere. Longwood's unsettling, stubborn silence is as eloquent as any other testimony. Listen to it and you will discover that it is a deep brooding silence, with a long startled echo lingering in a creaking floorboard, a shushing sound from under the door and a stifled moan near the windows.

During Napoleon's captivity, the somnolent atmosphere of the house was broken by the rats, which made an infernal din. These rodents were unbelievably daring. Bertrand received a very nasty bite on the hand while asleep. Ali relates that one day, when he was making a poultice in a saucepan, he went out of the room for a few moments. When he came back, the contents of the pan had disappeared, eaten by the rats. The spoon had also vanished. He found it four days later in a hole in the attic.[4]

The rat – acolyte of the Devil and of witches.

On 5 October 1853 at Marine Terrace, Victor Hugo gets Napoleon I to speak. The little table with the three claw feet, which has been lifted up on to the big table, now begins to turn. After Marat, then Robespierre, the spirit of the Emperor appears. Of course he begins to dictate. The poet records what he says. "Oh thought! Come to my aid!" exclaims Napoleon. Victor Hugo asks his guest, who always had a passion for definitions, to characterize God. "An infinite gaze in an eternal eye," the ghost replies forthwith.[5]

The look, the eye . . . There is no getting away from vision with a man like Napoleon. The distracted look of Eylau and *The Last Phase*. The study is indeed a copy of the dark room. The same two beds, the same deprivation, the same bareness. The double man slips from one room to the other in search of rest. The damp shroud . . . Strength sapped by the tropics. They say that Napoleon was poisoned, that Montholon fed him arsenic. The Longwood courtier didn't need to go to that bother. One only has to spend a few hours in the memory's tomb to realize that the prisoner poisoned himself with his past. Day after day for five-and-a-half years, he took the hemlock of regret, desperately seeking to recover the consistency of events and the essence of things.

The walled-up prisoner inoculated himself, day after day, with the venom of boredom, that aching emptiness which searches for meaning but cannot find it. In the glory days he had isolated himself. Michelet succinctly summed up the Empire as boredom. The brilliant centre of the world was no longer in Paris, but on the battlefields. He was already infected with this absence during his reign. "He received nothing. Emptiness, nothingness, nothingness was the only reply to this new king of the world," Michelet stresses once more. One side of him still remains at Longwood: the rigid, stiff, military, boring, formal side. The process of accumulation, which is typical of the dictations, is often marked by dull profusion, a series of boring details and strings of uninteresting anecdotes.

In *The Dispossessed*, Maurice Barrès has likened Napoleon on St Helena to King Lear pursued by his daughters and the elements. "Napoleon's daughters were his ideas, the memories of his great achievements. He was driven insane by his genius."

In much the same way, all the inhabitants of Longwood were full of calomel, a mercury-based purgative that O'Meara administered on a regular basis.

A statuette by Vela, *The Dying Napoleon*, stands on the occasional table. He is sitting in his armchair and is obviously not long for this world. His back is arched against the chair and his eyes roll grotesquely. The sculpture lends a comic note to the room, which certainly could do with it.

What a lot of occasional tables and console tables there are in Longwood! Do they speak, like those in Marine Terrace or Hauteville House? For Hugo, exile is full of dead souls; for Napoleon it is full of dead bodies. The two were made for each other. According to Péguy, "there was no one in the whole history of the world who did more for Victor Hugo than Napoleon Bonaparte".

A door slams somewhere near the dining room. The bad alignment of the rooms and corridors makes the smallest sound reverberate. I recognize the measured tread and the creak of new leather shoes on the floor. He appears, his face relaxed, his cigar gone out and his hair dishevelled.

"Well, what do you thinks of Napoleon in *The Last Phase*?"

"It's a really fascinating painting."

"I believe you saw it at Plantation House. Well! One governor at St Helena had the picture removed. He hated Napoleon. It happened not so long ago."

"It wouldn't be a certain John Massingham?"

"How did you know?"

"I know the story. He loathed Napoleon because, according to him, he had brought a new form of warfare to Europe . . . full-scale war. He wasn't entirely wrong on that point."

"I agree. But it's mean spirited. I knew Massingham well. Not a bad man really . . . I got into an argument with him over some swings. Did you see the play area at the entrance to Longwood? I let him know I wasn't at all happy about it."

His face changes.

"Tell me now. Are you looking for a clue to trigger something in your mind like Inspector Maigret?" he says in a theatrical voice, obviously amused.

"I'd like to have his intuition."

"I'm not joking . . . Sniffing around people's houses to get to know them better isn't a bad way to go about it. Can one play Beethoven properly if one hasn't mused for a while in the places where he lived?"

"You must know Napoleon better than anyone else, as you've lived in his house for 40 years."

"Oh! Napoleon isn't the only reason. It was mainly to leave France, that old world ossified in its own complacent well-being."

He speaks through clenched teeth, then pauses. His eyes are as impenetrable as ever.

"We're searching for what can make us wiser and better. If not, life's a farce!"

"Have you found what you're looking for in St Helena?"

"That's an extraordinarily indiscreet question. Ah, bipeds!" he sighs wearily.

"Bipeds?"

"Yes. You, me, human beings!"

He has that chilling look that I'm beginning to know well. Then he begins to recite.

"'I wrote silences, I wrote nights, I recorded the inexpressible. I stilled the giddiness.' That fits this study, don't you think? Do you know who wrote it?"

He sometimes pronounces words with the tip of his tongue and his mouth almost closed. This way of mispronouncing his consonants gives him an English accent.

"You can't guess?"

"Well, it's not Napoleon . . . 'The inexpressible', 'still the giddiness' . . . That's not his style."

"Not his style! You've read Bertrand's *Notebooks*. They're full of strange images, unknown metaphors, especially at the end. All right, it's not Napoleon . . . It's Arthur Rimbaud."

"Two visionaries after all . . ."

"Did you know that Arthur Rimbaud visited Longwood? He saw this study where you're standing now."

"How can that be? I've never heard of any such visit. What's more, he hated the Empire, Napoleon III . . ."

"It's true. Anyway, he came to St Helena in 1876. It was during the time when he was a deserter from the colonial army of the Dutch East Indies. He had boarded a British ship, the *Wandering Chief*, in Java to return to Europe. The boat had lost its mast in a terrible storm going around the Cape of Good Hope. It had to call in at St Helena for repairs."

Gilbert Martineau told me about the poet's stay in St Helena. When the *Wandering Chief* anchored in Jamestown Bay, Rimbaud slipped into the water, wanting to reach dry land unnoticed. He didn't have the £1 tax required to go on to the island. Once he reached land, the young man set out for Longwood.

"Is there any proof that he visited this place?"

"Yes, he signed the visitors' book. There was a French caretaker called Maréchal."

"May I see the visitors' book?"

"Unfortunately, no. It was stolen after the war, but I think I may have traced it to South Africa. It's the only proof we have. Rimbaud makes no mention of the visit, nor of calling at St Helena."

"Napoleon-Rimbaud, what a strange conjunction!"

"I don't agree with you. One can admire both of them. I'm one of that number . . . Does the name Jean Bourguignon mean anything to you?"

"Wasn't he the one who edited Marchand's *Memoirs*?"

"The same. He was Paul Painlevé's right-hand man during the Great War. He was also a great Malmaison Curator. Well! He had two passions: Napoleon and Rimbaud. He knew Isabelle, the poet's sister, very well. His book on Rimbaud is a major work. Mallarmé praised him to the skies!"

His tone, which has been detached until then, now becomes more and more animated. He seems almost inspired.

"Napoleon, Rimbaud: two Prometheuses. Two great spirits. Harar is the poet's St Helena. The only difference being he chose his exile."

"It's a rather surprising comparison. In any case, looking is fundamental to Napoleon. Rimbaud is also *the man who saw everything*."

Michel Martineau comes into the study.

"Forgive me for interrupting this interesting discussion. You can continue it in my studio, if you like . . ."

"I must go," the father murmurs. "There's work to be done . . . I've wasted too much time."

That's flattering. His voice has become morose again, he frowns, his eyes are very small and without the slightest glimmer of good-will. He turns his back with that surly look of his. And yet, he had been in full flight. I'd never seen him so loquacious and engaging.

"I'm sorry . . . The conversation seemed fascinating . . . Didn't he tell you that he was working on a biography of Rimbaud? My father can be quite dazzling when he wants to."

"That's true. But then he always seems to regret it afterwards."

"Ah, well. That's his way of cutting himself off from the contradictions of the outside world, of being both in it and outside it . . ."

"Is that why he chose St Helena?"

"You'd have to ask him that. But he won't give you an answer. He's a great anglophile and yet he behaves like a Frenchman. St Helena is one of the rare places in the world where he can live this double life. The British spirit still lives on here. You've probably noticed it: a respect for the proprieties, a self-confident placidity . . ."

"I've often heard it said since I arrived that St Helena is a museum. I've observed that you still have afternoon tea here, the Saturday night dance, the late afternoon drink at the wooden bar of the Consulate."

"My father rarely goes to the Consulate bar, you know," Michel Martineau says with a smile. "The fact is that he chose St Helena out of regret for the past. There is something missing in his life that he finds hard to come to terms with. For him I think it's the loss of greatness. He's very disillusioned. He feels that History has deserted Old Europe for ever. He doesn't believe in redemption. He says that one can only free oneself from things by accepting oneself. Perhaps he finds consolation for this disenchantment here."

"You mean that the two last vestiges of empire are hidden here on St Helena: the British Empire and the Napoleonic Empire . . ."

"It's a way of looking at it that my father would probably share. He's reached a certain truth here. What's more, he often says that truth is always stranger than fiction."

I had indeed noticed the Free French touch that the ex-naval officer had put into his private apartments: a photo of General de Gaulle, with pennant on the desk; a serious, muted, military, no-nonsense style that can still sometimes be seen in our far-flung embassies. The mystique of the State and the slightly overdone sobriety of symbols.

We've stopped for a few moments in the dining room, where the only window looks out on Ali's garden. "It's the darkest and most depressing room in the house," the Consul points out. There's a damp smell rather like wet wool. Added to that is a whiff of something pharmaceutical, vaguely peppery and heady, which seems to slightly darken the already heavy atmosphere of the room.

Here, more than anywhere else in Longwood, one has the feeling that a hidden disease is slowly eating at the walls. Its ravages can be seen in the poor state of the wallpaper and the mediocrity of the furniture. It's like the dwelling of a vegetating provincial notary who nonetheless wants to keep up appearances. The big table from New Longwood, the sideboard with the white marble top, are evidence of former opulence. These pieces of furniture only make it more obvious that this is a depressing home which gives the impression of having seen better days while rather pathetically trying to maintain its station in life. The Chinese wallpaper of gold flowers on a red background, an exact copy of the paper laid in 1819, darkens and accentuates the cave-like atmosphere of the room.

The small Longwood colony used to gather there in the evening. Dressed in full livery, Santini or Cipriani would open the door and solemnly announce that the Emperor was served. Napoleon sat in the middle with his back to the fireplace. The many pieces of silverware on the table shone in the light of four candelabras holding a multitude of candles, making the stifling humidity even less bearable. The ruby-red plates of the famous Sèvres dinner set, called "The Headquarters", were brought out for the dessert. Dinner was usually over and done with in a quarter of an hour. Napoleon did not like to waste time at the dining table. When guests were present, the meal rarely lasted more than 40 minutes. The menu consisted of soup, a spicy dish, two entrées, a roast and two sweets. As the unpredictable climate of the island did not allow oranges, apricots or lemons to fully ripen, fruit was rarely served. The Emperor's pastry-cook did however use bananas, which he prepared as fritters marinated in rum.[6]

Michel Martineau places the flat of his hand on something that looks like a radiator.

"Look at that. We've put them in everywhere. It's absolutely essential. Every night this dehumidifier absorbs two litres of water."

"Two litres! That's a lot."

"Damp is the disease that eats into Longwood for eight months of the year. It attacks everything. We have to repaint things all the time, just like boats. We've hardly finished the last wall when we have to start on the other end again."

"So it's damp that gives these rooms that particular smell."

"Partly . . . I know you're very interested in that. But more importantly, there's the treatment I administer with a syringe every three months."

"A treatment!"

"For termites. Look at the floorboards. Near the walls, there are holes every 30 centimetres. The injections are made into those holes."

"So, the medicinal smell I couldn't identify was only that product injected into the wood."

I would like to tell him about Ali's eau de Cologne, which I brought to St Helena with me, but something like consideration for other people's opinions prevents me. I've inflicted too many of my pet hobby-horses on him already.

"The Longwood smell is nothing but an anti-termite product. Mundane, isn't it?"

"And the wallpaper? I suppose you have to change it."

"The wallpaper is identical to that of Napoleon's time. It's an awful problem trying to replace it. On the walls, you can't have the new clashing with the old. Before I lay it, I leave the paper out in the sun to dull the colour. It's a very delicate operation that has to be constantly checked. But enough of that. We were on our way to see my studio."

We cross an inner courtyard and go up to the room where the silverware was once kept.

"Here's my little domain! It's more comfortable than in Napoleon's time. You went up to it by a wooden stepladder then."

A painting of a bouquet of flowers stands on the easel. As in all artists' studios, there's a jumble of brushes of all kinds, coloured rags, mixtures and tubes.

"You know, I'm rather like Marchand. I don't take myself seriously."

The still life has been painted delicately and with great attention to detail. The sense of light and shade renders it both realistic and mysterious. There is something dreamlike in the exact care for detail and the rigorous depiction of reality. The painter presents his flowers in half-light to make them more glowing.

"Well, what do you think of them?"

"You pretend to be a naïve painter."

"What do you mean?"

"Your simplicity . . . In actual fact, it's very carefully worked out."

"No. There is some clumsiness . . . I like it. That's the way I am."

He shows me some other pictures. The bouquets and baskets of fruit are nearly always placed on realistic accessories such as shelves, cabinets, untidy dressers. The contrast between this *bric-à-brac* and the perfect forms of the plants is rather reminiscent of seventeenth-century *vanitas* paintings.

"Well! I see you're puzzled."

"I was just thinking that this painting was very influenced by the period of Napoleon's captivity"

"I beg your pardon?"

"When he recollects his past, Napoleon likes to recall privileged moments. He was very sensitive to the pure moment of existence. Your pictures convey this texture of the instant very well. At the same time, they are very much part of time as a continuum."

"You're right. For me, painting is a way of fighting against time. When I redesigned the gardens to the original plan and the first flowers emerged, I wanted to paint them."

"There you are. You wanted to save these flowers from death and oblivion. But tell me. Human beings are conspicuously absent from your works."

"My 'works'! You're going a bit far there. What you say is rather amusing. I should tell you that those who worship Napoleon don't much care for my flowers."

"Why not?"

"It's easy to understand. The flowers of St Helena don't correspond to the image of suffering that should be the way Longwood is depicted. Look at these asters, these day lilies, these amaryllises . . . It's much too cheerful."

"Too cheerful? I wouldn't say that. There's something disturbing in these still lifes."

"Just paint what you see and you'll soon be dealing with the strange and unusual, you know."

"Who has influenced you?"

"I told you before. I'm self-taught. Although discovering the floral still life paintings in the Ashmolean Museum certainly had an effect on me. As you can see, the English have been very important to me. In 1993, they asked me to do an issue of five stamps for the island post."

"The French Consul designing St Helena's stamps! That's fairly unusual."

"All the more because one of the flowers is the everlasting daisy, a symbol of the captivity, since, as you know, it was Lady Holland who had the idea of sending these flowers to Napoleon in 1819. They have acclimatized remarkably well. You see them everywhere on the island."

The everlastings of St Helena never die . . . I remember what I felt in the Napoleon Museum of Havana, which has the finest collection of Empire memorabilia outside France. These objects were collected before the Cuban Revolution by an extremely wealthy man who was obsessed with the Emperor. They are housed in a Tuscan-style villa whose opulence stands in stark contrast to the decay of the old town. On the upper floor the attendant will show you a flask containing some everlastings picked on St Helena. The little golden heads still have quite a lot of their colour. I recognized the downy surface and the little leaves with their rolled edges. St Helena everlastings are also there in the La Pagerie Museum in Martinique, as in Châteauroux. It's the identification mark of Napoleon's exile as well as the symbol of compassion.

"You say that everlastings can be seen everywhere. Where are they? In the garden?"

"No. Not here. At Deadwood."

"Deadwood. Isn't that the place where the English garrison guarding Napoleon was stationed? Where is it?"

"It's to the west of the house. I'll show you. There's also a golf course there. It's a bit windy, as you'll see."

Longwood was formerly a farm on a bare plateau, but houses gradually appeared and then a village was born. When you are within the French compound, you are scarcely aware of its existence. The little oasis of greenery is not only protected from the outside world, it's also a blessed, inviolable place. The French Longwood stands apart from the mundane. The petrol pump, the grocery shop and the Paradise Bar at the entrance to the property are all carefully kept at a distance.

Paradise: an allusion to the hell of the Emperor's captivity? That would be too much to expect. There's nothing attractive about the bar. An old woman stands at the entrance, knitting with two needles. She has combed her fuzzy hair to make it stand on end. Her face looks to me like a Parca, one of the Three Fates. She looks at me maternally, but then curses when she realizes I don't want to go into that dark paradise.

We reach a lonely cottage with a huge camellia bush hiding the façade. The elegantly proportioned house is built on a base with a veranda.

"That's the Bertrand house," the Consul informs me. "The whole family took up residence here in October 1816. There's a very good view over Deadwood from the sitting room windows. Napoleon's house is only 150 metres away. The Emperor sometimes came to this house to look at parades or horse races organized by the English garrison. No one could see him. He had holes made in the shutters so that he could put the end of his spyglass in them, as he had done at Longwood."

Since Gourgaud's departure, Napoleon enjoys visiting the Bertrands. He is touched by the Grand Marshal's offspring, with their spontaneity, enthusiasm and gaiety, although it's often very noisy. This is one of the unexpected facets of his personality, which we glimpsed with Betsy Balcombe. He loves being with children. "Though one may accuse Napoleon of being hard, even calculating with his companions, at least he is very good-natured, really kind with little ones, children and servants. This is no doubt because with them he does not need to insist on his rank, shun familiarity or study his words and attitudes with an eye to the future."[7]

He is very indulgent with these little devils. He has his pastry-cook, Pierron, make them cakes and sweets, and spends considerable time having fun with them.

The mischievous, provocative side of Napoleon comes to the surface again in exile. He adores pretending he has company, or hiding, to annoy Hudson Lowe. One of his favourite distractions is to cause confusion among his servants by making them doubt the fidelity of their women. Moreover, the taste for jokes grows in proportion to his melancholy. The dark thoughts and the disenchantment that are often with him, sometimes release a kind of retaliatory verve, like a huge mockery thrown in the face of the world that had abandoned him. This stance no doubt allows him to conquer his helplessness and adopt a distant and dominating attitude to misfortune and human nature, which he despises. His jibes spare no one in his little court. Bertrand is a "fool", Montholon a "jackass". He makes fun of the way their wives dress, calling them "washer women". That does not mean he has turned nasty. He needles them out of boredom. He has always given people this harsh verbal treatment, which he alone finds amusing, to make them drop their masks. In Las Cases's time, he couldn't resist the temptation of playing tricks on him: for example, devising letters which left the former chamberlain quite perplexed. That was his aim. The mischievous great man would secretly watch his reactions. One day, when Bertrand refused to give in to his point of view, as a joke he leapt at his throat crying: "Your money or your life? Aristocrat!"

A swing, a jumble of toys on the steps and childish prattle are signs that the Bertrands' house has remained the children's domain. We walk around Longwood's low wall and pass by a school. The satiny green stream of the golf course faces the sea. It's actually a desolate sight, as the rushing wind accentuates how bare the lawn is. The harshness of the trade wind has mown down all vegetation here. The rocks are purple-black against an aubergine-coloured ocean bed: it's a land with no adornment, no veneer. Deadwood: an indistinct land's end, a sterile headland opening on to the still, sluggish sea.

The two massive shapes of The Flagstaff and The Barn, which the prisoner could see from his bedroom windows, close in the horizon. The Flagstaff was the spy-mountain, where the captive was kept under surveillance. A semaphore on its summit transmitted Bonaparte's slightest movements to Hudson Lowe. "All's well"; "The General is ill"; "He has broken the four-mile limit", and so on. The colour blue, the jailer's constant fear, meant "The General has disappeared". It was never used. The entablature of The Barn, which looks like a Cyclopean blockhouse, looms over the horizon. The moor is dotted with small golden tufts. I recognized Lady Holland's everlasting flowers and their little yellow heads. The Consul picks a flower and passes it to me to sniff. It has no perfume. I vainly try to capture the heady scent of Indian curry and honey that perfumes the Corsican scrub and the Breton island moors in summer. The heat and damp of the tropics have overwhelmed the piquant peppery smell. St Helena does not exterminate whatever comes from overseas: the island merely diminishes, disintegrates and sterilizes it. The sticky atmosphere rots everything in order to alter it all the more completely. In Napoleon's time, the death rate of soldiers stationed on Deadwood was four times higher than elsewhere.[8]

"Where are the famous gum trees that Las Cases talks about all the time during Napoleon's captivity?"

"They have almost disappeared from the island," the Consul replied. "I'll show you one of the last survivors."

In the middle of the golf course, a tree lying full length looks as though it is dying. The sparse foliage seems to hiccup in the wind. A cement block and a prop hold up the trunk lying horizontally in the direction of the trade wind. The sound of the waves crashing against the cliffs is like a dull boom in the distance.

A solitary golfer has set down his buggy and tries to tee up the ball, which keeps shaking and wobbling about as the winds batter it. We stop to look, fascinated by the strange sight. He manages to hit the ball between two gusts, but it whirls in the air, moves back and, with a sudden jerk, is sucked up towards the sky like a leaf. Then, after another jolt, it plunges straight into the sea.

The scared golfer quickly puts his club back into his bag. His face has turned very pale.

In 1676 the English astronomer Edmund Halley, who gave his name to the famous comet, landed at St Helena to write a major treatise on meteorology. His observations of the St Helena trade winds enabled him to detect the origin of winds and to posit the theory of the displacement of air on a world scale. He was fascinated by the strangeness of the weather and stayed two years on the island. The St Helena anti-cyclone, which is as elusive as the one in the Azores, affects the appearance of the rock. The various landscapes all cohabit, without one particular character managing to dominate.

Before going down to Jamestown again, it occurs to me to pay a visit to the Longwood police station, a modest little house with a tin roof and a wooden gate at the entrance. I'm greeted by a tanned man wearing a uniform. His chequerboard black and white cap is firmly wedged in the middle of his forehead. His name is George Merlin and he has no opinion about the illustrious neighbour who lived on the plateau. The only thing that really interests him is the building of the airport. He would like the site to be at Prosperous Bay, on the east side of the island.

"If the project comes off, Longwood will be the most important place on St Helena," he says enthusiastically.

Like all the people on the island, he pronounces it "Heleena", like the Portuguese. The Saints have a particular accent: for example, they say *dar* for *there*, *noin* for *nine* and *dour* for *door*.

"You know that your village didn't exist before Napoleon? There was only a farm. The township came into being because of his presence here with the soldiers who kept watch over him."

"You just say that because you're French," he says, bursting out laughing.

"No. No. It's the truth. You can check it out."

"Right. I don't know if he was miserable. I only know one thing:

206

Longwood's weather is miserable. I don't like these clouds . . ."

He's no longer smiling and stares at me without seeming to see me.

"We're out of the world here . . . But it's not a heavenly place to live."

1. Quoted by Suzanne de la Vaissière-Orfila, *Lettres à Fanny* (Albin Michel).
2. The title of a poem by Gérard de Nerval and before him, the motto of a knight in Walter Scott's *Ivanhoe*. It is a Spanish word meaning "The Dispossessed One". [Tr.]
3. *Sainte-Hélène, au temps de Napoléon et aujourd'hui* [*St Helena in Napoleon's Time and Today*], by Ernest d'Hauterive.
4. Jourquin Collection, unpublished.
5. *Victor Hugo* by Hubert Juin, vol. 2 (1844–70).
6. See *L'Art de la cuisine française au dix-neuvième siècle* [*The art of French Cuisine in the Nineteenth Century*] (Comptoir des Imprimeurs), 1847, vol. I.
7. Octave Aubry, *Sainte-Hélène*, vol. II.
8. Guy Godlewski, *op.cit.*

The Eighth Day

THE RISING SEA LAZILY PUSHES AT THE BLACK SHINGLE, shiny as nuts of coal. Three men are line fishing, facing Rupert's Bay near Jamestown. A fourth, sitting on the rocks not far from the ruined artillery batteries, watches the scene with a bored expression on his face. One could certainly make fun of the lack of enthusiasm shown by the three fishermen, who only show any sign of energy when their lines tangle. The three men are side by side and arguments frequently arise. The fish are biting in spite of their lack of enthusiasm, and the plastic bags they use in place of baskets fill up before my eyes.

The three fishermen are prisoners. The fourth is their warder. The Dutchman, who was the captain of the *Frontier* intercepted with its cargo of cannabis, is not one of the group. Prisoners don't usually look particularly joyful, but these three seem very morose. The one wearing a baseball cap can't manage to pull the hook out and impatiently tears the fish's head. I ask him about their conditions in custody.

"It's all right," he says, wearily summing up the situation.

"It's all right, but we're not free," adds the second.

"I gather you can go out of the prison whenever you like!"

"Yes . . . Well, there are rules."

"Is it true that you can also go swimming in the sea?"

"Yes, yes. That's all true. We have lots of advantages. We take swimming lessons in the municipal baths. We can play football on the school ground. You can call that privileges, but all the same we're still prisoners."

"Many people in custody would envy you though . . ."

He gets excited, stutters, makes a vague dispirited gesture in the direction of the ocean.

It has just occurred to me that these prisoners are in the same situation as Napoleon. The Emperor could go out wherever he wanted in St Helena – a permission he never wished to make use of. This freedom no longer seemed one as soon as he realized that the complete isolation of the island made it a veritable rat trap. These prisoners are condemned to freedom in a 122-square kilometre dungeon.

"Still, an island is much bigger than a cell," I say to them.

"We have a cell as well . . ."

"But you're not shut up in it during the daytime!"

"That depends . . . No, no, we can't complain," he stammers, but looks unhappy.

"Hello! What a surprise!"

The chuckle from that mellow, imperious voice comes from behind my back. My two lady friends greet me with evident delight. Amy's face is suntanned and she is wearing elegant sunglasses in the style of those Greta Garbo wore towards the end of her career. Her companion wears a turban. They seem in good spirits, even excited, and so thrilled to see me that I feel rather ashamed of giving them the cold shoulder.

"We're so happy . . . Tomorrow, it's goodbye St Helena. I've never known such a deadly dull place in all my life."

(I bet the other one will say: "Amy, you're exaggerating.")

"Amy, you're exaggerating again. We've had some good times. You're so impatient . . ."

"Oh, yes!" Amy replies with a nasty look. "She wanted to go back to Longwood. Can you imagine that? I let her go on her own.

See that old place again! . . . What's more, she didn't even dare go inside. What got into you?" she murmurs, talking to her companion as though she were a naughty child. "Oh! She's so sentimental! Heavens, how she annoys me with her Napoleon!"

The companion contains herself, then the expression on her face suddenly changes.

"Will you shut up!" she retorts, flaring up. "We've been going round the island for a week, and you've seen nothing! Oh, Amy! You're so selfish, so blind, so obnoxious . . ."

The three prisoners have stopped casting their lines and are watching the scene with amused astonishment. The warder no longer looks bored. I know the way these two elderly English ladies carry on by heart now. In the beginning, I was taken in by their false quarrels. When I try to slip away in the middle of their argument, Amy calls out to me: "Oh no! You're not going to escape like that. That's a cowardly thing to do! Do stay."

The curt tone gives way to the sly, wheedling little girl's voice.

"Please!"

"You see, the boat leaves tomorrow," I say. "All I've seen on the island is Longwood, Jamestown and Plantation House. Time's getting short. I'd like to take a quick trip to the Sandy Bay area and perhaps see Diana's Peak."

"Take us with you," the companion says, joining the conversation. (Her clear, rather shrill voice contrasts with Amy's theatrical expressions and affectations.) "We'll behave," she declares, addressing her friend, as if to shut her up. "I promise you."

"Yes. All right," I say, seeing no way out.

I smile at the companion, letting her know that I'm doing the favour for her alone.

This little game has not escaped Amy, who once more puts on her hypocritical, shrewish look. The aquiline nose and the little lines at the corners of her mouth give her a hard expression that manages to convey both self-control and anger.

"What are those men trying to catch?" she says in honeyed tones, pointing to the prisoners who have begun to cast their lines again.

"I haven't any idea . . . They fish mainly for something to do. They're prisoners."

"Prisoners? Not really!"

With her, the demon of curiosity takes the form of a greedy, almost avid facial expression. She eyes them curiously in a most indiscreet way, as if they were animals at a fair, or prey. In fact, she reminds me of a bird of prey. There is something inhuman in the lordliness of her manner and her aggressively friendly behaviour.

"They're lucky not to be behind bars. Prisoners who have freedom . . . that's something you don't see every day!"

"Freedom! I don't think so. Their luck is very relative."

"But just look at them all. They're really happy. It's extraordinary. The ocean, the warder asleep on the rocks . . ."

"Yes, but they're prisoners without hope. The warder can go to sleep because he knows that they can never escape."

"Well, what of it?" she cuts me off impatiently.

"A prisoner with no hope is like a dead man."

"Ah, yes! Mr Answer-for-everything. How would you know? You know everything about Napoleon and now you're holding forth pedantically about people in prison."

I refrain from answering and turn my back on Amy. Her companion has a strange look on her face as she looks intently at mine.

2

The *coup de grâce* will come from Aix-la-Chapelle, Charlemagne's former imperial capital. The first congress of the Holy Alliance meets there at the end of September 1818. France, represented by the Duke de Richelieu, secures the departure of the army of occupation. What is to be done with Bonaparte? This is the question faced by the European powers. The final blow will be dealt by a Corsican who joined the service of the Tsar, Pozzo di Borgo, a sworn enemy of the Bonaparte family. The delegates ratify recommendations of the Russian plenipotentiary, who justifies the measures taken against the prisoner. The jailer's harshness is approved by the participants, who go so far as to encourage the English to increase their vigilance.

Napoleon is devastated. He had placed great hopes in this conference, and had counted on the moderation of his father-in-law, the Emperor of Austria, as well as on the goodwill of Alexander I.

From January 1819, the newspapers arriving from London had given him some forewarning of the verdict. The protocol of the Congress of Aix is officially handed to him on 26 May 1819. Napoleon knows from that moment on that he is a doomed man and that he will never leave St Helena. He had cherished the dream of ending his days in Malta or at Belle-Île. He has been deprived of the most precious possession that every captive has and holds dear: hope. Hope, the only thing left, when a prisoner has lost everything. Now he has nothing. "Twenty breathtaking years led to this nothingness."[1]

He will be less and less interested in the work of reconstructing the past, which until then had enabled him to overcome misfortune. The gold of time has become permanently tarnished. The narrative impetus of the dictations has slackened. He becomes weary of reviving "the pure moment". Now he is nothing more than a man, a role, a cipher.

He immerses himself in his bath two or three times a day. Sluggishness has penetrated his very soul. He had once said to Gourgaud: "If you don't curb your imagination, you will go mad." The prisoner's nights are more and more disturbed. His health had begun to decline towards the middle of 1817; it now becomes much worse. The pain in his right side, symptomatic of liver trouble, worsens during the night of the 16–17 January 1819. He loses consciousness. This attack is all the more alarming as O'Meara was sent back by Hudson Lowe in July 1818, and Napoleon no longer has a doctor. Because of this latest attack, the sick man has to call on the services of Dr Stokoe, the ship's doctor on board the *Conqueror*, anchored in Jamestown harbour. The surgeon confirms O'Meara's diagnosis of hepatitis. However, after the doctor's fourth visit to Longwood, Lowe suspects him of being in league with the French, forbids him to see his patient again and has him sent back to England.

Captain Nicholls, the duty officer assigned to verifying the prisoner's presence, has great difficulty in carrying out his mission. Napoleon has become invisible. One day Bertrand shows him the Emperor in his bath through an open window. He is immersed in water up to his neck. Nicholls thinks he has "a face like a ghost". Sweating and lethargic after his bath, he lies on a sofa and watches the rain run down the window panes in his bedroom.

Mme de Montholon, whose health has always been delicate, manages to convince the Emperor that she needs to go back to France, but the captive manages to dissuade her husband from leaving with her. Albine is provided with numerous bills of exchange, payable by the imperial family. Napoleon also assures the Montholons of his generosity to them in the provisions of his will.

Her departure will grieve him. He has become used to Albine's familiar charm, her patience and her kindness. Aubry sums it up as "the last smile in Napoleon's captivity".

On the day she leaves Longwood (2 July 1819), Napoleon can scarcely conceal his confusion. Hidden behind a curtain, he watches Mme de Montholon leave. He sees her look at the house for the last time. Montholon affirms that on that day the Emperor cried, "for the first time in his life". With a sinking heart he exclaims to

Marchand: "You will go back to Europe! You will see your families again! Montholon will rejoin his wife and children, and you, your mother!" With an aching heart he adds: "I shall be dead, abandoned in this loneliness."

There is only one consolation for such sorrow: the bath. He undresses and lowers himself into the warm, calming water with a sigh of relief. After that he dines alone. In the evening, two rats run across the dining room and nearly trip him up. The rats are a plague that the people at Longwood have learned to live with. There are so many of them that they cover the paving stones "so that they look almost black" (Marchand).

Octave Aubry claims that the days that followed were "perhaps the darkest that Napoleon had experienced". Albine's escape has all the signs of a headlong flight from the place. It marks a new turning point in Napoleon's captivity. There are many turning points in the dénouement of the St Helena tragedy. Strangely enough, even though these reversals finally come to an end, they are characteristically circular and enclosed, as if these successive desertions invariably came back to their point of departure. Napoleon is locked in this vicious circle.

Nevertheless, in September 1819 it looks as though the exodus will stop with the arrival of "the little caravan", made up of the two abbés, Buonavita and Vignali, together with Dr Antommarchi. The Emperor soon sizes up these newcomers, sent from Rome by his uncle Cardinal Fesch. "My family sends me nothing but boors." Buonavita is 57 and a simple, slightly stupid man. Vignali looks more like a Corsican shepherd than a priest. As for Antommarchi, Napoleon finds him "young and brash". He is of the opinion that the surgeon does not have the necessary qualities to practise medicine. The prisoner is dreadfully disappointed. He thinks that his family is losing interest in what becomes of him.

There will, however, be a little excitement at Longwood. At the beginning of his exile, Napoleon regretted the absence of a church service on Sunday, an even drearier day than the rest. "If we had a priest . . . That would have occupied a moment of our day!" the prisoner would say with a sigh.

The Mass celebrated in the drawing room on the Sunday after the arrival of the two priests is a real event. After that it will be held in the dining room. When the Emperor is indisposed, he takes part in the service lying down in his study.

Antommarchi, who has noted the captive's inactivity, encourages him to go out and exercise. He suggests gardening. The young Bonaparte had tended the plot of land allotted to each pupil at Brienne with enormous enthusiasm. Could that memory have made him eager to take up the idea? From October to December 1819, Longwood is the scene of feverish activity. They dig the earth, they plant, they sow, they rake, they sow grass. Ali comments that "Longwood had never been as full of life as it was during this work on the garden." Napoleon designs the beds, plans the various gardens, keeps his workers up to the mark. The moment he likes best is the watering. He feels a childlike joy when he makes the water run along the channels. He loves to hold the pipe and send the jet of water where he wants it. Ali notices that the Emperor has never felt better. Then it gradually becomes apparent that the vegetables are not growing well. Then the drought and the insects play havoc with everything. Then the prisoner begins to lose interest in the work. Longwood falls back into its state of torpor.

As a New Year's gift for 1 January 1820, Marchand gives his master a watercolour that he has secretly been painting. Longwood in all its detail, transformed after the work on the garden, is carefully and faithfully reproduced. Napoleon is on the threshold of the veranda. On the right, the two priests Buonavita and Vignali are walking down a path, while on the left, Mme Bertrand is watching over her two children. It's a naïve work. Although the drawing is clumsy, Marchand has a real talent with colour. Why does this snapshot have such a feeling of strangeness about it? Beneath the reassuring appearance of the scene, disaster looms. Behind the bucolic decor lurks Death. Or else it could be the stranger in black who is making his way to the veranda. The presence of this figure is intriguing. He looks strangely like Napoleon.

This *other* that he glimpses, his double, is the messenger of death. In his own way, Marchand has tried to indicate Fate.

If we could read the prisoner's thoughts, what would we find during that year, 1820? Probably a feeling of emptiness, despondency and world-weariness. Shadows gradually fall in the small dark room. He had kept suffering at bay by giving a meaning to his ordeals. Now his enthusiasm has waned; time has become fossilized. The thoughtful eyes gazing at the blank wall or the flames in the fireplace become weary. The hours drift by, but he does not seem able to pick up the thread of the past again. An anniversary sometimes sets the wheels of memory in motion. On 18 June 1820, the day of Waterloo, he begins the battle again for the hundredth time. "I had 71,000 men in line; the Allies had nearly 100,000, and I was about to beat them." He cannot get used to the idea of having been defeated. Waterloo is the thing that has been lost, but is essential to him. He hates it, and takes pleasure in hating it in an obsessive, unhealthy way even though it hurts him and eats away at him. He complains to Antommarchi of feeling listless and queasy. Antommarchi mentions stomach trouble, which makes Napoleon angry.

The master of Longwood is worried not only about his health, but also about an all too familiar malaise that he feels lurking in the background: the desire to escape. Bertrand's wife can stand St Helena no longer and wants to leave. "Give her another child. That will postpone your departure for a year, and will also give her something to interest her," Napoleon advises bluntly. In July the Grand Marshal makes up his mind to go, then abandons the idea. Montholon also wants to leave Longwood, but, being more flexible, proceeds by dropping hints. Napoleon swears by him. One day he declares very hurtfully to poor Bertrand: "I place all my trust in Montholon."

He is more and more morose and persistently stays in his bedroom. When Antommarchi begs him to get up, he replies: "Oh, doctor! Let it be. One is so happy asleep!" He has no desire to walk in the garden.

"The air makes me sick," he says in a dolorous voice.

Of the six years that Napoleon spent as a prisoner, 1820 is the most difficult to investigate. The Longwood community has lost several members. Bertrand is no longer writing his diary. He will take it up again in 1821. The only reliable sources available for this period come from Marchand and Ali. Montholon's account, written much later, is more than dubious.

1820 is an empty, mysterious, morbid year. There is not a sound to be heard from the house now. The shutters are always closed. The gardens gradually become overgrown. Longwood is the realm of absence.

3

Sandy Bay. Bones, pebbles, wreckage, mounds of seaweed lie on the black sand. The sea has slowly broken up the tubular shape of the basalt rock. There is a sort of primitive disorder, historical zero, primeval indifference. All the gradations of black and grey are strewn in dull profusion. A dead beach and a leaden sea. Eternal, inhuman nature. The waves spew forth a thick foam as they unfurl on the shore. The milky water sticks to the pebbles and deposits a slimy trace on the sand. Bubbles of foam rise and then burst, leaving silvery threads.

Napoleon has never walked on the lonely inlet, but from Mount Pleasant he has gazed out on the monumental amphitheatre that descends to the black-bordered bay. On 4 October 1820, he finally decides to go out of Longwood. He wants to see the part of the island he discovered on 6 January 1816, when, with Gourgaud, he had inspected the coast and perhaps taken stock of the defence system set up by the English.

This time he goes off in full daylight with Bertrand and Montholon. They leave early in the morning. As Napoleon is soon feeling tired, he asks the owner of Mount Pleasant if he might rest there. A lunch is improvised in the shade of the cedars and cypresses. In his usual teasing way, the Emperor insistently asks his host whether he ever gets drunk. He gets Bertrand to ask the same question of the owner's wife. They drink champagne. The Englishman is struck by the prisoner's plumpness, "as round and fat as a Chinese pig". Napoleon is worn out when he comes back from this outing. It is the last time he will go beyond the walls of Longwood. He has only eight more months to live. He is now a shapeless, prematurely old man. His face is puffy and his complexion grows more and more yellow. He waddles as he walks and is quickly out of breath. Even his altercations with Hudson Lowe have lost their sting. Napoleon is weary. He suffers cruelly from a sharp pain in his side that he likens to a knifepoint. He vomits and has a dry cough. "I am dying. I can feel it. My hour has come . . . There is nothing left of me. My strength and my faculties are deserting me."

"Oh! Your story is dreadfully sad," exclaims the companion to whom I have described the visit to Mount Pleasant. She is visibly moved. Amy is sitting in the back seat, sulking. She hasn't opened her mouth since we left Jamestown. Her companion sitting beside me looks at the map and calmly and confidently gives directions. We are following the same route as Napoleon. Fairyland is well named. The fairies have at last deigned to turn their attention to St Helena – at least in this spot, which is like a basket of brightly coloured camellias, arum lilies and daturas. In the distance, the sea with its violet patches of deep water seems calm and peaceful once again, almost replete. Complete solitude. The crenellations on the mountain tops, the crumbling basalt towers, the sheer precipices, the booming of the sea nevertheless recalls the essential nature of the maritime prison.

The companion points out amphitheatre formations called The Gates of Chaos, Lot's Wife and The Devil's Garden. They are bare, wadi landscapes, wide stretches of split rock: the ruins of an earthly paradise, where a few flowers and petrified trees still manage to cling. I can see the babies' toes with their white flowers, looking like little jellyfish. Sandy Bay has two faces. The bright surface hides a dark Plutonian underside, burnt from within. Ecstasy and chaos.

On our way back, we stop at the foot of Diana's Peak, the highest point in the island (820 metres), covered with plants with long pointed leaves.

"Flax. We saw some in New Zealand, Amy," the companion says enthusiastically.

"Flax! What are you talking about? I don't remember," is Amy's chilly reply.

"Yes you do. You remember, *Phormium Tenax* is a plant used to make hemp."

"You know very well that I'm not interested in such things," Amy retorts, with a weary look.

Flax . . . I've already heard something about it in Jamestown. The golden age of St Helena. This textile plant, originally from New Zealand, brought prosperity to the island for a century. The leaves were cut, teased out, washed and dried. Then the fibres were pressed by machine. The hemp was used for making rope. After the war, the arrival of synthetic materials meant the end of flax mills. It's thought that this plant might be the cause of allergic reactions suffered by some of the population today. A large proportion of the Saints suffer from asthma. Not far from Longwood, the Consul had shown me the remains of a clay pipeline that came down from Diana's Peak. Hudson Lowe had organized it to supply water to Napoleon and his entourage. I try to find traces of the channel near a spring, but the vegetation is too dense. We get back in the car.

"What good would it do you to find the pipeline again?"

Amy decides to speak at last. She attacks with her usual mordant style and her ingratiating smile, which is becoming more and more automatic.

"I can't understand your – how can I put it? – fetishism for places, this obsession you have for relics. Oh yes! I've studied you from the beginning. You're so pretentious! Just who do you think you are? A kind of Hercule Poirot, investigating the past?"

"As far as a fetishism for places is concerned, you're right. But

221

you're wrong about Hercule Poirot. The thing that actually intrigues me is the past that I can never reach, the vividness I can never revive. It's this definitive, irreparable, irretrievable *never* that excites me. Do you understand? What's more, you're wrong. It's not clues that I'm looking for, but permeation. Do you know Inspector Maigret?"

She nods.

"Well, I belong more to his school. Feeling, smelling. Absorbing noises, odours, images. It's the deposit which forms on the past that I love. The colouring and the veneer that cover objects and places. But one can't remove the patina of the past. The very fact that it's materially impossible fascinates me. Do you grasp this contradiction?"

"No. But I like your Inspector Maigret. He's so French! What you've just been telling me is also very French. You must go against common sense at all costs. Your passion for paradox . . . It's the way you French people have of thinking you're intelligent."

"What do you mean?"

"Oh! You know very well. Claiming what is true is false, what is wrong is provisionally right. You French have quite a gift for it. Take your Napoleon! You seem to think that I'm only interested in his private life, that I'm just a rather empty-headed old trout. But I've studied your great man quite a lot. In the last analysis, he's an impostor. He deceived you, you're well aware of it, and you love it. It's true that we English contributed a lot to this myth by persecuting him."

She pauses a moment.

"The past bores me," she says, emphasizing the words in a sad voice. "Or rather, it pains me. Probably because it makes me face decline . . . my death. Yes, I do think about it. Now do you know why I hate Longwood? You can smell death there. The smell of melancholy! That's a laugh! I can't bear all this carrying on to preserve the old place! . . ."

Her tone changes and she claps her hands enthusiastically.

"Oh, look! There's Radio St Helena. Let's stop."

On the heights surrounded by pines, stands a building bristling with antennas. A number of cars are parked beside the small road.

"What kind of programmes could this station possibly broadcast? Nothing ever happens on St Helena," Amy declares scornfully.

Some young Rastafarians with dreadlocks are sitting on the steps in front of the entrance. We ask to speak to the manager who arrives straight away to welcome us.

"I'm Anthony Leo," he says.

The two English ladies, feeling intimidated, are standing in the corridor leading to his office. They don't dare introduce themselves. He looks at them somewhat perplexed, wondering who they are. He has some coffee brought in and asks us to sit down. The station manager decides straight away to talk on a serious level. He says he's very much taken up with the imminent arrival of television.

"We happen to be here at a crucial time in the life of St Helena," I say to him. "The building of the airport, television . . ."

"It's a problem," he sighs. "We're discussing broadcast times at the moment. It's quite a revolution. People's outlooks will certainly change. We'll see the sense of community disappear. The phenomenon already began with video. Paradoxically, this opening out to the world will close us in even more."

"That certainly is paradoxical. Can you explain what you mean?"

"We've always been spectators, never actors. We sit quietly on our rock watching the performance while forgetting who we are."

His expression becomes grim.

"Yes, who are we?" he says with mock solemnity.

"You're British citizens."

"Precisely. But we have to get a permit to work in Great Britain. People are worried that the Saints will arrive *en masse*, but it's not true."

He ponders in silence then declares sententiously: "We're like prisoners on our island."

"So, St Helena is still a prison."

"Yes . . . It's not a good thing, as every prisoner tries to escape. By any means possible . . . The British Government should understand that. The Crown wanted to keep St Helena as a relic of its former glory. Well then, let it take responsibility for it!"

Amy, who has been sitting there gesticulating for a while now, breaks into the conversation:

"Allow me to disagree with you, sir. Take responsibility . . . Why, if we hadn't taken responsibility, what would have happened? Would you have become an independent country? With 6,000 inhabitants! That's not a very serious proposal."

"We have never demanded independence, only the right to be treated like full British subjects – to be treated as you are."

I can feel tension in the air.

"And what about Napoleon?" I say as a diversion.

His hard eyes light up.

"Ah! Napoleon," he says cheerfully. "He's part of our island's identity. People at least know where to locate us."

Then he turns to Amy with a look on his face that is both amused and provocative: "England has definitely won all round. She made Napoleon submit to her, and now she lays down the law to us."

I look coldly at Amy, signalling her not to start up the discussion again. I can tell she has understood from the ingratiating, disagreeable look on her face.

As we are leaving, Anthony Leo gives me a discreet nod in Amy's direction. It's an irritated, mocking glance, but also understanding, I fancy. I can hear the two women arguing in whispers as we go back to the car. The companion is exasperated and her voice hisses as she speaks.

4

Day is dying in the dark room. A pale light comes through the shutters in intermittent spasms, as if the twilight was reluctant to give way to the darkness.

It's my last visit to Longwood. The RMS *St Helena* gets underway tomorrow. The shadows die; the engraving of *Napoleon Dictating* grows dark; on the mantelpiece, Marie-Louise's nose is still faintly shining. The house is full of creaks and liquid sounds like the dull blows that hit the tight hull of a ship.

In the last months of the Emperor's captivity, Ali describes an ordinary but deeply moving scene. Napoleon, the unstoppable talker, has long since ceased holding forth. All he needs is the presence of another human being. Bertrand is there, as silent as he. The shutters are closed. The room is quite dark. Ali relates that they stayed like that for hours on end "without a word from either of them".

The wind begins to sound like someone having difficulty breathing. I can hear it whistling under the doors, shaking the shutters, panting loudly in the corridors. The day ends very suddenly in the tropics. It's a mournful, agonizing time when the air loses its perfume and one is more than ever aware of universal disintegration. The stickiness that oppresses Longwood feels like a mass of spongy cottonwool. An atmosphere like that couldn't help but encourage the appearance of the microscopic mushroom the English call "mildew". The little colony watched helplessly as the grey, downy spots slowly grew on the walls. The house continues to stew in a sour, slightly stale sweatiness that gets into the skin. Longwood is still fighting the mildew. For Lord Rosebery, it was the symbol of Napoleon's captivity; in fact, he maintains that it had contaminated the objects, the people and, above all, their words. Here at dusk, I breathe the air of the famous "laboratory of legends" described by the author of *The Last Phase*. Its atmosphere is conducive to comedy rather than concealment, for the subtle art of *mise en scène*, as evidenced by Napoleon's two wives facing each other in the dark room.

Darkness has now completely engulfed Longwood. The room has become like a heart where no light can penetrate. The wind roars over the plateau and lashes the cardboard house. The gusts draw closer and sound like warning shots.

In the last months, the captive no longer wants to go out. The wind "hurts him and affects his nerves". He can no longer bear the light. A see-saw with a saddle is set up in the parlour so that the sick man can get a little exercise. He gives it up after about a fortnight. All day long he recites these two lines from Voltaire's *Zaïre*:

> *To see Paris again, I may no longer crave.*
> *As you can see, I go to my grave.*

He no longer eats anything but jellies and soup. Hegel notes that "Seeing a man of enormous genius destroy himself is an incredible and frightening sight. It is the most tragic thing there is."

On 17 March, the prisoner has violent bouts of vomiting. "It's as though someone has put a knife into me there," he says pointing to his abdomen. "They broke the blade in the wound." The Emperor's entourage knows then that he has entered the last phase of his illness. "I'm suffering terribly . . . I'm proud Napoleon no longer," groans the former icon.

Full of pity, I look round the simple room, lit up now and then by the white light of the moon. Its pale glow leaves silver streaks on the little bed and the furniture, briefly sweeping through the room like a revelation or a benign radiance.

I've brought the bottle of St Helena eau de Cologne with me. I decided to keep it for the end; the final olfactory impression of Napoleon's captivity; my way of going back up time's one way street. I'm weak enough to think this telescoping of time will produce something: if not a revelation, then at least some small impression that is lasting or perhaps amusing. A smell, a perfume, like wine, has the power to abolish the idea of time as unique and absolute, to live in an eternal present. The whole purpose of smells is to bring back lost memories.

The bottle is enclosed in an elegant cardboard tube. On the label with the imperial coat of arms is written: *Eau de Cologne de Napoléon Ier à Sainte-Hélène*. I go into the prisoner's bathroom and turn on the light. Many tiny gleams of light are reflected in the large battered copper tub. In a corner the Emperor's riding coat and hat are laid out. It's a disturbing effect created by a present that seems as though it should never end, and which is probably the ultimate truth of Longwood.

I found the sheet of paper on which Ali carefully wrote the formula. The eau de Cologne was made up of essences of lemon, citron, bergamot and rosemary. This information made it possible for the people at the Versailles Osmothèque, a living collection of perfumes from the past and present, to reconstitute the captive's eau de Cologne.

I pour a few drops on to my wrist . . . It smells like normal eau de Cologne. A fresh, bracing, familiar sensation, yet with an overtone of something heavy, indefinable. I was going to say oriental, sensual. I have the fleeting illusion of a smooth, continuous movement, a sort of slide. It's not in time or even space, but something, in short, like a misapprehension, a misunderstanding somewhere. There's been a mistake in casting. I suddenly feel ridiculous with my miraculous water. I was waiting for it to transport me. As far as sliding is concerned, I've simply gone into a skid.

What can one conjure up with a perfume that is both so familiar and so exotic? It's no good imagining that a body was soaked in it, and that the body was in this bath: no subterfuge can fulfil my expectation. All these ruses, all these pebbles that I've accumulated since Eylau, amount to nothing more than a heap of stones, which has never built a house. Admittedly, the perfume of the eau de toilette once more fills the room for the first time in 170 years. But what of that? There has, of course, been Proust and his madeleine in the meantime. Besides, what I've just done has nothing Proustian about it; it's more like bad Huysmans. Des Esseintes in the tropics: utter contrivance.[2]

In his *Journal*, Michelet relates that when inspiration left him, he would go into a foul-smelling public urinal. He breathed in the noxious fumes and went back to work. What a pity Amy is not here. Her feistiness would have been some consolation for the hoax that didn't come off.

The bathtub has intrigued me from the start. On each of my visits, I haven't been able to resist taking a look at the copper trough. It's deep, asymmetrical and pigmented with microscopic residue. It seems to me that it's the only memory of Napoleon's captivity that is still really alive, perhaps because of the verdigris which grows according to the ambient humidity. Gazing at the black, gaping cavity, makes one feel a little giddy. A rather rudimentary system of a firebox heating a copper coil produced fairly hot water that the Chinese servants brought in buckets.

The pale body lying in amniotic fluid ... Hairless pale skin. Remember Las Cases and Napoleon's reference to his "plumpness that is not typical of our sex"? When he shows his body to Antommarchi, he makes this disconcerting remark: "As you can see Doctor, beautiful arms, rounded breasts, soft white skin, not a hair, except for ... More than one beautiful lady would glory in a chest like that!"

I realize now why the bathtub fascinates me. The still body in the oak box ... It's a living representation of death. The water in the sarcophagus. The bath of purification, but also of passing over into the other world. Regeneration and the end ...

The end. He longs for it. He even awaits it with joy. The vanquished Caesar who has sought martyrdom surrenders his life to gain a redemption that he knows will transfigure him.

His last days begin on 17 March 1821. He starts vomiting. For weeks now he has been unable to absorb any nourishment. He brings up everything he eats. "He is as thin as he was in 1800," writes Montholon. The captive has no illusions about the outcome of his illness. He knows that he will die of stomach cancer like his father and his sister Elisa. On 15 April, as death is approaching, he dictates his will. It begins with these words: "I die in the Roman, apostolic faith into which I was born more than 50 years ago."

During the next and following days, he behaves strangely. He asks for the windows to be opened, crying: "Hello sun, hello sun, my friend!" His rapid, impatient way of speaking also returns. He hounds those close to him with continual, insistent questioning, especially Dr Arnott, the English doctor assisting Antommarchi. It's a barrage of questions on unimportant subjects, as if he felt the need to know right to the end. Bertrand recorded these mechanical dialogues, which in sequence are wildly chaotic, like something out of an Ionesco play:

"What do your sailors drink?"

"Beer."

"But when they receive their pay, they drink wine, don't they?"

"No, they drink brandy or beer."

"What kind of brandy? French?"

"Usually English brandy, grain alcohol."

"Does it taste very different?"

"Yes, very."

"Have you been to Paris?"

"Yes."

"When?"

"After the Peace of Amiens."

"How long did you stay?"

"Five weeks. I would have stayed longer, but the breakdown in relations was coming. I left in a hurry."

"Oh! You were afraid I might arrest you?"

"There would not have been time, ten days later."

"Did you visit Lord Whitworth?"

"Yes."

"Did you see Lady Dorset?"

"Yes."

"Did you dine with them?"

"No."

"Where did you stay?"

"At the Hôtel Saint-Thomas."

"Where did you eat?"

"At the establishments of various restaurateurs. I had friends. I dined here or there, depending on what they had to do. There were two restaurants in the Palais Royal which the English often frequented."

"How much did it cost you?"

"One or two dollars a day for food and lodging, all inclusive."

"Would it have cost you twice as much in London for the same fare?"

"Yes."

"Do you think that the proportion of expenses is double between Paris and London?"

"Yes. However I think that it would be closer to the truth to say that the kind of life you can live for three dollars in Paris costs four in London. The situation is different, if you go out of the two capital cities. In England the cost of living is double that of France.

"Ah! The market price list varies. In England there are outlets everywhere; in France, consumption decreases outside of the large towns. How much does it cost to dine in London?"

"In taverns it costs two dollars or a louis, wine included."

"And if one does not have wine?"

"One must have wine in these taverns. You cannot dine there without it. Their main profit is in wine."

"What wine do they drink? Claret?"

"No. Only the rich drink claret."

"What is the cost of claret, or of sherry?"

"Fifteen shillings a bottle."

"Your soldiers must have drunk a lot of it in France, where it cost two sols a bottle, or in Sicily."

"Yes, they were all drunk."

"How much does land in England yield?"

"Three to four per cent."

"I did not think it was as much as that."

"Land is increasing. It did not bring in as much in wartime, when the Income Tax was in force, but since it has been abolished, land generally yields that amount."

"Oh! I did not know that. Is it a worthwhile proposition at that price?"

"Yes. Leases last from seven to fifteen years, otherwise farmers cannot farm properly."

"Do they pay regularly?"

"Yes."

"Can they be forced to pay?"

"No doubt. The courts have the means to do it."

And so on.

These dialogues take place on 24 April. Bertrand records everything, down to the most improper details. He scrupulously notes the dying man's obsession concerning Mme Bertrand. "I hold it against her for not having been my mistress," Napoleon says with a groan.

* *

"Where on earth are you hiding?"

Gilbert Martineau's distant, but peremptory voice reaches me from the direction of the drawing room.

"What's happening? All the lights are out," he grumbles.

The footsteps are hesitant. I can hear him feeling his way.

"He's in the bathroom."

"Oh! There you are! But why are you standing here in the dark?"

Both of them are there in front of me, amused and knowing, the father looking sceptical, the son friendly and interested.

"So, now it's goodbye to Longwood! Well, you'll come back again. After Fontainebleau came the Hundred Days," the father says with a smile.

"Then Waterloo . . . No. After a voyage like this, one should never come back."

Coming back. Three weeks after the Emperor's death, the Bertrands and the St Helena survivors board the *Camel*, a cattle ship. In the filthy boat taking them away to England, the little group, deeply shocked by the tragic end of their hero, cannot know that it will mark the beginning of the most extraordinary *chanson de geste* of the nineteenth century.[3] The French are welcomed with curiosity and deference. Thus the real life of the vanquished hero begins . . . Like a dream.

One of the representations of this dream taking shape is actually called *Bertrand's Dream*. This work by Horace Vernet dated 1821, often copied and distorted, had an extraordinary fate. Every self-respecting Napoleon museum must have a version of it. The painting, also known as Napoleon's apotheosis, celebrates the exile's Passion and transfiguration. The sobbing figure of Montholon stands leaning towards the Bertrand family also in tears. A broken chain, symbolizing the martyr finally liberated by death, lies near the sword and famous hat placed on Napoleon's tomb. The fame of

the great leader is represented by a list of his exploits: Rivoli, the Pyramids, Marengo, Iéna. The Empire has become the wreck of a ship breaking against the prison rock. The sky opens, revealing the great figures of the epic who have already died: Lannes, Berthier, Brune, Desaix. These valiant men prepare to welcome their chief into the imperial Valhalla. It's an extraordinarily romantic vision of the Napoleonic epic, inspired by Girodet's picture in la Malmaison: *The Apotheosis of the French Heroes who Died for Their Country during the War of Freedom.* All the symbols of the legend, which is just beginning, are there in Vernet's work: suffering and redemption, fall and apotheosis, exile and the return in glory. The survivors of St Helena will come back to the accursed island as heroes. Fidelity and self-sacrifice will be rewarded at last. Nineteen years later comes the time for revenge.

I'm watching Gilbert Martineau. Solitude has given his face a hard, closed expression. To be alone – but to what end? He must have been an angry man. Was it disappointment at not having been able to realize the dreams and illusions of his youth? He has described the wound that never heals in Byron extremely well: the poet regarded life as a monstrous irony. Martineau, the inscrutable, wounded man. "When his youth had flown, he was alone in the world," he writes of the romantic poet. Proudly alone. Even more alone than Napoleon who had the illusion of reigning over his little court. Michel joined him in the mid-1980s.

He has reigned over the empty reliquary that is Longwood, over his cheerless, enclosed private life. In the gloom where these two men are standing, with the woodwork creaking in the wind, I realize that Longwood will never awaken from its saturnine nightmare. The tortured heart is forever sealed within these walls like an evil relic.

"Make the most of St Helena . . . It's a great empty page. You can fill it any way you like."

These are his last words . . . I never saw that solitary man again.

1. Octave Aubry, *op. cit.*
2. Des Esseintes is the hero of Joris-Karl Huysmans' novel of experiments in aesthetic decadence, *A Rebours* [*Against the Grain*], 1884. [Tr.]
3. The term was originally used for heroic mediaeval verse chronicles. [Tr.]

The Ninth Day

I

AT 3 A.M., IN POURING RAIN, THE SAPPERS' PICKAXE HITS the cement layer sealing the tomb. Six hours later, the mahogany coffin can be seen through two large cracks. Once the first casing has been opened, there are still three caskets to unseal: one lead, one wood and the third tin. The lid of the last one is lifted off carefully. The doctor parts the padded satin wrapped around Napoleon's body.

It's 16 October 1840. Prince de Joinville, Louis-Philippe's son, has been charged with the mission of bringing Napoleon's remains back to France. Down in the valley where the Emperor was buried stand Marchand, Bertrand, Gourgaud, Ali and also Emmanuel de Las Cases, son of the author of the *Memoirs*. When these men had left St Helena, they were convinced they would never see the island again. Standing in the front row of those present, they anxiously await the moment when the expedition's doctor raises the veil. Given the way everything decomposes in the tropics, they all expect to find the hideous remains of a dead body. They suddenly see Grand Marshal Bertrand rush forward as though he were going to throw himself into the Emperor's arms.

Nineteen years after his death, Napoleon is almost intact. Bertrand and Marchand, who sat with him until he breathed his last, are astonished to find that his face has the same expression as when he was dying. "His hands, which were so beautiful when he was alive, are in a perfect state of conservation. His skin still has the colour one only finds in the living," one of the witnesses notes.[1] A growth of beard has given a blue tinge to the face and the fingernails have grown. Marchand goes so far as to say that the body looks more like the Emperor than when he died in 1821. Emmanuel de Las Cases exclaims: "At the sight of what death had wrought – changes that were more like life than death, in spite of the time that had elapsed – we were all suddenly overcome with feelings impossible to describe."

The Consul told me that Las Cases had brought a daguerreotype with him. The process had been perfected in 1829, but he could not use it because of the considerable length of time the subject needed to pose. The emperor's remains were exposed to the air for only two minutes.

The caretaker of the tomb, Adrian Wade, shows me around his domain, three kilometres from Longwood. The captive was very taken by the tranquillity of Geranium Valley, as it was called in Napoleon's time. He thought the water from the spring was so good that he sent a servant there every day to get some for his personal use.

What a contrast between the tomb and Longwood! The joy of nature seems to be concentrated there so that it can radiate its peace and calm throughout the valley. The tall colonnade of trees with their tops bent over like buttresses form a cathedral whose arches echo softly with countless bird songs. Spider webs, wound around the bark like silver embroidery, glisten in the sunlight. Visitors, famous or not, have planted trees they brought with them here: an olive tree from the Prince of Wales, araucarias planted by the officers of the *Joan of Arc*.

Why do people still come here and meditate, when the tomb has been empty since 1840 and the Emperor's body was there for only 19 years? Perhaps because it is a place of *deliverance*! Freed for ever from the torments of captivity. Freed at last from the suffering of exile, dullness and degeneration. Freed most of all from the body, from the material being that has passed away. The Valley of the Tomb does not wear mourning. It's a moving, relaxing place that inspires a "voluptuous melancholy". As in one of the novels of Bernardin de Saint-Pierre, a writer Napoleon much admired, the tomb is one of those rare sites on St Helena where nature can be studied by quietly wandering around, just for the pleasure of it. That's the great difference from Longwood. You don't visit Longwood; Longwood visits you, as you are irresistibly drawn by the tragic power of the plateau and the old house. Here the wind has ceased its plaintive moan. Here it's a deep, harmonious breath, which idly stirs the branches as it gently blows over the valley.

"Many visitors say to me, 'I'd love to be buried in a place like this!'" Adrian Wade tells me.

He lives in a little house down in the valley. He keeps a discreet watch over the place and rushes up as soon as a tourist approaches. From 1821, visitors had the habit of removing leaves and branches from the three willows for souvenirs, so that they disappeared after a few years.

The tomb is a vision where the nightmare has vanished and nature celebrates the epiphany of renewal. The gravestone on which the Norfolk pine catkins lie is huge. The shrill noise of insects pierces the air in waves like a needle pricking into heavy material. There is no inscription. ("Here lies; no name; ask the earth," as Victor Hugo wrote.) Montholon had wanted "Napoleon 1769–1821" to be engraved there. Hudson Lowe insisted on adding "Bonaparte". The French preferred to leave the stone bare.

The spear-shaped iron railings surrounding the tomb are the same as those in the Place Sainte-Hélène at Châteauroux. A faded bouquet hangs from one of the bars: red and yellow gladioli tied with a tricolour ribbon on which the word "Association" can still be made out. A sharp, slightly camphorated smell from the freshly cut eucalyptus trees spreads over the valley.

2

The RMS *St Helena* is anchored in Jamestown Bay. We leave at midday. Amy and her companion were the first to arrive on the wharf. They're terrified of missing the boat. Amy is very light-hearted and talkative. Her companion makes me think of Martha in the Gospels. She's gentle, active, considerate, but she has not been given grace. Like Mary, the obnoxious Amy has chosen the better part. She shines quite undeservedly.

Two men are busy cleaning the old rusty cannon in front of the law court. I recognize one of the prisoners who were fishing at Rupert's Bay. The other is the Dutchman, the captain of the *Frontier*. He is rubbing the mounting without any great enthusiasm, one eye on the passengers and their families going down to the jetty. He has a grey beard and a wily look about him. He's been given the nickname "Captain Igloo", a reference to a brand of frozen fish symbolized by the picture of an old seadog who looks very like him, it seems.

Marian, the wife of the attorney, hails me in the main street.

"I told you so. People always bump into each other here."

She introduces a member of the island Executive Council called Bill Drabble. He talks to me at length about Napoleon, whose story he seems to know well. Of all the Saints I've met until now, he is the only one who has been really interested in him. He has even been to Paris to visit the Emperor's tomb.

"The future rests on the past. There's no future without the past. That's the tragedy of St Helena," he says solemnly as he leaves.

Marian walks a little way with me.

238

"The people here are very friendly."

"That's what you said the first time we met," she replies with a smile.

She continues: "The Saints are friendly. But what they like most is for people to take notice of them."

"Do you mean Great Britain?"

"Yes. The relations between the two are complex, rather like the relationship between child and adult. Like children, the Saints throw tantrums from time to time. They want London to take care of them, but at the same time they rage against this dependency. But look at the boat in the bay and the people strolling down towards the wharf. Idyllic, isn't it? That's the picture you should take away with you. Don't be too fond of the past."

She then declares in a subdued voice: "There's no hope to be found in the past."

Amy is waving frantically to me from the launch. I'm one of the last passengers to embark.

"The Prince has the coffin placed in the longboat, which sinks deeper into the water under its weight. The Emperor's mortal remains have touched the land of his exile for the last time. Henceforth and forever, they will be with the French. The flags are unfurled. The notes of The Dead March from Saul fade away. The rays of the setting sun form a halo of glorious crimson around the *Belle Poule*, like a coronation day at Notre Dame."[2]

1. Phillippe de Rohan-Chabot, the King's commissary, *Les Cinq Cercueils de l'Empereur* [*The Emperor's Five Coffins*] (France-Empire).
2. Philippe de Rohan-Chabot. *op. cit.*

Epilogue

Three years have elapsed since my voyage to St Helena.

Television arrived on the island two months after I was there. First there was CNN, then the Cartoon Network, Super Sport and Discovery.

Marian has left St Helena and is now living in England. A new governor has taken over from Alan Hoole.

I never saw Amy and her companion again. We said our final goodbyes when the ship called in at the Cape. They were two sisters, both widows. While we were on the boat, I never managed to get them to talk about their lives, to find out for example under what circumstances Amy had learned to speak our language.

I have vainly searched Mme de Montholon's *Memories* for any mention of the Dane's ghost. The last I heard, the cook at Longwood is reported to have come face to face with the apparition. It was wearing a white cravat. A resident of Jamestown claims to have caught sight of it recently while she was visiting Longwood.

Intrigued by James Sant's picture, *Napoleon: the Last Phase*, I tried to get some information about the work from the art gallery in Glasgow. They replied that the artist "in all probability" took his inspiration from a portrait by Paul Delaroche, *Napoleon in 1814*. I went to Les Invalides where this picture is hanging. It was painted in 1845, after Napoleon's death. Like Sant, Delaroche had never seen his model. The mystery is still unresolved.

Knowing that I was writing a book on St Helena, a friend passed on to me a study entitled *Napoléon en phase ou Pourquoi on ne peut pas le voir en peinture* [*Napoleon in phase or Why he cannot be seen in paintings*]. In this unpublished text, the author Michel Covin uses the "enigmatic strangeness" of Sant's picture to analyse the problem of Napoleon's "resemblance" to his portraits. "And what if that one was the real Napoleon, and all the other images were deceptive?" Covin asks, pointing out this paradox: "The eye witnesses are not the ones who produced the most realistic portraits of Napoleon." He explains the fact that the Emperor's contemporaries, like Baron Gros, were content to copy paintings in series. Napoleon himself cared little about verisimilitude or accuracy.

The Dutchman, the captain of the *Frontier* who was in jail for trafficking cannabis, escaped from St Helena six months after my visit. The circumstances surrounding this incident still remain something of a mystery. It seems that he took advantage of the Saturday night drinking session, and made his escape on board a sailboat. By the time they realized he had gone, he was far away from St Helena. The island has no patrol boats. In the whole history of the rock, he is the only captive to ever escape from the island prison. CAPTAIN IGLOO DID WHAT BONAPARTE NEVER SUCCEEDED IN DOING, ran the proud headline of a Dutch newspaper. The escapee is reported to be in Brazil and negotiating rights to a book about his exploits.

Gilbert Martineau died in France on 23 August 1995. His son brought back his ashes, which were scattered at sea off St Helena. Our consul now lives alone on the plateau. He is responsible to Foreign Affairs at the Quai d'Orsay, and their ruling is categorical: he will have to leave his post in three years' time. An exhibition of his paintings took place in Paris in February 1996. The flowers of Longwood were a great success.

Villa Jamot-Genthieu-Hoëdic, le Vieux Phare, November 1996

BIBLIOGRAPHY

Many of the works I have consulted have been cited in the footnotes. The first items to be mentioned from the impressive St Helena bibliography should be the accounts written by the four evangelists and eye-witnesses of Napoléon's captivity.

LAS CASES, Emmanuel de: *Mémorial de Sainte-Hélène*. Complete critical edition, edited by Marcel Dunan, 2 vols (Flammarion, 1951).

BERTRAND, General: *Cahiers de Sainte-Hélène*. Manuscript deciphered, edited and annotated by Paul Fleuriot de Langle, 3 vols (Sulliver et Albin Michel, 1949–59).

GOURGAUD, General Baron: *Journal de Sainte-Hélène*. Introduction and notes by Octave Aubry, 2 vols (Flammarion, 1944–47).

MONTHOLON, General de: *Récits de la captivité de l'Empereur Napoléon à Sainte-Hélène*, 2 vols (Paulin, 1847).

O'MEARA, Barry E.: *Napoléon dans l'exil*. Introduction and notes by Paul Ganière, preface by Jean Tulard, 2 vols (Fondation Napoléon, 1993).

MARCHAND, Louis: *Mémoires*. 2 vols (Tallandier, 1991).

ALI (Louis-Étienne Saint-Denis): *Souvenirs sur l'Empereur Napoléon* (Payot, 1926).

MONTHOLON, Comtesse de: *Souvenirs de Sainte-Hélène* (Émile Paul, 1901).

ABELL, (Betsy Balcombe): *Recollections of the Emperor Napoleon, during the First Three Years of his Captivity on the Island of St Helena* (London, 1844).

Napoléon à Sainte-Hélène by the four evangelists: LAS CASES, MONTHOLON, GOURGAUD and BERTRAND. Selected passages. Preface and notes by Jean Tulard (Robert Laffont, 1981).

AUBRY, Octave: *Sainte-Hélène*. 2 vols (Flammarion, 1935).

BERTHELOT, Michel: *Bertrand, grand-maréchal du Palais. Dans les pas d'un fidèle* (Châteauroux, published by the author, 1996).

BORDONOVE, Georges: *La Vie quotidienne de Napoléon en route vers Sainte-Hélène* (Hachette, 1977).

GANIÈRE, Dr Paul: *Invitation aux voyages* (Perrin, 1982).
   Napoléon à Sainte-Hélène. 3 vols (Perrin, 1957–61).

GUIBON, Alice: *Les Îles fatales*. (La Floride, Dieppe, 1956).

HAUTERIVE, Ernest d': *Sainte-Hélène au temps de Napoléon et aujourd'hui* (Calmann-Lévy, 1933).

MADELIN, Louis: *Vers l'Empire d'Occident*. Vol. VI: *De l'histoire du Consulat et de l'Empire* (Hachette, 1940).

MARTINEAU, Gilbert: *La Vie quotidienne à Sainte-Hélène au temps de Napoléon*, (Hachette, 1966).
   Le Retour des Cendres (Tallandier, 1990).
   Napoléon à Sainte-Hélène (Tallandier, 1981).

MASSON, Frédéric: *Autour de Sainte-Hélène*. 3 vols (Ollendorff, 1902–12).
   Napoléon à Sainte-Hélène (Ollendorff, 1912).

MOUGINS-ROQUEFORT, Joseph de: *Napoléon prisonnier vu par les Anglais* (Tallandier, 1978).

PAOLI, Dr François: *Le Docteur Antommarchi ou le Secret du masque de Napoléon*. Preface by Jean Tulard (Publisud, 1996).

QUENNEVAT, J. C.: *Atlas de la Grande Armée (1803–1815)* (Séquoia, 1966).

ROSEBERY, Lord: *Napoleon: The Last Phase* (Arthur L. Humphreys, 1900)

Bain, Kenneth: *St Helena* (Wilton 65, 1993).
GOSSE, Philip: *St Helena* (Anthony Nelson, 1990).

Le Général Bertrand, 1773–1844. Catalogue of the exhibition held at
the Musée Bertrand in Châteauroux, 1994.
Musée national des châteaux de Malmaison et de Bois-Préau.
Guidebook by Gérard and Nicole Hubert, 1986.
HUBERT, Nicole: "Regards sur Sainte-Hélène", Part III: "Le
mobilier de Longwood, hier et aujourd'hui" in the review
Le Souvenir napoléonien, March 1981.
MARTINEAU, Michel: *Le Souvenir de Napoléon à Sainte-Hélène.*
Brochure, 1994.

BAINVILLE, Jacques: *Napoléon* (Fayard, 1931).
GARROS, Louis, and TULARD, Jean: *Itinéraire de Napoléon au jour le
jour, 1769–1821* (Tallandier, 1992).
HILLEMAND, Dr P.: *Pathologie de Napoléon* (La Palatine, 1970).
TULARD, Jean: *Dictionnaire Napoléon.* Collective work (Fayard,
1988).
Napoléon ou le Mythe du sauveur (Fayard, 1987).

ACKNOWLEDGEMENTS

Without Éric Préau of the Sygma Agency, this voyage would never have taken place. Thanks go to him, and also to Yan Méot and the magazine *Géo*, and Jean-François Kahn of the *Événement du jeudi*, who made it possible. I certainly could not forget Stéphane Compoint, the photographer at the Sygma Agency, whose foresight and competence were invaluable to me.

Apart from the people mentioned in the book and, the first and foremost, Michel Martineau, my gratitude goes to Françoise Aujogue, Agnès Benetton, Philippe Béra and the Friends of the Napoleon Museum of Brienne-le-Château, Michel Berthelot, Gérard Boulitt, Michel Cantal-Dupart, Bernard Chevallier, Yvon Chotard, Jean Darnel, Victor Dust-Gonzalez, Édith Ganière, Annie Godefroy, Baron Gourgaud, Olivier Holdt, Yves Jeanpierre, Pierre-Yves Jourda, Annie Lorenzo, Éric Ollivier, François Paoli, Nata Rampazzo, Marjan Romain, Hélène Tavera, Jean-Luc Thomas, Jean Tulard and Henriette Walter.

I am grateful to Jacques Jourquin for having made my work so much easier. He introduced me to Ali's unpublished papers and reread the manuscript. I have taken note of his comments and am glad to have the opportunity to express my gratitude to him here.

I am also indebted to the team at La Table Ronde for having given me such a friendly reception. Denis Tillinac is a friend of long standing. His comments have been very valuable. Thanks to him I met Olivier Frébourg whose suggestions were invariably helpful in the editing stage. My thanks also to Marie-Thérèse

Caloni, Laurence Caracalla, Réjane Crouzet, Françoise Gaillard, Cécile Guérard, and Opere Citato.

What would I have done without Joëlle? She shared my time in the dark room with great patience.